THE OBSERVER'S BOOK
OF AUTOMOBILES ⌒ ⌒

The Observer's Books

THE OBSERVER'S BOOK OF

AUTOMOBILES

Edited by
L. A. MANWARING

With a Foreword by
STIRLING MOSS, O.B.E.

DESCRIBING 103 MAKES
with 263 half-tone photographs
and numerous line drawings

FREDERICK WARNE & CO. LTD.
FREDERICK WARNE & CO. INC.
LONDON · NEW YORK

© FREDERICK WARNE & CO. LTD.

LONDON ENGLAND

1965

First Edition	1955
Second Edition	1956
Third Edition	1957
Fourth Edition	1958
Fifth Edition	1959
Sixth Edition	1960
Seventh Edition	1961
Eighth Edition	1962
Ninth Edition	1963
Tenth Edition	1964
Eleventh Edition	1965

LIBRARY OF CONGRESS CATALOG CARD NO. 62–9807

Printed in Great Britain

FOREWORD

I AM happy, as always, to write, once again, the Foreword, to this, the 11th edition of *The Observer's Book of Automobiles*.

During 1964, British racing cars had similar sweeping successes to those which they enjoyed during the previous year, and we once more had the satisfaction of seeing a British driver, John Surtees, hailed as World champion. Enthusiasts will have also been heartened by the fact that Ferrari has begun a comeback on the Grand Prix scene and that this famous marque has won World championship honours.

In the sports car field, Ferrari supremacy has been seriously challenged by several cars, including the British A.C., now better known as a Cobra, which, in an effort to overcome the lack of a suitable engine to match the fantastic Ferrari-V-12's, are turning to the big American V-8 to provide the means of winning races. These engines can be tuned to produce a terrific amount of power and are, of course, relatively inexpensive. Several British G.T. cars, including the Bristol, Gordon Keeble, Jensen, Sunbeam and TVR, use these husky Yankee "mills" to provide powerful acceleration, effortless cruising and maximum speeds of 150 m.p.h. plus.

These G.T. cars and many more, including the new Austin 1800 saloon—the latest brain child of Alec Issigonis—are described and illustrated in this little book. Supplementing the descriptions are potted histories of some of the more famous manufacturers, drawings of some of the cars and of Company Badges. All this, together with details of British and foreign number plates, adds up to quite a lot of information which has been packed into a pocket-sized volume and which should prove of interest to car enthusiasts of all ages.

I close, as before, with an appeal for more safety and consideration on the road and to ask younger readers to remember their kerb drill and not to cross a road without first LOOKING RIGHT, LOOKING LEFT and then LOOKING RIGHT again. **STIRLING MOSS**

PREFACE

THIS edition—the 11th—of *The Observer's Book of Automobiles* follows the general pattern of previous years and sets out to provide a coverage of the world's cars that is as complete as possible. Every effort has been made to include details of as many different models as possible from the world's manufacturers. Many of these cars, of course, will not be seen in Britain but are included in order to widen the scope of this little book and to provide the reader with information that may not be readily available elsewhere.

To the publicity departments of the automobile manufacturers of the world go my thanks for their co-operative attitude towards my requests for information and for furnishing the material used in this book, as well as the many excellent photographs used as illustrations. Details of the cars described are as supplied by the manufacturers but are of necessity somewhat abbreviated due to considerations of space. However, the details presented represent the essential specifications of the vehicles described, and should more detailed information on a particular model be desired, then this can be obtained from the manufacturers' catalogues and leaflets.

My thanks are due also to Mr. Tuckfield of the Automobile Association for revising and bringing up to date the list of International Plates and to the Science Museum, South Kensington, for their permission to reproduce the photograph of the Benz car on page 7.

L. A. MANWARING

A BRIEF HISTORY OF THE AUTOMOBILE

THE ancestry of the motor-car or automobile goes back to the middle of the eighteenth century when, in 1770, Nicholas Cugnot built a steam carriage seating four passengers and running at a speed of $2\frac{1}{4}$ m.p.h.

After many years of experiments with steam carriages, culminating in Hancock's " Enterprise ", which worked

1885. Benz Three-wheeled Car. (Crown Copyright, from an exhibit in the Science Museum, South Kensington, London.)

in the streets of London in 1833, steam finally gave way to petrol as a form of road propulsion.

The two forms of power overlapped for some years, for the internal combustion engine, derived from Lenoir's and Dr. A. N. Otto's gas engines, came into being in 1886, as a result of independent experiments by Carl Benz and Gottlieb Daimler who worked in Mannheim and Cannstatt, in Germany.

Daimler's first attempt in 1885 was a motor bicycle, and Benz's effort of the same year concerned a three-wheeled vehicle, or "dog-cart".

The Daimler engine was eventually used by the French firm of Panhard and Levassor in their cars, this extremely profitable agency having been acquired for that company by a Belgian, one M. Sarazin, whose widow eventually went to see Daimler and persuaded him to allow her to carry on with her husband's interests, in conjunction with Panhard and Levassor. Romance combined with business when she married M. Levassor, who continued his experiments with Daimler engines and produced what might be termed the first "real" motor-car from a set of working drawings.

One of his most difficult problems was the finding of the correct position for the engine, and after having tried it in the centre and in the rear of the chassis, in 1891 he placed the little twin-cylinder Daimler engine in a vertical position in front, where it has remained almost universally ever since.

This was the first Panhard-Levassor car, one of a long line of petrol vehicles which were to add a brilliant contribution to motor-car history, but by this time other motor-car pioneers were appearing on the scene in France, including Comte De Dion (later De Dion-Bouton), Léon Serpollet, Amedée Bollée, Gautier Werhle, Peugeot and others, some of whom favoured steam propulsion, some electric and some petroleum; indeed, the motive power was one of the leading controversies of the day.

In 1895 in Britain the motor-car was still hampered by rules and regulations in which prosecution was risked if one was driven on the public highway without a man walking 20 yards ahead with a red flag. But the Frenchmen with their practical minds realized that there could be no progress without trial and error so certain public highways were closed on occasions so that motor-cars could be tested under practical conditions. The Paris to Bordeaux race of 1895 was such a trial and by it constructional errors were discovered and rectified. That first motor race in history was won by M. Levassor in a Daimler-engined Panhard-Levassor car, and it proved the superiority of petroleum as a fuel.

In 1888 William Steinway, the American piano manufacturer, visited Europe and obtained the rights to sell Daimler engines in the United States; by the 1890's the Duryea Brothers, Haynes and other Americans developed automobiles.

1907 Rolls-Royce Silver Ghost. This car had a 6-cylinder 40/50 h.p. engine and in that year completed 15,000 miles continuous running under Royal Automobile Club observation.

It is impossible to say to whom we owe the foundations of the motor industry in Great Britain, but there was no one in the early days who did more for the industry than F. R. Simms who met Gottlieb Daimler at the Bremen Exhibition of 1890, as a result of which he was given the opportunity of establishing Daimler motor-cars in Great Britain. Simms eventually acquired control of the patent rights for Great Britain, Ireland, and the Colonies.

Meanwhile the first Daimler car—a Panhard and Levassor car with a Daimler engine—had arrived in Britain, and in this historic car Simms and Evelyn Ellis made the first journey of any consequence in Britain by a petrol-driven motor-car from Micheldever in

Hampshire to Datchet, near Windsor, a distance of 56 miles in 5 hours 32 minutes (excluding stops)—at an average speed of 9·84 miles per hour.

In 1896 the crippling road regulations were lifted. Members of the Veteran Car Club of Great Britain drive their grand old motor-cars from London to Brighton annually to celebrate that memorable year.

Also in 1896 Miesse of Belgium did much to pioneer the motor-car in that country, as also did Martin in Switzerland two years later; while in a short time Spyker made a great impression in Holland and a motor-car appeared in Spain in 1902.

Some idea of the size of the motor industry in 1900 may be gathered from the fact that in that year there were 209 different makes of motor-cars, and just over half of them were American. It is incredible that in only twelve months this total had risen to 300 although the peak was not reached until 1905, when 700 makers were recorded. By 1906 Australia, Canada, Denmark, Hungary, Russia and Sweden were producing various makes.

By now the internal combustion engine was well established in principle and refinements continued to appear very rapidly. For example, the sliding-gear was brought out by the French Panhard company before the turn of the century. The fluid coupling and torque converter had been invented by 1902 and were later adapted for use in the car's transmission.

Some years later, in 1928, the American engineer Thompson invented synchro-mesh gears. The United States may also claim the adoption of free-wheeling and overdrive in 1932 and 1934, and Thompson was successful again in 1940 in perfecting hydromatic drive.

As these changes came about, reliability and convenience replaced uncertainty and discomfort. Weight was reduced and performance improved. Some makers advocated the rear as the rightful position of the engine, others employed air cooling, while some experimented with front-wheel drive. Strides were made in suspension systems, and the coil spring and independent road wheel springing were favoured by many makers. The Diesel engine was, and still is, fitted to a number of cars.

To ease the task of the driver, the steering column gear change became widely used, though soon pre-selector mechanisms and, later, automatic drives requiring only an accelerator and brake control became fairly common. Bodies of a smoother shape gave less wind resistance and, incidentally, reduced work when cleaning.

1961. Does this portray the shape of things to come? The experimental Chrysler Turboflite gas-turbine powered car which will run on petrol, paraffin or diesel fuel.

In 1950 the British Rover company produced the first turbine-engined car—the Turbocar JET 1. This represented a milestone in automotive engineering, for it marked the beginning of a new era in motor-car design. The gas-turbine form of power unit was conceived some thirteen years before, but it was not then applied to a road vehicle.

By 1952 France and the United States had experimental vehicles on the road employing this type of engine. Other British makers, including Austin, and other countries are now working along similar lines.

This system has been found to offer a number of advantages over the petrol engine, but many difficulties have to be overcome, such as the heavy fuel consumption, before the gas turbine becomes a practical and economical proposition for manufacturing and running.

However, with further experimenting and research the future may see a world populated with turbine cars and the petrol engine may recede into history as the steam engine did before it.

THE CHANGING SHAPE OF THE AUTOMOBILE

Up to 1900
Large road wheels, high seats variously placed and engines located under the seat or at the back, depending on whether they were steam, electric or petrol driven.
1901–1910
Cars began to assume a universal character with engines placed under a cover at the front.
1911–1914
At the end of this period mudguards or wings had become shaped for the motor-car. From the side view most contours were square.
1915–1920
The car by now consisted of three parts or masses: the engine housing, passenger area and wheels. Body-work became somewhat rounded, bonnets longer and wheels smaller. Wings became more shapely.
1921
There was evidence of a distinct tidying up of detail.
1922
Balloon tyres and bumper-bars were used.
1923
An effort was made to create new shapes for various major components but these were arrived at individually.
1924
Bodies became lower but not so the radiator, which still allowed under-engine details to be seen from the front.
1925
By this date a large percentage of cars had a fixed roof.

1926

In some cases, spare wheels were carried in a vertical position at the rear.

1927

The curving roof line gained favour.

1928

Several types of wheel in use. Most manufacturers favoured the wire spoked wheel, others disc wheels and wheels with wooden spokes.

1929

Body construction utilized a number of different materials; steel, wood and fabric. Sometimes a combination of all three was used.

1930

Bumpers at the front served to conceal under-engine and axle details. Front wings finished lower and were more domed. Running-boards began to disappear.

1931

Individuality was maintained by nation and maker.

1932

The pressed-steel body encouraged rounded edges.

1933

Aerodynamics were studied in the search for new body shapes. The pressed-steel type of coachwork encouraged the use of oversweep curves.

1934

In an effort to become " streamlined ", designs resulted in an over-statement. Wing valances increased in size.

1935

As the " square " and " elliptical " eras ended, bonnets became longer and higher, and front and rear overhang increased. Pressed wheels gave a neater look and some spare wheels were carried upright in the front wings.

1936

The uncompromising radiator began to disappear beneath a cowling or shell which in some cases gave a thrust-forward look.

1937

Bumpers increased in size. In some cases, where horizontal slats were incorporated in the radiator grille, they were also carried along the shallower bonnet sides.

1938

Shapes became well rounded, wing lines moved higher and some merged into body sides.

1939

Grilles and shells were quickly replacing the external radiator. The streamline form was now better understood; rounded contours, convex curves and faired wings were becoming more common.

1940–1945

World War II. In these years only the United States was still producing civilian passenger vehicles. A general accentuation of the horizontal rather than vertical began.

1946

Tests with bodies made from plastics indicated a further encouragement for designs with gentle curves.

1947–1948

Major alterations in appearance were evident due to post-war re-organization, though some manufacturers continued with modifications of 1939 designs. Gradually world design assumed a common basic shape.

1949

Curved windscreens and larger rear windows appeared.

1950

Front wings became part of the bonnet and body sides and rear wings merged into the luggage boot. Radiator and bonnet lines became lower.

1951

Most manufacturers now featured a grille over the radiator air-intake. Front and rear wings were becoming part of the main body mass.

1952

With the merging of front and rear wings by many manufacturers, the car-body designers featured three main areas: the window area, the oblong wing mass and the wheels.

1953

As the amount of window space increased, windscreens became more curved and their slope increased.

1954

The "hardtop" and "estate car" styles became increasingly popular.

1955

Marked accentuation of length and a wider range of body colours available.

1956

The two-piece "vee" windscreen had almost disappeared and bodies were becoming lower and wider. "Hooded" headlamps were a feature of some designs.

1957

"Fins" formed by an extension of the rear wing line popular especially in the U.S. Wrap-around windscreens and rear windows found increasing favour.

1958

Twin headlamps used extensively and "fins" more accentuated. Stainless steel used by some designers for bright trim.

1959

"Fins" less prominent and some cases became "flattened". Italian influence played a large part in the styling of many cars. Window areas became larger.

1960

The "wrap-around" windscreen began to lose favour. Body styles generally remained as for 1959.

1961

Use of bright trim became more restrained. Twin headlamps beginning to find favour in Europe.

1962

Little change generally in body design. "Fins" had virtually disappeared.

1963

Body styling more restrained and angular. Designs generally sleeker with lack of unnecessary ornamentation. Many cars featured wide radiator air-intakes.

1964

Trend of simplified, uncluttered body styling continued. Paired headlamps mounted vertically in one or two makes.

A *camshaft*, which opens and closes the valves as required; this being driven from the engine-crankshaft.

A definite series of movements has to be gone through in order to admit the gas to the cylinder, to compress it into the combustion chamber, to allow it to expand when it explodes, and to expel the burnt gas from the cylinder. These various movements make up what is called the " cycle of operation ". Two strokes of the piston, one down and one up, take place to every one revolution of the crankshaft; thus one stroke of the piston equals half a revolution. But the complete cycle of operation in an ordinary four-cycle petrol engine occupies two revolutions of the crankshaft, which means that between explosions (in any one cylinder of the engine) the piston goes up and down twice each way, or four times altogether; these four strokes being:

1. Downward—suction stroke.
2. Upward—compression stroke.
3. Downward—explosion (power) stroke.
4. Upward—exhaust stroke.

Obviously, after each cycle of operation the cylinder must be refilled with gas from the carburettor, which is done on the downward suction stroke of the piston. Almost immediately after the piston begins to descend, the inlet valve is opened by means of a cam and a charge of gas is drawn in from the carburettor. Shortly after the piston reaches the bottom of the suction stroke, the inlet valve is made to close.

The piston now rises in the cylinder, compressing the gas into a small space termed the combustion chamber and whilst on this stroke both inlet and exhaust valves remain closed. When the piston has reached the top of its stroke and the gas is fully compressed the latter is ignited by an electric spark across the points of the sparking plug.

The effect of the explosion is to cause a great increase in the volume of the gas and the additional pressure in the small space acts on the top of the piston, driving it down the cylinder, thereby rotating the crankshaft.

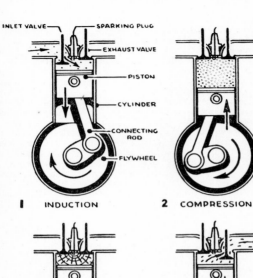

THE FOUR-STROKE CYCLE

When the piston is approaching the bottom of the explosion stroke the exhaust valve is opened by means of another cam, thereby allowing the burnt gas to escape into the silencer.

The piston now rises in the cyclinder, sweeping the burnt gas before it, and when it reaches the top of its stroke is ready to descend on another suction stroke and start the whole cycle over again.

Thus is described the complete sequence of events making up one cycle of operation. Owing to the fact that only one explosion takes place to every four strokes of the piston, the engine described is called a four-stroke engine, and in order that the events mentioned should continue smoothly, a flywheel is fitted to the crankshaft which, by the energy it accumulates from the action of rotation, keeps the piston moving during the idle strokes of exhaust, suction and compression. It absorbs the jerky action of the engine (in the case of single and twin-cylinder types) and keeps the crankshaft running at a smooth and uniform speed. In the case of a four-cylinder engine, in which an explosion takes place for every half revolution of the crankshaft, such a heavy flywheel is not necessary.

THE CLUTCH

This is placed between the engine and the gearbox and consists usually of a series of discs which, when pressed together in their normal position, form a solid driving coupling between the engine and the gearbox, but which, when separated by the depression of the clutch pedal, disconnect the drive from the engine to the gearbox, to allow the engine to idle when the car is stationary and to facilitate a change of speed.

THE GEARBOX

When a petrol-driven vehicle encounters a hill, its speed will begin to slow down even though the engine is still developing its full power, and as the speed of the vehicle decreases, so will the engine run slower, because the two are connected together by means of gearing.

As the power which a petrol engine develops depends upon the number of explosions which take place in a given time, and as the number of explosions depends upon the number of revolutions per minute, the power of the engine falls off as its speed decreases, until at last the vehicle would come to a standstill.

This is avoided by altering the gearing between the engine and the road wheels, thereby enabling the engine to maintain its normal speed even though the road wheels may be revolving at a much slower rate.

In a gearbox, if two gear wheels of equal size engage with each other their two shafts will revolve at the same speed, but should one wheel be larger than the other they will revolve at different speeds; this difference being denoted by the term *gear ratio*, a low gear ratio indicating a considerable difference between the driving shaft and the driven shaft.

When the first speed, or low gear, is in mesh inside the gearbox, the engine will make a large number of revolutions compared with the road wheels, but when high gear is used the difference in speed between the engine and the road wheels will not be so great; so that if the engine speed remains constant the vehicle will travel at a greater speed.

THE BACK AXLE

This consists of a casing which houses the toothed wheels necessary to change the direction of the drive supplied by the engine, through the transmission shaft, to two short axles or half shafts which carry the road wheels. Also by an additional arrangement of meshed wheels within the " gearbox " or differential, the two half axles are permitted to rotate at varying speeds though transmitting power continuously. In cornering, the outer wheel is required to travel a greater distance than the inner wheel and therefore revolves a greater number of times. If this latter provision were not made the inner wheel would skid on the road and cause great strain to the axle.

In a motor-car an electric current is required to provide a spark for ignition. This energy is generated by a dynamo driven by the engine which charges an accumulator. This also supplies the current required to operate the self-starter motor. The accumulator also provides electric current for the lamps, horn, trafficators, and sometimes for the windscreen wiper, radio, heater and fuel pump. On some cars, particularly those of earlier make, ignition is brought about by a spark produced by an engine-driven magneto, instead of by an induction coil fed with electricity from an accumulator.

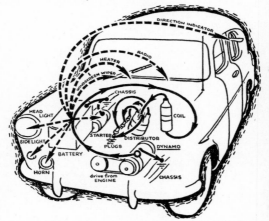

DIAGRAM OF THE ELECTRICAL SYSTEM

The *Coil* converts 6 or 12 volts supplied by the battery into the 10,000 (approx.) volts necessary to jump the gap at the sparking plugs.

The *Distributor* is a device which conveys the current to the sparking plugs in a fixed sequence.

GLOSSARY OF TECHNICAL TERMS NOT DESCRIBED IN THE TEXT

MEASUREMENTS

h.p.	The unit of work used to calculate the power output of an engine. 1 horse-power = 33,000 ft.lb./min. (1 French horse-power = 32,549 ft.lb./min.)
b.h.p.	Brake horse-power. The power delivered at the engine flywheel without frictional losses in transmission. (Due to a difference in the method of calculation, U.S. figures are slightly higher than those of Great Britain. Also some U.S. makers give the figure with the engine " stripped " of some components, therefore raising their figure above others.)
R.A.C.h.p.	(Not now used.) A horse-power rating figure obtained by the use of a formula for taxation purposes. $\dfrac{b^2 n}{2 \cdot 5}$ where b = bore (diameter of the cylinders in inches) and n = number of cylinders.
k.p.h.	Kilometres per hour.
m.p.g.	Miles per gallon of fuel.
m.p.h.	Miles per hour.
Compression ratio	The expression for the difference between the enclosed volume left above the piston when it has reached its lowest position of travel, and the volume of the combustion chamber when the piston has arrived at its highest position.
Cubic capacity	This is the volume left above the piston when at its lowest position, but not including the volume of the combustion chamber. This is expressed in cubic centimetres or cubic inches and is sometimes known as piston displacement or swept volume.

To convert cubic inches to cubic centimetres multiply by 16·39.

Wheel-base	The distance between the centres of the front and rear wheel axles as seen from the side of the car.

Track	The distance from the centre of one front tyre to the centre of the other or the measurement between the centres of the rear tyres.
Turning circle	The diameter of the circle described by a car when the steering is fully over one way (full " lock ").
Dry weight	Weight of a car without fuel, oil and water.
Kerb weight	Weight of a car with full amount of fuel, oil and water.
1 millimetre	= ·03937 of an inch (or $\frac{1}{25}$ of an inch approx.).
1 inch	= 25·4 millimetres (or ·025 metre).
1 kilometre	= ·6214 of a mile (or $\frac{5}{8}$ of a mile approx.).
1 litre	= 1·76 pints.
1 Imperial gallon	= 4·546 litres.
1 U.S. gallon	= ·832 Imperial gallon.

ENGINE

Diesel engine	Termed a compression-ignition engine, it depends upon the heat generated by compression to fire the fuel, which in this case is diesel oil.
Gas-turbine engine	This engine is still in an experimental stage. It may be powered by a number of fuels and relies upon continuous combustion and expansion, the results of explosion being directed on to vaned wheels or rotors. (See Rover historical notes.)
" F " Head	An engine cylinder block with side exhaust valve and overhead inlet valve.
" L " Head	An engine cylinder block with both valves on one side of the engine block.
" T " Head	Exhaust valve on one side of engine, inlet on the other.
" Straight " engine	An engine whose cylinders are arranged in line.
" V " engine	An engine whose cylinders are arranged in two banks at an angle to the crankshaft.

O.H.V.	Overhead valve.
O.H.C.	Overhead camshaft.
Crankshaft	The shaft which carries the cranks to which the pistons are joined by their connecting rods.
Fluid drive or coupling	A form of clutch which depends for its drive on the close proximity of two vaned wheels housed in an oil bath.
Pre-selector gearbox	A device which enables the driver to select a gear before needing it and then merely to depress the clutch pedal when he requires to bring it into operation.
Automatic gearbox	Of this there are many variations, some electrical, some hydraulic, which select the necessary gear according to the prevalent speed, load and road conditions.
Poppet valve	A valve consisting of a mushroom-shaped head on the end of a stem of metal, operated by a cam.
Slide or Sleeve valve	Consists of one or more concentric sliding sleeves placed between the cylinder and the piston, which, by sliding up and down, open and close the intake and exhaust ports.

COACHWORK

Aerodynamics	The study of the behaviour of wind as it passes round a body—usually carried out with the aid of a wind-tunnel.
Air-intake	The opening at the front of the car, allowing air to enter the radiator.
Louvre	A slatted air-intake or orifice.
Razor edge	The description given to a bodywork which is designed with square edges.
Rubbing-strip	The chromium strip sometimes fitted along the sides of a body.
Running-board	A long flat board which serves as a foot-step for passengers.

ABARTH

ITALY

Abarth and Co.,
Corso March N 38,
Turin,
Italy.

Current Models: *Fiat Abarth 595 & 595/34.* 2-door Saloons. *Fiat Abarth 695 & 695 SS.* 2-door Saloons. *Fiat Abarth 700.* Bialbero GT Coupé. *Fiat Abarth 850 TC Corsa.* 2-door Saloon. *Fiat Abarth OT 850/150.* 2-door Saloon. *Fiat Abarth 1000.* 2-door Saloon, Bialbero GT Coupé. *Fiat Abarth OT 1000.* 2-door Saloon. *Fiat Abarth OT 1600.* 2-door Saloon. *Abarth Simca 1150 SS.* 4-door Saloon. *Abarth Simca 1300.* GT Coupé. *Abarth Simca 2000.* GT Coupé.

Fiat Abarth 1000 Bialbero GT Coupé: Number of cylinders 4 (Fiat with twin overhead camshafts). Cubic capacity 982·216 c.c. Compression ratio 10·8 : 1. B.H.P. 104. Max. m.p.h. 135. Overall length 11 ft. 5 in. Overall width 4 ft. 7½ in. Height 3 ft. 9 9/10 in. Wheel-base 6 ft. 6¾ in. Track 3 ft. 11⅗ in.

(front and rear). Fuel tank capacity 9·9 Imp. gals. (other capacities available). Weight 1254 lb.

Appearance: Small car with tiny, oval intake in nose set low and flanked by headlamps beneath large, transparent fairings. Rounded tail with small, oblong tail-lamps and louvres for cooling air outlet. Twin exhaust pipes project from beneath tail. Cast wheels are spoked, have large slots and no hub-caps.

Fiat Abarth OT 1600 Saloon: Number of cylinders 4 (Fiat with twin overhead camshafts). Cubic capacity 1591·611 c.c. Compression ratio 9·5 : 1. B.H.P. 154. Max. m.p.h. 135. Overall length 11 ft. 8¾ in. Overall width 5 ft. 5⅖ in. Height 4 ft. 5½ in. Wheel-base 6 ft. 8 in. Track 3 ft. 9$\frac{7}{10}$ in. (front), 4 ft. 4 in. (rear). Weight 1672 lb.

Appearance: Bodywork is basically Fiat 850 but note distinctive frontal intake. Headlamps set into body front with side/indicator lamps below. Straight-through wing line to squared off tail-panel with high-set, circular tail-lamps. Note large flanges on rear wheel arches to clear massive tyres. Cast, spoked wheels.

Abarth Simca 1300 GT Coupé: Number of cylinders 4 (Simca with twin overhead camshafts). Cubic capacity 1288·364 c.c. B.H.P. 138. Max. m.p.h. 142. Overall length 11 ft. 8 in. Overall width 4 ft. 10$\frac{9}{10}$ in. Height 3 ft. 8½ in. Wheel-base 6 ft. 10$\frac{9}{32}$ in. Track 4 ft. 1⅗ in. (front and rear). Fuel tank capacity 6·6 Imp. gals. (other capacities available). Weight 1397 lb.

Appearance: Small, low-set oval intake with further intake below is flanked by twin scoop intakes. Headlamps beneath transparent fairings, straight-through wings to rounded tail and further scoop intakes behind windows. Large, almost flat rear window in roof line. Large section tyres at rear, cast, spoked wheels.

Abarth Simca 2000 Coupé: Number of cylinders 4 (Simca with twin overhead camshafts). Cubic capacity 1946·272 c.c. B.H.P. 202. Max. m.p.h. 167. Overall length 11 ft. 10$\frac{1}{10}$ in. Overall width 4 ft. 10$\frac{1}{4}$ in. Height 3 ft. 11$\frac{3}{5}$ in. Wheelbase 6 ft. 10$\frac{9}{32}$ in. Track 4 ft. 2 in. (front), 4 ft. 3$\frac{1}{5}$ in. (rear). Fuel tank capacity 9·9 Imp. gals. (other capacities available). Weight 1463 lb.

Appearance: Low-set, slot intake in nose, " bonnet " slopes gently down between headlamps behind transparent fairings. Note " turned-up " deflector at rear tip of body. Fuel tank filler set in almost horizontal rear window. Distinctive cast wheels.

A.C.

GREAT BRITAIN

A.C. Cars Limited,
  Thames Ditton,
  Surrey, England.

History: The A.C. company commenced operations with a small three-wheeled commercial vehicle known as the " Autocarrier ", not making its first passenger model, the A.C. " Tricar " with a single-cylinder air-cooled engine, until 1909.

The first four-wheeled model appeared just before the First World War and its four-cylinder Anzani engine was soon replaced by a six-cylinder engine largely designed by S. F. Edge. Many records were taken by this model, including a speed of 104·19 m.p.h. in 1924, and a car driven by Gillett covered 2000 miles at an average speed of 82·58 m.p.h. Aluminium was largely used in the 1919 six and this proved so successful that it has remained the basic type of A.C. power unit ever since.

Four models were offered in 1928, powered by four- and six-cylinder engines, and in 1930 the " Royal " and " Magna " models were produced, using the 1991 c.c. six-cylinder engine. In 1934 the " Ace " and " Ace Sports " appeared.

In 1939 four models were offered, including the 16/80 Sports which was also available with a supercharger. By 1955 six models were in production and the " Ace " and " Aceca " Coupé were made available fitted with the Bristol 2-litre engine.

Current Model: *Cobra*. 2-seater Sports.

A.C. Cobra Sports: Number of cylinders V8 (Ford). Cubic capacity 4727 c.c. Compression ratio 11 : 1. B.H.P. 280. Max. m.p.h. 153. Overall length 12 ft. 7½ in. Overall width 5 ft. 1 in. Height 4 ft. 1 in. (to top of hood), 2 ft. 11 in. (to top of scuttle). Turning circle 34 ft. Wheel-base 7 ft. 6 in.

Track 4 ft. 3½ in. (front), 4 ft. 4½ in. (rear).   Fuel tank capacity 13 Imp. gals.   Kerb weight 2020 lb,

Appearance: Sleek, sporting lines.   Small, oval radiator air-intake is thrust forward and is flanked by vertical "overriders". Prominent headlamps.   Flowing wing line rises over rear wheels. Rounded tail. Wheel-arches have prominent flanges to cover large-section tyres.   Wire wheels have "knock-off" hub-caps.

ACADIAN

CANADA

General Motors of Canada,
Oshawa,
Ontario,
Canada.

Current Models: *Beaumont.* 2- and 4-door Sedans, Convertible. ***Beaumont De Luxe.*** 2- and 4-door Sedans, Station Wagon. ***Beaumont Custom.*** 4-door Sedan, Sport Coupé, Convertible, Station Wagon. ***Beaumont Sport De Luxe.*** Coupé, Convertible. ***Invader.*** 2- and 4-door Sedans, Station Wagon. ***Canso.*** 4-door Sedan, Sport Coupé, Station Wagon. ***Canso Sport De Luxe.*** Coupé.

Acadian Beaumont Custom Sport Coupé: 6 or V8. Cubic capacity 194 cu. in. (6), 283 cu. in. (V8), (230 cu. in. (6), 327 cu. in. (V8) optional). Compression ratio 8·5 : 1 (6), 9·25 : 1 (V8), (8·5 : 1 (6), 10·5 : 1 (V8) optional). B.H.P. 120 or 195, (140 (6), 250 and 300 (V8) optional). Overall length 16 ft. 4⅜ in. Overall width 6 ft. 2⅗ in. Height 4 ft. 4⅘ in. Turning circle 41·9 ft. Wheel-base 9 ft. 7 in. Track 4 ft. 10 in. (front and rear). Fuel tank capacity 16⅔ Imp. gals.

Appearance: Full-width divided radiator air-intake with inset horizontally barred grille and paired headlamps. Plain bumper has long slots and side/indicator lamps at ends. Broad, flat

31

bonnet, straight-through, flowing wing line to long rear deck. Slightly curved windscreen, narrow roof line and well-raked rear window. Horizontal tail-lamps and rear bumper echoes frontal treatment. Wheel discs have long radial slots.

Acadian Invader 2-door Sedan: Number of cylinders 4 (6 and V8 optional). Cubic capacity 153 cu. in. (194 cu. in. (6), 283 cu. in. and 327 cu. in. (V8) optional). Compression ratio 8·5 : 1 (8·5 : 1, 9·25 : 1 and 10·5 : 1 optional). B.H.P. 90 (120, 195 and 250 optional). Overall length 15 ft. 2 $\frac{9}{10}$ in. Overall width 5 ft. 9 $\frac{9}{10}$ in. Height 4 ft. 7 in. Turning circle 38·4 ft. Wheel-base 9 ft. 2 in. Track 4 ft. 8 $\frac{1}{5}$ in. (front), 4 ft. 8 $\frac{3}{10}$ in. (rear). Fuel tank capacity 13 $\frac{1}{2}$ Imp. gals.

Appearance: Neat, uncluttered styling. Full-width radiator air-intake with inset grille is divided by central bar and has headlamps at ends. Simple bumper mounting side/indicator lamps. Straight-through wing line to " wedge " shaped rear styling. Deep windscreen and rather angular passenger area. Disc wheels have large, domed hub-caps

ALFA ROMEO

ITALY

Alfa Romeo s.p.a.,
Via Gattamelata, 45,
Milan,
Italy.

Current Models: *Giulietta t.i.* 4-door Berlina. *Sprint 1300.* Coupé. *Giulia 1300.* 4-door Berlina. *Giulia 1600.* 4-door Berlina t.i., 4-door Berlina t.i. Super, Sprint Coupé, Sprint G.T. Coupé, Spider 2-seater Sports, SS Coupé, TZ Coupé. *2600.* 4-door Berlina, Sprint Coupé, Spider 2 + 2 Sports.

Alfa Romeo Giulia 1600 Berlina t.i.: Number of cylinders 4. Cubic capacity 1570 c.c. Compression ratio 9 : 1. B.H.P. 92 (112 Super). Max. m.p.h. 105 (115). Overall length 13 ft. 10 in. Overall width 5 ft. 1 in. Height 4 ft. 8 in. Turning circle 35 ft. 9 in. Wheel-base 8 ft. 3 in. Track 4 ft. 3½ in. (front), 4 ft. 2 in. (rear). Fuel tank capacity 10 Imp. gals. Dry weight 2184 lb. (2016 lb.).

Appearance: Angular and unusual styling. Full-width radiator air-intake features paired headlamps and small, vertical " grille " in centre. Large, upright passenger area. Squared-off rear panel is slightly inset and tail-lamps are large and rectangular. Perforated disc wheels have large, domed hub-caps.

C   33

Alfa Romeo Giulia 1600 Sprint G.T. Coupé: Number of cylinders 4. Cubic capacity 1570 c.c. Compression ratio 9 : 1. B.H.P. 106. Max. m.p.h. 112 plus. Overall length 13 ft. 5 in. Overall width 5 ft. 2 in. Height 4 ft. 4 in. Turning circle 32 ft. Wheel-base 7 ft. 9 in. Track 4 ft. 3½ in. (front), 4 ft. 2 in. (rear). Fuel tank capacity 10¼ Imp. gals. Dry weight 2094 lb.

Appearance: Full-width radiator air-intake which includes headlamps and has vertical side-lamps at ends. Note rather "sculptured" look of bodywork. Straight-through wings to large almost square tail-lamp clusters mounted on slightly concave tail-panel. Deep windscreen and narrow roof line. Perforated disc wheels.

Alfa Romeo Giulia 1600 SS Coupé: Number of cylinders 4. Cubic capacity 1570 c.c. Compression ratio 9 : 1. B.H.P. 112. Max. m.p.h. 125 plus. Overall length 13 ft. 6 in.

Overall width 5 ft. 5 in.   Wheel-base 7 ft. 4 in.   Track 4 ft. 3 in. (front), 4 ft. 2 in. (rear).   Fuel tank capacity 17¼ Imp. gals. Dry weight 2097 lb.

Appearance: Well streamlined bodywork.   Thrust-forward, narrow radiator air-intake with small central " grille ".   Flat bonnet slopes down between large headlamps.   Well-raked, wrap-around windscreen; rear body line with large window slopes gently down.   Flat rear panel is slightly inset and mounts paired, circular tail-lamps.   Perforated disc wheels.

Alfa Romeo Giulia 1600 TZ Sports/Racing Coupé: Number of cylinders 4.   Cubic capacity 1570 c.c.   Compression ratio 9 : 1.   B.H.P. 112.   Max. m.p.h. 137 plus.   Overall length 12 ft. 7 in.   Overall width 4 ft. 11 in.   Height 4 ft.   Wheel-base 7 ft. 2 in.   Track 4 ft. 3 in. (front and rear).   Fuel tank capacity 21 Imp. gals.

Appearance: Narrow, thrust-forward radiator air-intake in rounded nose is flanked by headlamps beneath transparent fairings.   Streamlined, well-raked windscreen to gently rounded roof line—rear window is almost flat.   Note slight " lip " at tail; rear panel is flat and inset, has circular tail-lamps.   Perforated disc wheels do not have hub-caps.

Alfa Romeo 2600 Sprint Coupé: Number of cylinders 6. Cubic capacity 2584 c.c.   Compression ratio 9 : 1.   B.H.P. 145.   Max. m.p.h. 125.   Overall length 14 ft. 4 in.   Overall width 5 ft. 7 in.   Height 4 ft. 4 in.   Turning circle 38 ft. Wheel-base 8 ft. 5 in.   Track 4 ft. 7 in. (front), 4 ft. 6 in. (rear).   Fuel tank capacity 13 Imp. gals.   Dry weight 2550 lb.

Appearance: Full-width radiator air-intake with inset horizontally barred grille and paired headlamps at ends.   Small, pointed " Alfa Romeo " radiator air-intake centrally mounted on grille.   Straight-through wings to oval tail-lamps.   Flat bonnet with small slot air-intake.   Well-raked windscreen and

rear window. Short tail. Rear wheels partially enclosed.
Small, oblong side-lamps mounted on front bumper.

Alfa Romeo 2600 Spider: Number of cylinders 6. Cubic
capacity 2584 c.c. Compression ratio 9 : 1. B.H.P. 145.
Max. m.p.h. 125. Overall length 14 ft. 4 in. Overall width
5 ft. 5 in. Height 4 ft. 4½ in. Turning circle 36 ft. Wheel-
base 8 ft. 2 in. Track 4 ft. 7 in. (front), 4 ft. 6 in. (rear).
Fuel tank capacity 13 Imp. gals. Dry weight 2530 lb.

Appearance: Low and sporting. Tiny vertical radiator air-
intake is flanked by large, horizontally barred intakes having
spot-lamps at ends. Straight-through wing line to large,
vertical tail-lamp clusters. Bumpers front and rear are plain.
Bonnet has narrow intake and flows down between slightly
thrust-forward headlamps. Perforated disc wheels have large
hub-caps.

ALPINE

FRANCE

Société des Automobiles Alpine,
13, rue Forest,
Paris, 18,
France.

Current Models: *Type A.108.* Cabriolet, Coupé Sport,
Coupé GT 4, Berlinette " Tour de France ". ***Type A.110.***
Cabriolet, Coupé Sport, Coupé GT 4, Berlinette " Tour de
France ".

Alpine Type A.110 Coupé GT 4. Number of cylinders 4
(Renault). Cubic capacity 1108 c.c. Compression ratio
9·6 : 1. B.H.P. 66. Max. m.p.h. 96. Overall length 13 ft.
3½ in. Overall width 4 ft. 11 in. Height 4 ft. 1⅓ in. Turning
circle 30 ft. Wheel-base 7 ft. 5⅖ in. Track 4 ft. 1⅕ in. (front),
4 ft. (rear). Weight 1320 lb. (approx.).

Appearance: Small, shapely car with generally rounded contours. Note lack of frontal air-intake due to rear-mounted
engine. " Bonnet " is flat and slopes gently down to wrap-
around bumper with raised central portion. Headlamps set
beneath transparent fairings; straight-through wing line to
flat tail panel on which are mounted large, horizontal tail-
lamps. Deep, curved windscreen and well-raked rear window.
Perforated disc wheels have triple-eared " knock-off " hub-caps.

ALVIS

GREAT BRITAIN

Alvis Limited,
Holyhead Road,
Coventry, England.

History: The Alvis company was founded by the late Mr. T. G. John, a naval architect and experienced engineer, in Coventry in 1919; the first car—a four-cylinder known as the " 10/30 "—was produced the following year, being successively increased in power, first to " 12/40 " and then to " 12/50 ".

From the beginning the Alvis car followed the ideal of its creator, Captain G. T. Smith-Clarke. Two years after the first Alvis had been made, the company decided to enter for racing and reliability trials. In 1921 Alvis won twelve trophy cups and thirty-five gold medals.

The real fame of Alvis as a successful sports car may be said to have begun with the famous " Twelve-fifty " model, which had an overhead-valve four-cylinder engine, giving the car a maximum speed of over 70 m.p.h. This car was introduced in 1923.

A reputation for technical enterprise was rapidly gained, and the first British front-wheel-drive car, the first British production model with independent front suspension, and the first British all-synchro-mesh four-speed gearbox were later produced by the firm.

In 1928 three four-cylinder 12/60 models and one six-cylinder 14/75 model were produced. In 1929 five four-cylinder models and one six-cylinder rated at 14·75 h.p. were offered. In 1930 one 12/50 four-cylinder, two six-cylinders each of 16·95 h.p. and one eight-cylinder of 15·0 h.p. were available.

For 1931 seven types were produced, including one eight-cylinder model. The following year the famous " Speed Twenty " series was commenced, the eight-cylinder car being dropped. In 1937 the very fast 3½-litre " Speed Twenty-five " was introduced and by 1953 production was concentrated on a 3-litre six-cylinder model.

Current Models: *TE 21 3-litre (Series III).*   2-door Saloon, Coupé.

Alvis 3-litre (Series III) Saloon: Number of cylinders 6. Cubic capacity 2993 c.c.   Compression ratio 8·5 : 1.   B.H.P. 130.   Max. m.p.h. 100 plus.   Overall length 15 ft. 8½ in. Overall width 5 ft. 6 in.   Height 5 ft.   Turning circle 39 ft. Wheel-base 9 ft. 3½ in.   Track 4 ft. 7⅝ in. (front), 4 ft. 6⅛ in. (rear).   Fuel tank capacity 14·3 Imp. gals.   Dry weight 29 cwt. (approx.).

Appearance: Vertically paired headlamps flank traditional radiator shell blended into modern coachwork. Straight-through wing line to vertical tail-lamp clusters. Note lack of bright trim to bodywork. Faintly " suggested " rear wings. Rounded passenger area with curved windscreen.   Disc wheels standard, wire wheels with " knock-off " hub-caps optional.

AMPHICAR

GERMANY

ACV Amphicar Vertriebsgesellschaft mbH,
56 Wuppertal-Elberfeld,
Hofaue 81,
West Germany.

Current Model: *Model 770.* 2-door Amphibious Vehicle.

Amphicar Model 770: Number of cylinders 4 (Triumph). Cubic capacity 1147 c.c. Compression ratio 8 : 1. B.H.P. 38·3. Max. m.p.h. 75 (on land), 7·5 (on water). Overall length 14 ft. 3 in. Overall width 5 ft. 1 in. Height 5 ft. Turning circle 36 ft. 10 in. Wheel-base 7 ft. Track 4 ft. (front), 4 ft. 1 in. (rear). Fuel tank capacity 10½ Imp. gals. Kerb weight 2315 lb.

Appearance: Slightly pointed front, sharply cut-away beneath. Note rather high ground clearance. Slightly hooded headlamps, straight-through wing line to canted fins and vertical tail-lamp clusters. High-set bumpers front and rear wth twin propellers beneath tail. Rows of louvres across tail. Curved windscreen and convertible fabric top. Perforated disc wheels have large hub-caps.

APAL

BELGIUM

Application Polyestere Armé Liège S.p.r.l.,
25, rue de la Fontaine,
Blegny-Trembleur,
Belgium.

Current Models: *1200, 1200 S.* 2 + 2 2-door Saloon.
1300 TVS. 2 + 2 2-door Saloon.

Apal 1200 Saloon: Number of cylinders Flat-4 (Volkswagen).
Cubic capacity 1192 c.c. Compression ratio 7 : 1. B.H.P. 40.
Max. m.p.h. 80. Overall length 13 ft. $11\frac{3}{10}$ in. Overall width
5 ft. $3\frac{4}{5}$ in. Height 4 ft. $1\frac{1}{5}$ in. Turning circle 36 ft. Wheel-
base 7 ft. $10\frac{1}{2}$ in. Track 4 ft. $3\frac{2}{5}$ in. (front), 4 ft. $2\frac{7}{10}$ in. (rear).
Fuel tank capacity 8·8 Imp. gals. Weight 1496 lb.

Appearance: Attractive-looking car based on Volkswagen.
Thrust-forward nose with inset lamps; divided front bumper
and headlamps set into wings. Straight-through wing line rises
over rear wheels. Well-raked, curved windscreen, gently
sloping roof line and large rear window. Air outlet in rounded
tail; divided rear bumpers. Perforated wheel discs and prominent hub-caps.

ASA

ITALY

Autocostruzioni Societa per Azioni,
Via S. Faustino 65,
Milan,
Italy.

Current Model: *1000 G.T.* Coupé Bertone.

ASA 1000 G.T. Coupe Bertone: Number of cylinders 4. Cubic capacity 1032 c.c. Compression ratio 9·1 : 1. B.H.P. 97. Max. m.p.h. 118. Overall length 12 ft. 8 in. Overall width 4 ft. 11 in. Height 3 ft. 11¼ in. Turning circle 32 ft. Wheel-base 7 ft. 2½ in. Track 4 ft. ¼ in. (front), 4 ft. ¾ in. (rear). Fuel tank capacity 13·2 Imp. gals. Dry weight 1720 lb.

Appearance: Graceful, well proportioned lines. Low-set, divided slot radiator air-intake has sidelamps at ends and inset grille. Headlamps very slightly inset, straight-through wing line to narrow flat tail-panel with large, paired tail-lamps. Gently sloping bonnet. Deep, well-raked windscreen, domed roof line and large rear window. Perforated disc wheels have triple-eared " knock-off " hub-caps.

ASTON MARTIN

GREAT BRITAIN

Aston Martin Lagonda Ltd.,

    Newport Pagnell,

      Buckinghamshire,

        England.

History: The Aston Martin history began with a small, fast sports car made by W. Bamford and Lionel Martin in 1914. After 1918 the car was put into production and achieved immediate success in racing circles.

As early as 1921, when the first Aston Martin car was driven by H. Kensington-Moir at a rate of 86·21 m.p.h., a very high standard was set up by the firm. In the late 1920's it changed hands, and under racing driver A. C. Bertelli produced a new 1½-litre model with an overhead camshaft engine, which achieved a grand series of successes at Le Mans.

The company was re-incorporated in 1947 in the David Brown group, and its immediate post-war production centred on a 2-litre model with push-rod-operated overhead valves and independent suspension, the chassis constructed from square-section steel tubing. Later, a six-cylinder twin overhead-camshaft Lagonda engine was mounted in this chassis, and thus was born the famous Aston Martin " DB-2 " which has piled up successes in international races ever since. It was later supplanted to some extent by the " DB-3 ", which appeared in 1951, to re-appear two years later as the " DB-3S ", and as the " DB2-4 " in 1954.

Current Models: *DB.5*. 2-door Saloon, Convertible.

Aston Martin DB5 Convertible: Number of cylinders 6. Cubic capacity 3995 c.c. Compression ratio 8·9 : 1. B.H.P. 282. Max. m.p.h. 150 plus. Overall length 15 ft. Overall width 5 ft. 6 in. Height 4 ft. 5 in. Turning circle 34 ft. Wheel-base 8 ft. 2 in. Track 4 ft. 6 in. (front), 4 ft. 5½ in.

(rear). Fuel tank capacity 16 Imp. gals. Kerb weight 3233 lb.

Appearance: Lines are sleek, sporting. Wide radiator air-intake has thinly barred grille. Headlamps beneath transparent fairings; straight-through wing line to vertical tail-lamps. Note air-intake on bonnet top. Convertible fabric top —may be seen fitted with hardtop having large rear window. Longish rear deck. Wire wheels have " knock-off " hub-caps.

AUSTIN

AUSTRALIA

British Motor Corporation (Aus.) Pty. Ltd.,

Joynton Avenue,

Zetland,

Sydney, N.S.W.,

Australia.

Current Models: *Freeway.* 4-door Saloon, Station Wagon.

Austin Freeway Saloon: Number of cylinders 6. Cubic capacity 2433 c.c. Compression ratio 8·2 : 1. B.H.P. 85. Overall length 14 ft. 10 in. Overall width 5 ft. 3½ in. Height 4 ft. 11 in. Turning circle 37 ft. Wheel-base 8 ft. 4 3/16 in. Track 4 ft. 2½ in. (front), 4 ft. 3⅜ in. (rear). Fuel tank capacity 10 Imp. gals.

Appearance: Generally similar to A.60 but note differing frontal treatment. Full-width radiator air-intake with grille of thin bars and incorporating oblong side/indicator lamps. Headlamps are high-set; straight-through wing line rises slightly at rear to form " fins "; pointed vertical tail-lamp clusters. Angular styling of bumpers; those at rear wrap around to wheel arches. Disc wheels have plain hub-caps.

AUSTIN

The Austin Motor Co., Ltd., Longbridge Works, Northfield, Birmingham, England.

History: Herbert Austin (later Lord Austin) emigrated to Australia as a youth. Subsequently he met Frederick Wolseley, and joined the Wolseley Sheep-shearing Company. In 1893, on his return to England, he designed his very first car—on behalf of the Wolseley company—a three-wheeler. Other Wolseley cars followed, but in 1905 he started his own car manufacturing business at Longbridge, near Birmingham, where, forty years later, the millionth Austin car left the production line. Austin's first car was a 25/30 h.p. model with some very interesting features, several of which were to be widely adopted in the future. The chassis frame incorporated the engine sub-frame, and the four-cylinder vertical engine had separate cylinders with " T " type heads in which detachable valve-covers allowed the valves to be easily withdrawn for grinding-in. The car was chain-driven, as was the method in those far-off days, and had a four-speed gearbox controlled by a lever on the right-hand side of the driver.

Austin's very first car made a non-stop run in the dramatic Scottish Reliability Trial of 1906, whilst the second car made won the Hundred Guinea Dunlop Challenge Cup in the Irish Reliability Trial, and another Austin won the Wolverhampton Hill Climb.

Perhaps the most famous models produced between the two wars were the " Twelve-fours " and, of course, the immortal " Seven ". There were also the Austin " Tens " which went into production again in 1946 and remained among the most popular of small British cars until they were superseded by the " A.40 ".

The four-cylinder Cambridge and six-cylinder West-minster were introduced in 1955. In 1956 the high-performance A.105 saloon was introduced.

Current Models: *Mini.* Standard and Super De Luxe 2-door Saloons, Countryman. *Mini-Cooper.* 2-door Saloon. *Mini-Cooper "S" 1000.* 2-door Saloon. *Mini-Cooper "S" 1275.* 2-door Saloon. *A.40 Mk. II.* Standard and Super De Luxe 2-door Saloons, Countryman. *1100.* Standard and De Luxe 4-door Saloons. *A.60 Cambridge.* Standard and De Luxe 4-door Saloons, Countryman. *1800.* Standard and De Luxe 4-door Saloons. *A.110 Westminster Mk. II.* Standard, De Luxe and Super De Luxe 4-door Saloons. *Gipsy.* Short and Long Wheel-base Utilities and Hardtops.

Austin Mini Saloon: Number of cylinders 4. Cubic capacity 848 c.c. (998 c.c. Cooper, 970 c.c. and 1275 c.c. "S"). Compression ratio 8·3 : 1 (9 : 1 Cooper, 10 : 1 and 9·75 : 1 "S"). B.H.P. 34 (55, 65 and 76). Max. m.p.h. 73 (87, 92 and 100). Overall length 10 ft. $\frac{1}{4}$ in. Overall width 4 ft. 7$\frac{1}{2}$ in. Height 4 ft. 5 in. Turning circle 31 ft. 7 in. Wheel-base 6 ft. 8 in. Track 3 ft. 11$\frac{1}{2}$ in. (front), 3 ft. 9$\frac{4}{5}$ in. (rear), (3 ft. 10$\frac{3}{10}$ in. (rear) Cooper). Fuel tank capacity 5$\frac{1}{2}$ Imp. gals. Weight (unladen) 11$\frac{1}{2}$ cwt. (12$\frac{1}{2}$ cwt. Cooper) (approx.).

1098 c.c. Compression ratio 8·5 : 1. B.H.P. 48. Overall length 12 ft. 2¾ in. Overall width 5 ft. ⅖ in. Height 4 ft. 5 in. Turning circle 34 ft. 9 in. Wheel-base 7 ft. 9½ in. Track 4 ft. 3½ in. (front), 4 ft. 2$\frac{9}{10}$ in. (rear). Fuel tank capacity 8½ Imp. gals. Weight (unladen) 16¼ cwt. (approx.).

Appearance: Familiar Austin " rippled " grille in oblong air-intake. Large, high-set headlamps; broad, flat bonnet. Deep windscreen; rear body panel raked forward between vertical tail-lamp clusters. Large passenger area. Simple bumpers. Disc wheels have projecting centres.

Austin A.60 Cambridge Saloon: Number of cylinders 4 (petrol or diesel). Cubic capacity 1622 c.c. or 1489 c.c. Compression ratio 8·3 : 1 (7·2 : 1 available) or 23 : 1. B.H.P. 61 or 40. Overall length 14 ft. 6½ in. Overall width 5 ft. 3½ in. Height 4 ft. 10$\frac{1}{10}$ in. Turning circle 37 ft. Wheel-base 8 ft. 4¼ in. Track 4 ft. 2⅗ in. (front), 4 ft. 3⅖ in. (rear). Fuel tank capacity 10 Imp. gals. Weight (unladen) 22¼ cwt. (approx.).

Appearance: Full-width radiator air-intake, with mesh grille incorporates side/indi-cator lamps; headlamps slightly hooded. Straight-through wing line to vertical, pointed tail-lamp units. Sim-ple bumpers with tiny over-riders. Broad, flat bonnet, deep windscreen and rear window. Disc wheels have plain, flat hub-caps.

Austin 1800 Saloon: Number of cylinders 4. Cubic capacity 1798 c.c. Compression ratio 8·2 : 1. B.H.P. 84. Overall length 13 ft. 8$\frac{3}{16}$ in. Overall width 5 ft. 7 in. Height 4 ft. 7$\frac{1}{2}$ in. Turning circle 37 ft. Wheel-base 8 ft. 10 in. Track 4 ft. 8$\frac{1}{2}$ in. (front), 4 ft. 7$\frac{1}{2}$ in. (rear). Fuel tank capacity 10$\frac{3}{4}$ Imp. gals. Weight (unladen) 22·6 cwt. (approx.).

Appearance: Bears strong family likeness to 1100 but note generally sleeker appearance. Narrow, full-width air-intake has inset mesh grille. Headlamps are high and inset. Short, broad bonnet has shallow intake. Curved windscreen, long passenger area and curved rear window with slight " peak " over. Well-raked tail panel. Wheel trims are perforated, hub-caps plain.

Austin A.110 Westminster Mk. II Saloon: Number of cylinders 6. Cubic capacity 2912 c.c. Compression ratio 8·3 : 1 (7·3 : 1 available). B.H.P. 120. Overall length 15 ft. 7$\frac{1}{4}$ in. Overall width 5 ft. 8$\frac{1}{2}$ in. Height 4 ft. 10$\frac{1}{2}$ in. Turning circle 41 ft. Wheel-base 9 ft. 2 in. Track 4 ft. 7 in. (front), 4 ft. 5$\frac{1}{4}$ in. (rear). Fuel tank capacity 16 Imp. gals. Weight (unladen) 30 cwt. (approx.).

Appearance: Oblong radiator air-intake has simple, slightly inset mesh grille. Flat bonnet with small intake flows down between slightly thrust-forward headlamps. Straight-through wing line with slight rise behind rear doors to vertical tail-lamps. Well curved windscreen and rear window. Plain bumpers wrap-around. Disc wheels have large, flat hub-caps.

AUSTIN HEALEY

GREAT BRITAIN

The Austin Motor Co., Ltd.,
Longbridge Works, Northfield,
Birmingham, England.

Current Models: *Sprite Mk. III.* 2-seater Sports. *3000 Mk. III.* Sports Convertible.

Austin Healey Sprite Mk. III Sports: Number of cylinders 4. Cubic capacity 1098 c.c. Compression ratio 8·9 : 1 (8·1 : 1 available). B.H.P. 59. Max. m.p.h. 90 plus. Overall length 11 ft. 5$\frac{3}{5}$ in. Overall width 4 ft. 6$\frac{9}{10}$ in. Height 3 ft. 7 in. (to top of screen), 4 ft. $\frac{1}{2}$ in. (to top of hood). Turning circle 32 ft. Wheel-base 6 ft. 8 in. Track 3 ft. 9$\frac{3}{10}$ in. (front), 3 ft. 8$\frac{3}{4}$ in. (rear). Fuel tank capacity 6 Imp. gals. Weight (unladen) 14 cwt. (approx.).

Appearance: Full-width oblong radiator air-intake with mesh grille slightly inset. Flattish bonnet slopes gently down between large, rather thrust-forward head-lamps. Straight-through wing line to vertical tail-lamps. Rounded front and square-styled rear wheel arches. Perforated disc wheels or wire wheels with " knock-off " hub-caps.

Austin Healey 3000 Mk. III Sports Convertible: Number of cylinders 6. Cubic capacity 2912 c.c. Compression ratio 9·03 : 1. B.H.P. 150. Max. m.p.h. 120 (approx.). Overall length 13 ft. 1½ in. Overall width 5 ft. Height 3 ft. 10 in. (to top of screen), 4 ft. 2¾ in. (to top of hood). Turning circle 34 ft. 9 in. Wheel-base 7 ft. 8 in. Track 4 ft. 1 in. (front), 4 ft. 2 in. (rear). Fuel tank capacity 12 Imp. gals. Weight (unladen) 22¾ cwt. (approx.).

Appearance: Smoothly lined car of well balanced appearance. Oval radiator air-intake has grille of thin, outwardly " veed " vertical bars. Straight-through wings rising slightly at cockpit over rear wheels. Rounded tail, fluted bumpers with vertical overriders. Perforated disc wheels standard, " knock-off " wire wheels available.

AUTOBIANCHI

ITALY

Autobianchi S.p.A.,
Via Fabio Filzi, 24,
Milan.
Italy.

Current Model: *Primula.* 2-door Saloon.

Autobianchi Primula Saloon: Number of cylinders 4 (Fiat—transversely mounted, F.W.D.). Cubic capacity 1221 c.c. Compression ratio 8·1 : 1. B.H.P. 57. Overall length 12 ft. 5 in. Overall width 5 ft. 2$\frac{1}{10}$ in. Height 4 ft. 4$\frac{3}{4}$ in. Turning circle 34 ft. Wheel-base 7 ft. 6$\frac{1}{2}$ in. Track 4 ft. 4$\frac{2}{5}$ in. (front), 4 ft. 2$\frac{4}{5}$ in. (rear). Fuel tank capacity 8$\frac{3}{4}$ Imp. gals. Kerb weight 15$\frac{1}{2}$ cwt.

Appearance: Full-width, oblong radiator air-intake flanked by high-set headlamps. Straight-through wing line to projecting vertical tail-lamps. Short bonnet and large passenger area. Note how rear body panel is raked sharply forward and has large window. Plain bumpers have vertical, rubber-tipped overriders. Disc wheels have four perforations and plain hub-caps.

AUTO UNION

GERMANY

Auto Union G.m.b.H.,

Ingoldstadt, Düsseldorf 10,

Germany.

Current Models: *D.K.W. F.11.* 2-door Saloon. ***D.K.W. F.12.*** 2-door Saloon, Roadster. ***D.K.W. F 102.*** 2-door Saloon. ***Auto Union 1000 Sp.*** Roadster, Coupé.

D.K.W. F.11 Saloon: Number of cylinders 3. Cubic capacity 796 c.c. Compression ratio 7–7·25 : 1. B.H.P. 34. Overall length 13 ft. $\frac{11}{16}$ in. Overall width 5 ft. $2\frac{13}{64}$ in. Height 4 ft. $9\frac{1}{5}$ in. Turning circle 32 ft. 9 in. Wheel-base 7 ft. $4\frac{3}{5}$ in. Track 3 ft. $11\frac{1}{5}$ in. (front), 4 ft. $2\frac{2}{5}$ in. (rear). Fuel tank capacity 7·7 Imp. gals. Weight (unladen) 1609 lb. (1640 lb. with Saxomat automatic clutch and sunshine roof).

Appearance: Car appears to " sit on " its wheels. Narrow, full-width air-intake flanked by high-set headlamps. Straight-through wing line to vertical tail-lamp clusters. Prominent passenger area with large windows. Simple bumpers. Disc wheels have plain hub-caps.

D.K.W. F.12 Roadster: Number of cylinders 3. Cubic capacity 889 c.c. Compression ratio 7·25–7·5 : 1. B.H.P. 45. Overall length 13 ft. 3/10 in. Overall width 5 ft. 2 in. Height 4 ft. 2⅕ in. Turning circle 32 ft. 9 in. Wheel-base 7 ft. 4¾ in. Track 3 ft. 11⅜ in. (front), 4 ft. 2⅖ in. (rear). Fuel tank capacity 7·7 Imp. gals. Weight (unladen) 1624·4 lb.

Appearance: Very similar to F.11 Saloon but note body with convertible fabric top. Headlamps rather thrust-forward; rounded bonnet line and thick framing to rounded windscreen. Prominent flange over front wheel-arches and along lower edges of body is carried straight back over rear wheels. Simple, wrap-around bumpers front and rear.

D.K.W. F.102 Saloon: Number of cylinders 3. Cubic capacity 1175 c.c. Compression ratio 7·25–7·5 : 1. B.H.P. 60. Over-

all length 13 ft. 11½ in. Overall width 5 ft. 3⅜ in. Height 4 ft. 8 10/16 in. Turning circle 36 ft. Wheel-base 8 ft. 1⅜ in. Track 4 ft. 4 3/10 in. (front), 4 ft. 3⅕ in. (rear). Fuel tank capacity 11 Imp. gals. Kerb weight 1900 lb.

Appearance: Well-proportioned design. Full-width radiator air-intake has horizontally barred grille and headlamps at ends. Straight-through wing line; long, horizontal tail-lamp clusters. Simple, square-section bumpers wrap around. Plain, disc wheels.

Auto Union 1000 Sp. Coupé: Number of cylinders 3. Cubic capacity 981 c.c. Compression ratio 8 : 1. B.H.P. 55. Max. m.p.h. 90 (approx.). Overall length 13 ft. 8⅔ in. Overall width 5 ft. 6 1/10 in. Height 4 ft. 4⅕ in. Turning circle 36 ft. Wheel-base 7 ft. 8½ in. Track 4 ft. 3 in. (front), 4 ft. 5 3/32 in. (rear). Fuel tank capacity 11·2 Imp. gals. Weight (unladen) 2094 lb.

Appearance: Very low, rakish-looking car with narrow, wide air-intake having mesh grille. Narrow slot intake on rounded bonnet top. Straight-through wings to long, canted tail-fins and large, circular tail-lamps. Plain, divided front bumpers, one-piece rear bumper. Headlamps slightly thrust forward. Perforated disc wheels with large, domed hub-caps.

BENTLEY

GREAT BRITAIN

Bentley Motors (1931) Ltd.,
    14–15, Conduit Street,
    London, W.1, England.

History: A well-known designer of aircraft engines in the First World War, W. O. Bentley produced his first 3-litre cars in time to participate in the T.T. Races of 1922, where they swept their way into second, fourth and fifth places.

Subsequent models, the 6½-litre six-cylinder and the 8-litre six-cylinder, each gained fame in its own way. The 4½-litre four-cylinder, in its supercharged form, also performed amazing feats in the hands of Sir Henry Birkin. The company's reputation was built up on its racing successes such as those at the 1929 Le Mans Race, when the first four places were taken by Bentley cars.

In 1931 their entire assets were purchased by Messrs. Rolls Royce. Thereafter the accent was placed on silent and smooth running rather than speed alone; the first model produced under the new régime was the 3½-litre six-cylinder introduced in 1933 as the " silent sports car ".

This new model became very popular with the specialist coach-builders; but inevitably the need for more power arose, and by 1936 the size of the engine was increased to 4¼ litres, an overdrive being subsequently added which permitted cruising speeds of 80 m.p.h.

After the war the 4¼-litre Mark VI was introduced, having an " F " head with side exhaust and overhead inlet valves. From this model was developed the " Continental " with streamlined bodywork and a maximum speed of 120 m.p.h. An aluminium V8 engine was introduced in 1959.

Current Models: *Series S3.* 4-door Saloon, L.W.B. Saloon (with division), James Young L.W.B. Saloon, H. J. Mulliner Park Ward Convertible Coupé. ***Continental.*** H. J. Mulliner Park Ward 2-door Sports Saloon, " Flying Spur " 4-door

Sports Saloon and Convertible Coupé, James Young 4-door Saloon.

Bentley S3 Saloon: Number of cylinders V8. Cubic capacity 6230 c.c. Compression ratio 9 : 1 (8 : 1 available). B.H.P. not disclosed. Overall length 17 ft. 7¾ in. Overall width 6 ft. 2¾ in. Height 5 ft. 4 in. Turning circle 41 ft 8 in. Wheel-base 10 ft. 3 in. Track 4 ft. 10½ in. (front), 5 ft. (rear). Fuel tank capacity 18 Imp. gals. Kerb weight 40¾ cwt.

Appearance: Large car with slight razor-edge styling to bodywork. Traditional vertical radiator with winged " B " mascot. Paired headlamps faired into body between wings and radiator. Large, domed front wings sweep across doors to blend into rear wings. Wraparound bumpers with vertical overriders. Shapely luggage boot. Plain disc wheels.

Bentley Continental Convertible Coupé: Number of cylinders V8. Cubic capacity 6230 c.c. Compression ratio 9 : 1 (8 : 1 available). B.H.P. not disclosed. Overall length 17 ft. 7¾ in. Overall width 6 ft. ½ in. Height 5 ft. 1 in. Turning circle 41 ft. 8 in. Wheel-base 10 ft. 3 in. Track 4 ft. 10½ in. (front), 5 ft. (rear). Fuel tank capacity 18 Imp. gals.

Appearance: Bodywork by H. J. Mulliner Park Ward. Paired headlamps slightly inset into front wings; direction lamps on front-wing " corners ". Straight-through wing line to vertical tail-lamp clusters; note uncluttered body sides. Wrap-around windscreen and convertible fabric top. Plain disc wheels.

Bentley Continental " Flying Spur " Sports Saloon: Number of cylinders V8. Cubic capacity 6230 c.c. Compression ratio 9 : 1 (8 : 1 available). B.H.P. not disclosed. Overall length 17 ft. 7¾ in. Overall width 6 ft. ½ in. Height 5 ft. 1 in. Turning circle 41 ft. 8 in. Wheel-base 10 ft. 3 in. Track 4 ft. 10½ in. (front), 5 ft. (rear). Fuel tank capacity 18 Imp. gals.

Appearance: Frontal details similar to Bentley S3 but lower. Sleek line to passenger area—note narrow roof line. Curved windscreen and rear window. Front wing line merges into passenger area; " suggested " rear wings with tail-lamps in trailing edges. Plain bumpers have large, vertical overriders.

61

B.M.W.

GERMANY

Bayerische Motoren Werke,

Munich, Germany.

Current Models: *700 Cabrio*. Convertible. **700C and 700CS.** Coupé. **LS.** Standard and De Luxe 2-door Saloons. **1500.** 4-door Saloon. **1600.** 4-door Saloon. **1800 and 1800 TI.** 4-door Saloons.

B.M.W. LS De Luxe Saloon: Number of cylinders Flat-2. Cubic capacity 697 c.c. Compression ratio 7·5 : 1. B.H.P. 38. Overall length 12 ft. 8 in. Overall width 4 ft. 10½ in. Height 4 ft. 5½ in. Turning circle 32 ft. Wheel-base 7 ft. 5¾ in. Track 4 ft. 2 in. (front), 3 ft. 11¼ in. (rear). Fuel tank capacity 7·3 Imp. gals. Kerb weight 1500 lb.

Appearance: Small car with rather angular styling. Note lack of frontal air-intake (rear engine); high-set headlamps and indicator lamps on front body "corners". Deep windscreen and rear window, flattish roof line. Flat bonnet and rear deck. Plain bumpers wrap-around front and rear. Disc wheels have large, flat hub-caps.

B.M.W. 1500 Saloon: Number of cylinders 4. Cubic capacity 1499 c.c. Compression ratio 8·8 : 1. B.H.P. 80. Overall length 14 ft. 8 in. Overall width 5 ft. 7¼ in. Height 4 ft. 9 in. Turning circle 31 ft. 6 in. Wheel-base 8 ft. 4½ in. Track 4 ft. 4 in. (front), 4 ft. 6 in. (rear). Fuel tank capacity 11½ Imp. gals. Dry weight 2196 lb.

Appearance: Rather angular. Unusual frontal treatment—tiny central traditional B.M.W. twin-oval grille flanked by long oblong intakes having horizontally barred grilles and incorporating headlamps. Indicator lamps on front body "corners". Straight-through wings to wide, high-set rear lamps—prominent "lip" along top of rear body panel. Passenger area has large windscreen and rear window and big side windows. Angular section bumpers with vertical overriders. Disc wheels have oblong perforations.

B.M.W. 1800 Saloon: Number of cylinders 4. Cubic capacity 1773 c.c. Compression ratio 8·6 : 1 (9·5 : 1 TI). B.H.P. 90 (110). Overall length 14 ft. 9⅛ in. Overall width 5 ft. 7⅜ in. Height 4 ft. 9⅛ in. Turning circle 31 ft. 6 in. Wheel-base 8 ft. 4½ in. Track 4 ft. 4 in. (front), 4 ft. 6 in. (rear). Fuel tank capacity 11½ Imp. gals. Dry weight 2238 lb.

Appearance: Generally similar to 1500 model. Note almost flat roof line. Large tail-lamp clusters are vertical. Wheels have large, almost flat hub-caps.

In 1960 Bristol Siddeley disposed of Bristol Cars Limited and the Company was acquired by Mr. George White and Mr. Anthony Crook with Mr. F. S. Derham as third member of the board. Production continued at Filton.

Current Model: *408*. 2-door Saloon.

Bristol 408 Saloon: Number of cylinders V8 (Chrysler) Cubic capacity 5130 c.c. Compression ratio 9 : 1. B.H.P. 250. Max. m.p.h. 122. Overall length 16 ft. 1½ in. Overall width 5 ft. 8 in. Height 4 ft. 11 in. Turning circle 39 ft. 6 in. Wheel-base 9 ft. 6 in. Track 4 ft. 5 in. (front), 4 ft. 6½ in. (rear). Fuel tank capacity 18 Imp. gals. Kerb weight 3584 lb.

Appearance: Long-looking car with smoothly lined body-work. Large, thrust-forward radiator air-intake has slightly inset grille and incorporates second pair of headlamps. Straight-through wing line to vertical, elliptical tail-lamps. Curved windscreen and wrap-around rear window. Plain bumpers. Perforated disc wheels with domed hub-caps.

BUICK

UNITED STATES OF AMERICA

Buick Motor Division,
General Motors Corp., Flint 2,
Michigan, U.S.A.

History: The first Buick car appeared in
1903. It had a twin-cylinder engine of
18 h.p. and a five-seater body, and was
continued with minor modifications for some years
before the 24/40 h.p. four-cylinder model appeared on
the market in 1908, when Buicks became a division of
the then newly formed General Motors Corporation.

In 1909 a 15/20 h.p. model was marketed, followed in
1914 by a small 14 h.p. car; after which six-cylinder, then
eight-cylinder models, were produced, the latter alone
being offered after 1931. Buick introduced the vacuum-
operated clutch in 1932, rear coil springs in 1938 and two
dual-downdraught carburettors in 1940. The 1948/9
Roadster featured a torque-converter combined with a
two-speed planetary " Dynaflow " transmission, and
power-operated steering in its 1952 version.

In 1954 the 188 b.h.p. of the V8 engine of the
" Super " model was increased to 200 b.h.p. for use in
the " Skylark " model of that year. The following
year, the V8 engine produced 236 b.h.p. In 1956 the
range consisted of four series, the Special, Century,
Super and Roadmaster with sixteen models available.

Current Models: *Special.* Standard and De Luxe 4-door
Sedans, Coupé, Convertible, Standard and De Luxe 6-seat
Station Wagons, 6- and 9-seat Sports Wagons. *Skylark.*
4-door Sedan, Coupé, Sports Coupé, Convertible, 6- and 9-seat
Sports Wagons. *Le Sabre.* 4-door Sedan, 2-door Hardtop
Coupé, 4-door Hardtop. *Le Sabre Custom.* 4-door Sedan,
2-door Hardtop Coupé, 4-door Hardtop, Convertible. *Wild-
cat.* 4-door Sedan, 2-door Hardtop Coupé, 4-door Hardtop.
Wildcat De Luxe. 4-door Sedan, 2-door Hardtop Coupé,
4-door Hardtop, Convertible. *Wildcat Custom.* 2-door
Hardtop Coupé, 4-door Hardtop, Convertible. *Electra*

" *225* ". 4-door Sedan, 2-door Hardtop Coupé, 4-door Hardtop. ***Electra " 225 " Custom.*** 4-door Sedan, 2-door Hardtop Coupé, 4-door Hardtop, Convertible. ***Riviera.*** Sports Coupé.

Buick Skylark Coupé: Number of cylinders V6 or V8. Cubic capacity 225 cu. in. (V6) or 300 cu. in. (V8). Compression ratio 9:1 (11:1 V8 optional). B.H.P. 155 or 210 (250 optional). Overall length 16 ft. 11⅖ in. Overall width 6 ft. 1 9/10 in. Height 4 ft. 6 in. Turning circle 40·6 ft. Wheelbase 9 ft. 7 in. Track 4 ft. 10 in. (front and rear). Fuel tank capacity 20 U.S. gals.

Appearance: Angular, full-width radiator air-intake has horizontally barred grille and incorporates paired headlamps. Oblong side/direction lamps in under-bumper. Broad, flat bonnet and rear deck, razor-edged styling to passenger area which has curved windscreen and rear window. Tail-lamps in flat rear panel extend full width of car. Wheel-discs have perforated centre portion and " knock-off " hub-caps.

Buick Skylark Sports Wagon: Number of cylinders V8. Cubic capacity 300 cu. in. Compression ratio 9:1 (11:1 optional). B.H.P. 210 (250). Overall length 17 ft. 4½ in. Overall width 6 ft. 1 9/10 in. Height 4 ft. 10 3/10 in. Turning circle 40·6 ft. Wheel-base 10 ft. Track 4 ft. 10 in. (front and rear). Fuel tank capacity 20 U.S. gals.

Appearance: Frontal details as for Skylark Coupé but note unusual utility styling with raised rear portion of roof. Long rear side windows and rear panel raked forward. Note characteristic Buick " venti-ports " behind front wheels. Wheel discs have thinly spoked effect to projecting centre portion.

Buick Wildcat Coupé: Number of cylinders V8. Cubic capacity 401 cu. in. (425 cu. in. optional). Compression ratio 10·25 : 1. B.H.P. 325 (340 and 360 optional). Overall length 18 ft. 3$\frac{9}{10}$ in. Overall width 6 ft. 8 in. Height 4 ft. 7$\frac{1}{5}$ in. Wheel-base 10 ft. 6 in. Track 5 ft. 3$\frac{9}{5}$ in. (front), 5 ft. 3 in. (rear). Fuel tank capacity 25 U.S. gals.

Appearance: Sleek lines generally but note unusual frontal treatment. Oblong radiator air-intake has paired headlamps at ends but centre portion is "veed" sharply outwards. Grille consists of inwardly curving bars. Under-bumper is slotted and mounts side/direction lamps. Frontal styling is echoed at rear—tail-lamps are large and oblong. Passenger area has flowing styling and large rear window. Wheel discs are dished and feature five-spoked effect.

Buick Electra "·225·" Hardtop Coupé: Number of cylinders V8. Cubic capacity 410 cu. in. (425 cu. in. optional). Compression ratio 10·25 : 1. B.H.P. 325 (340 and 360 optional). Overall length 18 ft. 6 9/10 in. Overall width 6 ft. 8 in. Height 4 ft. 8 in. Wheel-base 10 ft. 6 in. Track 5 ft. 3 3/5 in. (front), 5 ft. 3 in. (rear). Fuel tank capacity 25 U.S. gals.

Appearance: Styling generally as for other Buicks but note that oblong radiator air-intake is divided by horizontal and vertical bars and has inset mesh grille. Smallish passenger area with thin roof line and long side windows. Rear window is slightly " veed " outwards. Sharply angular line to trailing wing edges. Rear wheels partially concealed—discs have spoked effect.

Buick Riviera Sports Coupé: Number of cylinders V8. Cubic capacity 425 cu. in. Compression ratio 10·25 : 1. B.H.P. 340 (360 optional). Overall length 17 ft. 4 in. Overall width 6 ft. 4⅗ in. Height 4 ft. 5 in. Turning circle 43·6 ft. Wheelbase 9 ft. 9 in. Track 5 ft. ⅖ in. (front), 4 ft. 11 in. (rear). Fuel tank capacity 20 U.S. gals.

Appearance: Styling unique to this model. Full-width radiator air-intake has cellular grille and is flanked by vertical grilles which open to disclose vertically mounted paired headlamps. Straight-through, flowing wing line to rather angular tail—rear lamps mounted below narrow bumper. Razor-edged styling to passenger area, narrow roof line. Wheels have five-spoked effect.

CADILLAC

UNITED STATES OF AMERICA

 Cadillac Motor Car Division,
General Motors Corporation,
Detroit 32, Michigan, U.S.A.

History: Henry Leland, as founder of the Cadillac Company, produced the first model in 1902 and it had a horizontal, single-cylinder engine of 7 b.h.p. It was chain driven and exceedingly popular until its discontinuance in 1909 when Cadillac became a division of General Motors.

Because Cadillac policy favoured catering for the more expensive market, from 1905 until 1908 a four-cylinder engine of 30 b.h.p. was manufactured. The first electric starter was introduced by Cadillac in 1911.

In 1915 the four was replaced by a V8. This was the first production V8 engine to be seen in the U.S.A. The early Cadillac V8 developed 60 b.h.p., but by the time the last one was produced in 1937, the output had been raised to 87 b.h.p. V16 engines were installed in Cadillacs from 1930 to 1940 while V12's were used from 1931 to 1937.

Hydromatic drive was adopted in 1941 and the V8 engine, re-designed in 1936, was continued until 1948 with improved power from 135 b.h.p. to 150 b.h.p.

In 1954 the power of the Series 60, 62 and 75 was increased to 230 b.h.p. and in 1955 to 250 b.h.p., the Eldorado engine delivering 270 b.h.p. Power output of the V8 engine was again raised in 1956, the Series 60, 62 and 75 engine delivering 285 b.h.p. and the Eldorado 305 b.h.p. The compression ratio was raised to 9·75 : 1.

Current Models: *Calais Series.* Sedan, Hardtop Sedan, Coupé. *de Ville Series.* Sedan de Ville, Hardtop Sedan de Ville, Coupé de Ville, de Ville Convertible. *Fleetwood Series.* Sixty Special Sedan, Seventy-Five Sedan, Seventy-Five Limousine, Eldorado Convertible.

Cadillac Calais Coupé: Number of cylinders V8. Cubic capacity 429 cu. in. Compression ratio 10·5 : 1. B.H.P. 340. Overall length 18 ft. 8 in. Overall width 6 ft. 7$\frac{9}{16}$ in. Height 4 ft. 6$\frac{3}{4}$ in. Turning circle 44·7 ft. Wheel-base 10 ft. 9$\frac{1}{2}$ in. Track 5 ft. 2$\frac{1}{2}$ in. (front and rear). Fuel tank capacity 26 U.S. gals.

Appearance: The outwardly "veed" radiator air-intake is flanked by projecting vertically mounted paired headlamps. Note large cornering lamps forward of front wheel arches. Straight-through wing line—no "fins" this year—to large, vertical tail-lamp clusters. Broad, flat bonnet and rear deck. Narrow roof line. Dished wheels have prominent centre portions.

Cadillac Fleetwood Sixty Special Sedan: Number of cylinders V8. Cubic capacity 429 cu. in. Compression ratio

10·5 : 1.   B.H.P. 340.   Overall length 18 ft. 11½ in.   Overall width 7 ft. 7 9/10 in.   Height 4 ft. 7 9/10 in.   Turning circle 45·8 ft. Wheel-base 11 ft. 1 in.   Track 5 ft. 2½ in. (front and rear). Fuel tank capacity 26 U.S. gals.

Appearance: Note low, wide appearance of Cadillacs.   Sixty Special Sedan may be seen with vinyl covered padded roof and known as Fleetwood Brougham. Side/indicator lamps mounted in massive under-bumper.   Generally angular styling, rear wheels partially enclosed.

Cadillac Fleetwood Eldorado Convertible: Number of cylinders V8.   Cubic capacity 429 cu. in.   Compression ratio 10·5 : 1.   B.H.P. 340.   Overall length 18 ft. 8 in.   Overall width 7 ft. 7 9/10 in.   Height 4 ft. 6⅔ in.   Turning circle 44·7 ft. Wheel-base 10 ft. 9½ in.   Track 5 ft. 2½ in. (front and rear). Fuel tank capacity 26 U.S. gals.

Appearance: Generally as for other Cadillacs but note convertible fabric top.   Dummy " grille " at rear forms tail panel. Note large tail-lamps and bright trim strips along lower body edges.   Windscreen is well raked.

CHAIKA

U.S.S.R.

GAZ Motor Works,
Moscow,
U.S.S.R.

Current Models: *Chaika GAZ-13*. 4-door Limousine, Cabriolet.

Chaika GAZ-13 Limousine: Number of cylinders V8. Cubic capacity 5500 c.c. Compression ratio 8·5 : 1. B.H.P. 195. Overall length 18 ft. 4½ in. Overall width 6 ft. 6$\frac{7}{10}$ in. Height 5 ft. 3$\frac{2}{5}$ in. Turning circle 48 ft. Wheel-base 10 ft. 8 in. Max. track 5 ft. $\frac{3}{5}$ in. Fuel tank capacity 17·6 Imp. gals. Dry weight 4079 lb.

Appearance: Rather dated, angular styling. Oblong radiator air-intake with unusual grille. Deeply hooded headlamps with side-lamps below; strip indicator lamps continue around body " corners ". Straight-through wing line to cut-away trailing edges containing tail-lamp clusters. Note how bright side trim strips accentuate " suggested " rear wings. Plain bumpers with " bullet " overriders. Wrap-around windscreen and rear window. Plain disc wheels and hub-caps.

CHEVROLET

UNITED STATES OF AMERICA

Chevrolet Motor Division,
General Motors Building,
Detroit 2, Michigan, U.S.A.

History: Louis Chevrolet was a racing driver who designed and produced his first automobile for the public in 1912, and, in the same year, bought the Little Company. In 1913, therefore, the six-cylinder Model C and Little Six Chevrolets were offered together with the Little Four. At the end of the same year the Little Six was abandoned but the Model C was continued until 1915.

From 1914 to 1929 Chevrolet produced four-cylinder models developing 24 b.h.p. In 1916 the same engine was offered in a less expensive model and two years later the original car had the engine stroke lengthened. In 1917 a V8 engine appeared but was continued only for two years, Chevrolet becoming a division of General Motors in 1918. A change was made from four-cylinder to six-cylinder engines in 1929. These delivered 46 b.h.p. In 1932 it was 60 b.h.p., the following year 80 b.h.p. and by 1937, with greater piston displacement, 85 b.h.p. was obtained. 1948 saw the Fleetline and Styleline range of models with 90 b.h.p.

Powerglide automatic gear change was introduced with an engine giving 105 b.h.p. In 1953 the same power unit was offered, developing 108 b.h.p. for models fitted with the manual gear change and 115 b.h.p. for those cars fitted with Powerglide. The " One-Fifty ", " Two-Ten " and " Bel-Air " models developed 115 b.h.p. or 125 b.h.p. with Powerglide in 1954, and 123 or 136 b.h.p. in 1955. 1956 saw the b.h.p. raised to a maximum of 225.

Current Models: *Corvair 500.* 4-door Sport Sedan, Sport Coupé. *Corvair Monza.* 4-door Sport Sedan, Sport Coupé, Convertible. *Corvair Corsa.* Sport Coupé, Convertible. *Greenbrier.* Sports Wagon, Sports Wagon De Luxe. *Chevy II 100.* 2- and 4-door Sedans, Station Wagon.

Chevy II Nova. 4-door Sedan, Sport Coupé, Station Wagon. ***Chevy II Nova SS.*** Sport Coupé. ***Chevelle 300.*** 2- and 4-door Sedans, Station Wagon. ***Chevelle 300 de Luxe.*** 2- and 4-door Sedans, Station Wagon. ***Chevelle Malibu.*** 4-door Sedan, Sport Coupé, Convertible, Station Wagon. ***Chevelle Malibu Super Sport.*** Sport Coupé, Convertible. ***Biscayne.*** 2- and 4-door Sedans, Station Wagon. ***Bel-Air.*** 2- and 4-door Sedans, Station Wagon (6- and 9-passenger). ***Impala.*** 4-door Sedan, 4-door Sport Sedan, Sport Coupé, Convertible, Station Wagon (6- and 9-passenger). ***Impala Super Sport.*** Sport Coupé, Convertible. ***Corvette.*** Stingray Convertible, Stingray Sport Coupé.

Chevrolet Corvair Corsa Sport Coupé: Number of cylinders Flat-6. Cubic capacity 164 cu. in. Compression ratio 9·25 : 1 (8·25 : 1 optional). B.H.P. 140 (180 Turbocharged optional). Overall length 15 ft. 3$\frac{3}{10}$ in. Overall width 5 ft. 9$\frac{7}{10}$ in. Height 4 ft. 3$\frac{3}{10}$ in. Turning circle 38·2 ft. Wheelbase 9 ft. Track 4 ft. 7 in. (front), 4 ft. 9$\frac{1}{5}$ in. (rear). Fuel tank capacity 14 U.S. gals. Kerb weight 2545 lb.

Appearance: Paired headlamps slightly inset into plain frontal panel—note lack of frontal air-intake due to rear-mounted air-cooled engine. Centrally placed passenger area; curved windscreen and large, well-raked rear window. Rear deck has outlets for cooling air; flat tail-panel with paired taillamps. Plain, high-set bumpers. Wire wheels with " knock-off " hub-caps.

Chevrolet Chevy II Nova SS Sport Coupé: Number of cylinders 6 or V8. Cubic capacity 194 cu. in. and 230 cu. in. (6), 283 cu. in. (V8), (327 cu. in. V8 optional). Compression ratio 8·5 : 1 (6), 9·25 : 1 (V8), (10·5 : 1 optional). B.H.P. 120 and 140 (6), 195 (V8), (250 and 300 optional). Overall length 15 ft. 2$\frac{9}{10}$ in. Overall width 5 ft. 9$\frac{9}{10}$ in. Height 4 ft. 6 in. Turning circle 38·4 ft. Wheel-base 9 ft. 2 in. Track 4 ft. 8$\frac{4}{5}$ in. (front), 4 ft. 8.$\frac{3}{10}$ in. (rear). Fuel tank capacity 16 U.S. gals. Kerb weight 2815 lb. (6), 2970 lb. (V8).

Appearance: Simple frontal styling—full-width radiator air-intake with flat grille of thin bars standing slightly proud of headlamps. Side/direction lamps mounted in simple bumper. Straight-through wing line to slightly wedge-shaped rear contours. Oblong tail-lamps on slightly inset rear panel. Rather angular passenger area, curved windscreen and long side windows. Wheel discs feature row of oblong perforations and central triple-eared motif.

Chevrolet Chevelle Malibu Super Sport Coupé: Number of cylinders 6 or V8. Cubic capacity 194 cu. in. and 230 cu. in. (6), 283 cu. in. (V8), (327 cu. in. V8 optional). Compression ratio 8·5 : 1 (6), 9·25 : 1 (V8), (10·5 : 1 optional). B.H.P. 120 and 140 (6), 195 (V8), (250 and 300 optional). Overall length 16 ft. 4$\frac{3}{5}$ in. Overall width 6 ft. 2$\frac{3}{5}$ in. Height 4 ft. 4$\frac{4}{5}$ in. Turning circle 41·9 ft. Wheel-base 9 ft. 7 in. Track 4 ft. 10 in. (front and rear). Fuel tank capacity 20 U.S. gals. Kerb weight 3125 lb. (6), 3275 lb. (V8).

Appearance: Full-width radiator air-intake with grille of thin bars is " veed " slightly outwards and incorporates paired headlamps. Slotted under-bumper mounts side/direction lamps. Broad, flat bonnet; straight-through wing line rises

78

CITROËN

FRANCE

S. A. André Citroën,
117–167 Quai de Javel, Paris, 15e,
France
(also Citroën Cars Ltd.,
Trading Estate,
Slough, Bucks.,
England).

Current Models: *2CV AZL.* 4-door Convertible Saloon.
2CV AM. De Luxe 4-door Convertible Saloon. ***2CV
4 × 4 "Sahara".*** 4-door Convertible Saloon. ***Bijou.***
De Luxe 2-door Saloon. ***AMI 6.*** 4-door Saloon, Estate
Car. ***ID.19.*** 4-door Saloon, Drop-head Coupé. ***DW.*** De
Luxe 4-door Saloon. ***DS.19.*** De Luxe 4-door Saloon,
Drop-head Coupé. ***"Prestige".*** De Luxe 4-door Saloon.
DS "Pallas". De Luxe 4-door Saloon. ***"Safari"*** and
"Tourmaster". Estate Cars.

Citroën 2CV AZL Convertible Saloon: Number of cylinders
Flat-2. Cubic capacity 425 c.c. Compression ratio 7·5 : 1.
B.H.P. 18. Overall length 12 ft. 4¾ in. Overall width 4 ft.
10⅚ in. Height 5 ft. 3 in. Turning circle 35 ft. 3 in. Wheel-
base 7 ft. 9⁵⁄₁₆ in. Track 4 ft. 1⅝ in. (front), 4 ft. (rear). Fuel
tank capacity 4·4 Imp. gals. Weight (dry) 1120 lb.

Appearance: Stark, utilitarian car with nose-down attitude. Rounded bonnet slopes sharply down to small air-intake; fabric roof and straight-down back. Separate front wings, rear wheels enclosed. Plain, disc wheels.

Citroën AMI 6 Saloon: Number of cylinders Flat-2. Cubic capacity 602 c.c. Compression ratio 7·75 : 1. B.H.P. 25. Overall length 12 ft. 8⅝ in. Overall width 4 ft. 11⅞ in. Height 4 ft. 10½ in. Turning circle 36 ft. Wheel-base 7 ft. 10½ in. Track 4 ft. 1⅝ in. (front), 4 ft. (rear). Fuel tank capacity 5½ Imp. gals. Weight (laden) 2090 lb.

Appearance: Note the unusual "leaning back" side aspect of this car due to sharply raked windscreen and reverse-slope rear window with prominent peak over. Large, oblong head-lamps set into bonnet front; small air-intake and bonnet has "dip" in centre. Sculptured body sides. Disc wheels have narrow tyres. Large window area and narrow roof line.

Citroën DS.19 Saloon: Number of cylinders 4. Cubic capacity 1911 c.c. Compression ratio 8·5 : 1. B.H.P. 83. Overall length 15 ft. 11 in. Overall width 5 ft. 10½ in. Height 4 ft. 11⅞ in. Turning circle 36 ft. Wheel-base 10 ft. 3 in. Track 4 ft. 11 in. (front), 4 ft. 3¼ in. (rear). Fuel tank capacity 14 Imp. gals. Weight (unladen) 2632 lb.

Appearance: 4-door saloon of modern conception with un-usual appearance due to large amount of overhang at front and practically none at the rear. Bonnet slopes gently down to

thrust-forward radiator air-intake incorporated in wrap-around bumper. Front wings merge into body sides. Extremely large window area, wrap-around windscreen and rear window, thin pillars. Rear lights high on rear quarters. Disc wheels.

Citroën "Safari" Estate Car: Number of cylinders 4. Cubic capacity 1911 c.c. Compression ratio 8·5 : 1. B.H.P. 83. Overall length 16 ft. 6 in. Overall width 5 ft. 10½ in. Height 5 ft. Turning circle 36 ft. Wheel-base 10 ft. 3 in. Track 4 ft. 11 in. (front), 4 ft. 3¼ in. (rear). Fuel tank capacity 14 Imp. gals. Kerb weight 2850 lb.

Appearance: Note how DS frontal styling has been mated to utility type body. Car appears long and low and has large window area. Vertically mounted triple-rear-lamp clusters. Front of car thrust well forward and rear wheels placed well aft. Plain disc wheels.

DAF

HOLLAND

Van Doorne's Automobielfabriek N.V.
Eindhoven,
Holland.

Current Models: *Daffodil*. Standard and De Luxe 2-door Saloons.

DAF Daffodil Saloon: Number of cylinders Flat-2. Cubic capacity 746 c.c. Compression ratio 7·5 : 1. B.H.P. 30. Overall length 11 ft. 10$\frac{1}{10}$ in. Overall width 4 ft. 9 in. Height 4 ft. 6$\frac{3}{10}$ in. Turning circle 30 ft. 6 in. Wheel-base 6 ft. 9 in. Track 3 ft. 10$\frac{1}{2}$ in. (front and rear). Fuel tank capacity 7 Imp. gals. Kerb weight 1460 lb.

Appearance: Small car with neat angular styling. Full-width air-intake with side/direction lamps at ends. High-set headlamps with " hoods " carried over intake. Bonnet slopes sharply down between headlamps. Deep, well-raked windscreen, large side windows and almost flat rear window. Straight-through wings to high-set tail-lamp clusters. Plain disc wheels.

DAIMLER

GREAT BRITAIN

The Daimler Co., Ltd.,

    Radford Works,

    Coventry, England.

Daimler

History: The Daimler Motor Syndicate was formed in 1893 and in 1896 the Daimler Motor Co., Ltd., was registered.

A Daimler completed the first motor-car journey from John o' Groats to Land's End in 1897 and between that year and 1903 twelve models were produced, ranging from 6·9 to 27·34 R.A.C.h.p. The 22·8 R.A.C.h.p. Silent-Knight, sleeve-valve engine was introduced in 1909.

From a very early date Daimlers have served as Royal vehicles. The Prince of Wales (later King Edward VII) had his first motor ride in 1896 in the Canstatt-Daimler belonging to F. R. Simms, who introduced the German Daimler patents into this country.

In 1919 two new 30 and 45 R.A.C.h.p. models were produced and during World War I many Daimler products were used by our Forces. The Double-Six appeared in 1927 and three years later the world's first fluid flywheel and pre-selector self-change gear was offered by Daimlers. The poppet-valve engine was re-adopted in 1933, the sleeve-valve system being finally abandoned three years later, when the vast Straight 8 was produced. Independent front suspension was fitted to the Fifteen in 1938. Automatic transmission was introduced in 1956 in addition to the traditional Fluid Transmission on all models except the DK.400 Limousine. In 1960 the Company was acquired by Jaguar Cars Limited.

Current Models: *SP250.* 2-seater Sports. *2½-litre.* 4-door Saloon. *4½-litre " Majestic Major ".* 4-door Saloon. *4½-litre Limousine.* 8-seater Saloon.

Daimler SP250 2-seater Sports: Number of cylinders V8. Cubic capacity 2548 c.c. Compression ratio 8·2 : 1. B.H.P.

140. Max. m.p.h. 120. Overall length 14 ft. $\frac{3}{4}$ in. Overall width 5 ft. $\frac{1}{2}$ in. Height (to top of hood) 4 ft. $2\frac{1}{4}$ in. Turning circle 33 ft. Wheel-base 7 ft. 8 in. Track 4 ft. 2 in. (front), 4 ft. (rear). Fuel tank capacity 12 Imp. gals. Dry weight 2090 lb.

Appearance: Low-set elliptical radiator air-intake; rounded bonnet sweeps down between thrust-forward headlamps with small side-lamps above. Prominent " fins " with tail-lamp clusters in trailing edges; squarish tail, vertical overriders flank rear number plate. Perforated disc wheels with large, domed hub-caps standard, wire wheels optional.

Daimler 2½-litre Saloon: Number of cylinders V8. Cubic capacity 2548 c.c. Compression ratio 8·2 : 1. B.H.P. 140. Max. m.p.h. 112. Overall length 15 ft. $\frac{3}{4}$ in. Overall width 5 ft. $6\frac{3}{4}$ in. Height 4 ft. 9 in. Turning circle 33 ft. 6 in. Wheel-base 8 ft. $11\frac{3}{8}$ in. Track 4 ft. 7 in. (front), 4 ft. 5 in. (rear). Fuel tank capacity 12 Imp. gals. Dry weight 3046 lb.

Appearance: Traditional fluted Daimler radiator blended with Jaguar body. Generally rounded contours. Headlamps faired into body between wings and bonnet; spotlamps flank radiator air-intake. Well-rounded roof line and tail. Car tapers towards rear. Perforated disc wheels have large hub-caps.

Daimler " Majestic Major " Saloon: Number of cylinders V8. Cubic capacity 4561 c.c. Compression ratio 8 : 1. B.H.P. 220. Overall length 16 ft. 10 in. Overall width 6 ft. 1¼ in. Height 5 ft. 2¾ in. Turning circle 42 ft. Wheelbase 9 ft. 6 in. Track 4 ft. 9 in. (front and rear). Fuel tank capacity 16 Imp. gals.

Appearance: Upright radiator shell flanked by small circular intakes. Headlamps faired into wings which merge into front doors. Full-length styling line running rearward forms line of rear wings; triple tail-lamp clusters. Rounded boot line, rather prominent passenger area. Disc wheels have large hub-caps.

DODGE

UNITED STATES OF AMERICA

 Dodge Division, Chrysler Corp.,
Detroit, Michigan, U.S.A.

History: In 1915 John and Horace Dodge produced
the first car of their new company, then known as Dodge
Bros. It was of simple design, an open model, and had
a 35 b.h.p. four-cylinder engine. It was the first passenger
car with an all-steel body and was continued until 1928,
when the firm became a division of the Chrysler Corporation.

The successful Four was replaced in 1928 by the
Standard Six, the Victory Six and the Senior Six. The
first two of these cars, which were continued for the
next two years, had engines of 58 b.h.p. The Senior
Six developed 60 b.h.p. which by 1930 had been raised
to 78 b.h.p. A new selection of Sixes were then offered,
but they were all discontinued some years later, in 1942.
In 1930 a straight Eight appeared, but it was discontinued
after three years' production.

1948 saw the introduction of an improved 4-speed
two-range semi-automatic transmission. The " Way-
farer ", " Meadowbrook " and " Coronet " ranges were
presented in 1949 with six-cylinder engines. In 1953
came a 140 b.h.p. V8 engine with torque converter.
Also, overdrive was available on models featuring the
3-speed transmission. The 140 b.h.p. of the 1953
" Coronet " was increased to 150 b.h.p. in 1954. By
1955 the V8 was delivering 175 b.h.p. or 183 b.h.p.
With a compression ratio of 8 : 1, the cubic capacity
of the V8 engine was increased to 315 cubic inches for
1956.

Current Models: *Dart.* 2- and 4-door Sedans, Station
Wagon. *Dart 270*. 2- and 4-door Sedans, 2-door Hardtop,
Convertible, Station Wagon. *Dart GT.* 2-door Hardtop,
Convertible. *Coronet.* 2- and 4-door Sedans, Station
Wagon. *Coronet 440*. 4-door Sedan, 2- and 4-door
Hardtops, Convertible, Station Wagon (6- and 9-passenger).

Coronet 500. 2-door Hardtop, Convertible. **Polara.** 4-door Sedan, 2- and 4-door Hardtops, Convertible, Station Wagon (6- and 9-passenger). **Polara Custom 880.** 4-door Sedan, 2-door Hardtop, Convertible, Station Wagon (6- and 9-passenger). **Monaco.** 2-door Hardtop.

Dodge Dart GT Hardtop: Number of cylinders 6 or V8. Cubic capacity 170 cu. in. (6), 273 cu. in. (V8) (225 cu. in. (6), 273 cu. in. (V8) optional). Compression ratio 8·5 : 1 (7·1 : 1 available) (6), 8·8 : 1 (7·5 : 1 available) (V8), (8·4 : 1 (7·3 : 1 available) (6) optional, 10·5 : 1 (V8) optional). B.H.P. 101 (6), 180 (V8), (145 (6), 235 (V8) optional). Overall length 16 ft. 4⅘ in. Overall width 5 ft. 9¼ in. Height 4 ft. 6⅖ in. Turning circle 38·7 ft. Wheel-base 9 ft. 3 in. Track 4 ft. 7⁹⁄₁₆ in. (front), 4 ft. 7⅜ in. (rear). Fuel tank capacity 18 U.S. gals.

Appearance: Narrow, full-width radiator grille of five vertical and three horizontal bars is high-set and has headlamps at ends. Headlamps slightly inset and thrust-forward. Bumpers, high-set front and rear, have vertical overriders. Curved, well-raked windscreen and large rear window. Large, oblong tail-lamp units and dummy " grille " forming rear panel. Wheels have dished hub-caps.

Dodge Coronet 500 Convertible: Number of cylinders V8. Cubic capacity 273 cu. in. (318 cu. in., 361 cu. in., 383 cu. in.

and 426 cu. in. optional). Compression ratio 8·8 : 1 (7·5 : 1 available), (9 : 1 (7·5 : 1 available), 9 : 1, 10 : 1 and 10·3 : 1 optional). B.H.P. 180 (230, 265, 330 and 480 optional). Overall length 17 ft. $\frac{1}{5}$ in. Overall width 6 ft. 3 in. Height 4 ft. 7$\frac{1}{5}$ in. Wheel-base 9 ft. 9 in. Track 4 ft. 11$\frac{1}{2}$ in. (front), 4 ft. 10$\frac{1}{2}$ in. (rear). Fuel tank capacity 19 U.S. gals.

Appearance: Neat, well-balanced appearance; full-width radiator air-intake has grille of thin, inwardly curving bars and carries paired headlamps. Broad, flat bonnet and long rear deck; squared-off tail line with lamps at ends of panel. Note full-length body moulding following top line of wings and three long " ports " mounted high, behind headlamps. Deep well-raked windscreen. Disc wheels have " triple-eared " hub-caps.

Dodge Polara Custom 880 Sedan: Number of cylinders V8. Cubic capacity 383 cu. in. (383 cu. in., 413 cu. in. and 426 cu. in. optional). Compression ratio 9·2 : 1 (8 : 1 available), (10 : 1 and 10·3 : 1 optional). B.H.P. 305 (340 and 470 optional). Overall length 17 ft. 8$\frac{3}{10}$ in. Overall width 6 ft. 7 in. Height 4 ft. 9$\frac{1}{10}$ in. Wheel-base 10 ft. 1 in. Track 5 ft. 2 in. (front), 5 ft. $\frac{7}{10}$ in. (rear). Fuel tank capacity 25 U.S. gals.

Appearance: Note how full-width radiator air-intake " opens out " at ends to accommodate paired headlamps. Grille consists of slightly " veed " vertical bars. Massive bumper mounts

side/direction lamps. Note prominent, low-set body moulding which runs full-length of car; rear wheels partially concealed. Rather angular styling to passenger area and narrow
roof line. Wheel discs are dished.

Dodge Monaco Hardtop: Number of cylinders V8. Cubic
capacity 383 cu. in. (413 cu. in. and 426 cu. in. optional).
Compression ratio 10 : 1 (8 : 1 available), (10 : 1 and 10·3 : 1
optional). B.H.P. 330 (340 and 470 optional). Overall length
17 ft. 8$\frac{3}{8}$ in. Overall width 6 ft. 7 in. Height 4 ft. 6$\frac{9}{10}$ in.
Wheel-base 10 ft. 1 in. Track 5 ft. 2 in. (front), 5 ft. $\frac{7}{10}$ in.
(rear). Fuel tank capacity 25 U.S. gals.

Appearance: Generally similar to Polara Custom 880 but
note padded roof to Hardtop body; long side windows and
well-raked rear line of side windows. Car has long, low appearance generally. Flat, full-width tail-panel widens at ends to
accommodate tail-lamps. Wheels feature " triple-eared "
hub-cap motif.

ELVA

GREAT BRITAIN

Trojan Limited,
Trojan Works,
Purley Way,
Croydon,
Surrey,
England.

Current Models: *Courier Mk. IV T-Type.* 2-seater Sports.
G.T. Coupé.

Elva Courier Mk. IV T-type Sports: Number of cylinders 4
(M.G. or Ford). Cubic capacity 1798 c.c. or 1498 c.c. Compression ratio 8·8 : 1 or 9 : 1. B.H.P. 98 or 83·5. Max.
m.p.h. 100 plus. Overall length 12 ft. 5½ in. Overall width
5 ft. 1 in. Height 3 ft. 8½ in. Turning circle 25 ft. Wheelbase 7 ft. 6 in. Max. track 4 ft. 2½ in. (front), 4 ft. 1 in. (rear).
Fuel tank capacity 6½ Imp. gals. Dry weight 12½ cwt.

Appearance: Low-set, slot radiator air-intake with inset mesh
grille is flanked by downswept integral bumpers beneath inset
headlamps. Bonnet sweeps gently down between front wings.
Flowing wing line rises behind cockpit to squared-off tail line.
Small, horizontal tail-lamps. Well-raked windscreen has thick
framing. Disc wheels standard, wire wheels with "knock-off" hub-caps optional.

ratio 9·7 : 1.   B.H.P. 330.   Max. m.p.h. 190.   Overall length
13 ft. 6 in.   Overall width 5 ft. 6 in.   Height 3 ft. 9 in.   Wheel-
base 8 ft.   Track 4 ft. 6 in. (front), 4 ft. 5⅝ in. (rear).   Fuel
tank(s) capacity 28½ Imp. gals.   Weight 1792 lb.

Appearance: Note unusual styling—tiny passenger area set
amidships with engine at rear.   Low-set, narrow radiator air-
intake; flat "bonnet" flows down between headlamps set
beneath transparent fairings.   Straight-through wing line rises
over rear wheels to flat, slightly inset rear panel.   Sharply
raked windscreen is wrapped well round; rear window is deeply
inset beneath roof line.   Wire wheels have triple-eared "knock-
off" hub-caps.

FIAT

ITALY

Fiat S. A.,

Corso G. Marconi, 10,

Turin, Italy.

Current Models: *500D*. 2-door Sunroof Saloon. ***500*.**
Giardiniera Station Wagon. ***600D*.** 2-door Saloon, Con-
vertible, Multipla 4/5-seater and 6-seater. ***850*.** Standard
and Super 2-door Saloons. ***1100D*.** 4-door Saloon, Station
Wagon. ***1300*.** 4-door Saloon, Family Saloon (Station
Wagon). ***1500*.** 4-door Saloon, Family Saloon (Station
Wagon), Cabriolet. ***1500L*.** 4-door Long Wheel-base Saloon.
***1600S*.** Cabriolet. ***1800B*.** 4-door Saloon, Station Wagon.
***2300*.** de Luxe 4-door Saloon, Coupé, Station Wagon. ***2300S*.**
Coupé.

Fiat 850 Saloon: Number of cylinders 4. Cubic capacity
843 c.c. Compression ratio 8 : 1 (8·8 : 1 Super). B.H.P. 40
(42). Overall length 11 ft. 8¾ in. Overall width 4 ft. 8 3/32 in.
Height 4 ft. 6 17/32 in. Turning circle 29·2 ft. Wheel-base
6 ft. 7 31/64 in. Track 3 ft. 9⅛ in. (front), 3 ft. 11 43/64 in. (rear).
Fuel tank capacity 6·6 Imp. gals. Kerb weight 12¾ cwt.

Appearance: Small car of rounded appearance but note flat front panel with inset headlamps. Deep, almost flat windscreen, largish passenger area and sloping rear window. Rounded tail with outlets for cooling air; round tail-lamps. Bumpers have rubber-tipped overriders; flanged wheel arches. Small, disc wheels with simple hub-caps.

Fiat 1300/1500 Saloon: Number of cylinders 4. Cubic capacity 1295 c.c. or 1481 c.c. Compression ratio 8·8 : 1. B.H.P. 72 or 80. Overall length 13 ft. 2⅝ in. Overall width 5 ft. ⅞ in. Height 4 ft. 7⅞ in. Turning circle 33 ft. 5 in. Wheel-base 7 ft. 11⁹⁄₃₂ in. Track 4 ft. 3 in. (front), 4 ft. 2⁹⁄₆₄ in. (rear). Fuel tank capacity 9·9 Imp. gals. Kerb weight 19 cwt.

Appearance: Rather angular styling. High-set paired headlamps flank oblong radiator air-intake with grille of thin bars. Broad flat bonnet; line of headlamp hoods is carried rearward in form of crease line around bodywork. Passenger area has similar contours front and rear. Simple bumpers have rubber-tipped overriders. Perforated disc wheels with large, flat hub-caps.

Fiat 1800B Saloon: Number of cylinders 6. Cubic capacity 1795 c.c. Compression ratio 8·8 : 1. B.H.P. 97. Overall length 14 ft. 8⅝ in. Overall width 5 ft. 3¾ in. Height 4 ft. 9⅞ in. Turning circle 37 ft. 8¾ in. Wheel-base 8 ft. 8⅜ in. Track 4 ft. 5 in. (front), 4 ft. 3½ in. (rear). Fuel tank capacity 13 Imp. gals. Kerb weight 24·9 cwt.

Appearance: Headlamps beneath pointed hoods and large oblong side/indicator lamps flank full-width radiator air-intake with thinly barred grille and broad central, horizontal bar.

Leading edges of bonnet form prominent " lip " over air-intake.
Straight-through wing line to vertical tail-lamp clusters.
Sturdy, wrap-around bumpers. Curved windscreen and
smallish windows to passenger area. Large, flat hub-caps.

Fiat 2300/2300S Coupé: Number of cylinders 6. Cubic
capacity 2279 c.c. Compression ratio 8·8 : 1 or 8·9 : 1. B.H.P.
117 or 150. Max. m.p.h. 109 plus or 118 plus. Overall
length 15 ft. 1$\frac{57}{64}$ in. Overall width 5 ft. 4$\frac{1}{2}$ in. Height
4 ft. 3$\frac{27}{64}$ in. Turning circle 37 ft. 8$\frac{1}{4}$ in. Wheel-base 8 ft.
8$\frac{11}{32}$ in. Track 4 ft. 5$\frac{5}{32}$ in. (front), 4 ft. 3$\frac{21}{32}$ in. (rear). Fuel
tank capacity 15·4 Imp. gals. Kerb weight 24·2 cwt.

Appearance: Beautifully sleek design. Full-width, angularly
styled radiator air-intake with grille of thin bars. Straight-
through wing line to squarish tail, having rounded top line and
tail-lamps on body " corners ". Deep, well-raked windscreen,
thin roof line, very large, wrap-around three-piece rear window.
Plain bumpers, those at rear wrap well round. Perforated disc
wheels have plain, domed hub-caps.

FORD

GERMANY

Ford Werke A.G.,
Henry-Ford Strasse,
Koln-Niehl, Germany.

Current Models: *Taunus 12M.* Standard and De Luxe 2- and 4-door Saloons, Kombi Station Wagon. *Taunus 12M 1·5 litre.* Standard and De Luxe 2- and 4-door Saloons. *Taunus 12M TS.* 2- and 4-door Saloons, Coupé. *Taunus 17M.* 2- and 4-door Saloons, 2- and 4-door Kombi Station Wagons. *Taunus 20M.* 2- and 4-door Saloons, Hardtop Coupé, 2- and 4-door Kombi Station Wagons. *Taunus 20M TS.* 2- and 4-door Saloons. Hardtop Coupé.

Taunus 12M 2-door Saloon: Number of cylinders V4. Cubic capacity 1183 c.c. or 1498 c.c. Compression ratio 7·8 : 1, 8 : 1 or 9 : 1 (TS). B.H.P. 40, 50 or 65. Overall length 13 ft. 11½ in. (14 ft. 2 in. TS). Overall width 5 ft. 2⅘ in. Height 4 ft. 9⅞ in. Turning circle 37 ft. 9 in. Wheel-base 8 ft. 3½ in. Track 4 ft. 1 in. (front and rear). Fuel tank capacity 8½ Imp. gals. Kerb weight 1859 lb. (1914 lb. TS).

Appearance: Simple, restrained styling. Largish headlamps, plain bumpers front and rear. Note tapering moulding on body sides fairing into elliptical tail-lamps. Squarish styling of prominent passenger area and tail-line. Plain disc wheels.

Taunus 12M TS Coupé: Number of cylinders V4. Cubic capacity 1498 c.c. Compression ratio 9 : 1. B.H.P. 65. Overall length 14 ft. 2 in. Overall width 5 ft. 2⅘ in. Height

4 ft. 7$\frac{9}{10}$ in.   Turning circle 37 ft. 9 in.   Wheel-base 8 ft. 3$\frac{1}{2}$ in.
Track 4 ft. 1 in. (front and rear).   Fuel tank capacity 8$\frac{1}{2}$ Imp.
gals.   Kerb weight 1892 lb.

Appearance: Details mostly as for Saloon—note simple oblong
radiator air-intake with thinly barred grille and high-set headlamps.   Straight-through wing line has prominent leading
edges.   Smallish passenger area with thin roof line.   Curved
windscreen and almost flat rear window.   Wheel discs have
row of very thin radial slots.

Taunus 17M 4-door Saloon: Number of cylinders V4.   Cubic
capacity 1498 c.c. or 1699 c.c.   Compression ratio 8 : 1 or
9 : 1.   B.H.P. 60 or 70.   Overall length 15 ft. $\frac{1}{2}$ in.   Overall
width 5 ft. 7$\frac{1}{2}$ in.   Height 4 ft. 11$\frac{1}{4}$ in. Turning circle 33 ft. 6 in.
Wheel-base 8 ft. 10$\frac{1}{2}$ in.   Track 4 ft. 8$\frac{3}{10}$ in. (front), 4 ft. 7$\frac{9}{10}$ in.
(rear).   Fuel tank capacity 9·9 Imp. gals.   Kerb weight
2127 lb. or 2171 lb.

Appearance: Shapely, well balanced design. Narrow, full-width oblong radiator air-intake with thinly barred grille incorporates headlamps. Indicator lamps in leading edges of wings with bumper curving upwards to meet wings. Broad bonnet, deep, curved windscreen and squarish styling to passenger area. Straight-through wing line to vertical tail-lamps. Wheel-arches slightly cut-back. Plain hub-caps and radially slotted wheel-discs.

Taunus 20M 4-door Kombi Station Wagon: Number of cylinders V6. Cubic capacity 1998 c.c. Compression ratio 8 : 1. B.H.P. 85. Overall length 15 ft. 2½ in. Overall width 5 ft. 7½ in. Height 4 ft. 11 in. Turning circle 33 ft. 6 in. Wheel-base 8 ft. 10½ in. Track 4 ft. 8-⅜ in. (front), 4 ft. 7-¹⁄₁₀ in. (rear). Fuel tank capacity 9·9 Imp. gals. Kerb weight 2436 lb.

Appearance: Generally similar to 17M Saloon but note good looking utility type body. Well-raked rear panel and angular window styling. Note how bumpers front and rear form lower edges of wing line. Unusual headlamp styling on these cars.

FORD

GREAT BRITAIN

Ford Motor Co., Ltd.,
Dagenham, Essex,
England.

History: The Ford organization in England goes back a good deal further than 1928 when the present Company was established, for it was in 1904 that the first Ford car arrived from the United States. The cars were handled by agencies until 1911, when the Ford Motor Company (England) Ltd. was formed with works in Manchester.

It is interesting to recall that whereas, in those days, Manchester was assembling an American car, by 1954 seventeen countries were assembling the British vehicle from Dagenham.

Manchester saw the heyday of the Model T (15,000,000 of which were built in England and America between 1st October, 1908, and 26th May, 1927) and when, in 1925, Manchester produced the 250,000th British-built model, the car was toured throughout the kingdom.

Up to that time, assembly had been carried out in improvised shops adapted from some old carriage works. The existing works at Dagenham was then contemplated and eventually the enormous plant on the River Thames was built in order to deal with the " flow " production methods pioneered by Henry Ford in America. In 1931, 4569 passenger cars were built, by 1937 the production figure was 112,863 and in August, 1946, the millionth vehicle was driven off the end of the assembly lines. By 1954 the daily output was over 1000 units and, in addition, an average of 200 tons of spare parts. Briggs Motor Bodies Limited was acquired by the Ford Motor Company in 1953.

The range of cars offered in 1954 comprised the new " Popular ", the " Anglia " and " Prefect " both completely re-designed, and the " Consul ", " Zephyr " and " Zephyr Zodiac ". In 1955 the " Escort " and " Squire " Estate Cars were added to the " Anglia " and " Prefect " ranges respectively.

Current Models: *Anglia.* Standard and De Luxe 2-door Saloons, Super 2-door Saloon, Standard and De Luxe Estate Cars. ***Cortina.*** Standard and De Luxe 2- and 4-door Saloons, Super 2- and 4-door Saloons, G.T. 2- and 4-door Saloons, Lotus Cortina 2-door Saloon, De Luxe and Super Estate Cars. ***Corsair.*** Standard and De Luxe 2- and 4-door Saloons, G.T. 2- and 4-door Saloons. ***Zephyr 4.*** 4-door Saloon, Estate Car. ***Zephyr 6.*** 4-door Saloon, Estate Car

Zodiac Mk. III. 4-door Saloon, Executive Saloon, Estate Car.

Ford Anglia Saloon: Number of cylinders 4. Cubic capacity 997 c.c. (1198 c.c. Super—optional De Luxe). Compression ratio 8·9 : 1 (8 : 1 optional), 8·7 : 1 (7·3 : 1 optional) 1198 c.c. engine. B.H.P. 39 (48·5). Overall length 12 ft. 9½ in. Overall width 4 ft. 9½ in. Height 4 ft. 8½ in. Turning circle 32 ft. Wheel-base 7 ft. 6½ in. Track 3 ft. 10 in. (front), 3 ft. 9¾ in. (rear). Fuel tank capacity 7 Imp. gals. Kerb weight 14½ cwt.

Appearance: Unusual rear roof line; note how rear window is raked forward. Rounded bonnet, thrust-forward headlamps, straight-through wing line. Drawing shows frontal treatment on Standard model, illustration shows Super version—note radiator air-intake grille on Super and De Luxe versions, also side trim on Super. Disc wheels have large, plain hub-caps.

Ford Cortina Saloon: Number of cylinders 4. Cubic capacity 1198 c.c. (1499·9 c.c. optional De Luxe, standard in Super and G.T.). Compression ratio 9·1 : 1 (7·8 : 1 optional) 1198 c.c., 9 : 1 (7·5 : 1 optional) 1499·9 c.c. B.H.P. 54, 65 and 83·5. Overall length 14 ft. ¼ in. Overall width 5 ft. 2½ in. Height 4 ft. 8½ in. Turning circle 33 ft. 9 in. Wheel-base 8 ft. 2 in. Track 4 ft. 2 in. (front), 4 ft. 1½ in. (rear). Fuel tank capacity 8 Imp. gals. Kerb weight 15½ cwt., 16 cwt. and 16·7 cwt.

Appearance: Full-width grille of very thin vertical bars has thick framing and central bar and incorporates side/direction lamps. Largish headlamps, straight-through wing line to circular tail-lamps. Angular styling to passenger area—rear window is almost vertical. Sculptured body panels outlined in bright trim on Super. Disc wheels have large, plain hub-caps.

Ford Cortina Estate Car: Number of cylinders 4. Cubic capacity 1198 c.c. (1499·9 c.c. Super—optional De Luxe). Compression ratio 9·1 : 1 (7·8 : 1 optional) 1198 c.c., 9 : 1 (7·5 : 1 optional) 1499·9 c.c. B.H.P. 54 (65). Overall length 14 ft. ½ in. Overall width 5 ft. 2½ in. Height 4 ft. 9¾ in. Turning circle 33 ft. 9 in. Wheel-base 8 ft. 2 in. Track 4 ft. 2 in. (front), 4 ft. 1½ in. (rear). Fuel tank capacity 8 Imp. gals. Kerb weight 18½ cwt.

Appearance: Generally similar to Cortina Saloon. Note simulated wood trim on Super model. Shapely, van-like body. Deep, curved windscreen, almost flat roof line. Plain bumpers front and rear. Vertical tail-lamp units.

Ford Corsair Saloon: Number of cylinders 4. Cubic capacity 1499·9 c.c. Compression ratio 8.3 : 1 (7·5 : 1 optional), 9 : 1 G.T. B.H.P. 65 (83·5 G.T.). Overall length 14 ft. 8¾ in. Overall width 5 ft. 3½ in. Height 4 ft. 7¾ in. Turning circle 36 ft. Wheel-base 8 ft. 5 in. Track 4 ft. 2 in. (front), 4 ft. 1½ in. (rear). Fuel tank capacity 8 Imp. gals. Kerb weight 17½ cwt.

Appearance: Shapely, well-balanced design. Flat bonnet slopes down to horizontal leading edge. Headlamps inset into bonnet. Narrow, oblong radiator air-intake with high-set front bumper below. Straight-through wing line to vertical tail-lamps. Deep body sides. Rather angular passenger area. Longish rear deck. Disc wheels have plain hub-caps.

Ford Zephyr 4 Saloon: Number of cylinders 4. Cubic capacity 1703 c.c. Compression ratio 8·3 : 1 (7 : 1 optional). B.H.P. 73·5. Overall length 15 ft. ¾ in. Overall width 5 ft. 9¼ in. Height 4 ft. 9¼ in. Turning circle 36 ft. Wheelbase 8 ft. 11 in. Track 4 ft. 5 in. (front), 4 ft. 5½ in. (rear). Fuel tank capacity 12½ Imp. gals. Kerb weight 23 cwt.

Appearance: Simple, restrained styling. Wide, oblong radiator air-intake with grille of inwardly curved bars flanked by headlamps. Side/direction lamps project from front body corners. Broad, slightly curved bonnet. deep windscreen, thin roof line and large rear window. Tail-lamps canted slightly outwards. Disc wheels have plain hub-caps.

Ford Zephyr 6 Estate Car: Number of cylinders 6. Cubic capacity 2555 c.c. Compression ratio 8·3 : 1 (7 : 1 optional). B.H.P. 106. Overall length 15 ft. $\frac{3}{4}$ in. Overall width 5 ft. $9\frac{1}{4}$ in. Height 4 ft. 9 in. Turning circle 36 ft. Wheel-base 8 ft. 11 in. Track 4 ft. 5 in. (front), 4 ft. $5\frac{1}{2}$ in. (rear). Fuel tank capacity $12\frac{1}{2}$ Imp. gals. Kerb weight 26 cwt.

Appearance: Note differing frontal treatment from Zephyr 4. Radiator air-intake extends full-width of car, has inwardly curved grille with central bar and includes headlamps. Shapely utility type body with sharply raked forward rear panel and narrow roof line. Angular window styling.

Ford Zodiac Mk. III Saloon: Number of cylinders 6. Cubic capacity 2555 c.c. Overall length 15 ft. $2\frac{3}{4}$ in. Overall width 5 ft. 9 in. Height 4 ft. $8\frac{3}{4}$ in. Turning circle 36 ft. 6 in. Wheel-base 8 ft. 11 in. Track 4 ft. 5 in. (front), 4 ft. $5\frac{1}{2}$ in. (rear). Fuel tank capacity 12 Imp. gals. Kerb weight $25\frac{1}{4}$ cwt.

Appearance: As for Zephyr 4 and 6 but full-width radiator air-intake has grille of thin, inward curving bars and paired headlamps at ends. Narrow, slot intake above has thinly barred grille. Note small rear quarter lights on Zodiacs. Bumpers have small over-riders. Wheel trims have spoked effect.

FORD

Ford Motor Co.,

3000 Schaefer Road,

Dearborn, Michigan,

U.S.A.

History: A chain-drive model was the first car manufactured by Henry Ford in 1903. It had two opposed cylinders, giving 8 h.p. In 1904 and 1905 two four-cylinder air-cooled units with shaft transmission were offered, though the original two-cylinder model was continued until 1906. In that year a four-cylinder roadster, the Model N, appeared and also a Six, the latter remaining on the market until 1909. In that year the famous 20 b.h.p. Model T was introduced. This popular model continued for eighteen years. The Model A of 1927 to 1932 had a similar engine to the Model T, but larger, producing 40 b.h.p.

A 65 b.h.p. V8 followed in 1932 and remained unaltered for the next ten years, and from 1937 to 1940 a 60 b.h.p. V8 unit was made. The year 1941 saw the 90 b.h.p. six-cylinder engine, but this was discontinued in 1952. In 1949 the Ford " Custom Tudor " and " Fordor " models had coil spring suspension at the front and leaf springs at the back, having adhered to single transverse springs since 1929.

An automatic torque converter and a 2-speed and reverse planetary transmission was adopted in 1951, and in 1952 a 101 b.h.p. six-cylinder engine was manufactured. Two new engines were introduced in 1954: the 130 b.h.p. V8 in the " Mainline " and " Customline " models and the 115 b.h.p. Six in the " Crestlines ". In the following year the V8 produced 162 b.h.p. and the Six 120 b.h.p.; the " Crestlines " were replaced by the " Fairlanes " and the " Thunderbird " Sports was included in the range.

Current Models: *Falcon.* 2- and 4-door Sedans, 2- and 4-door Station Wagons, Squire Station Wagon. *Falcon Futura.* 2- and 4- door Sedans, 2-door Hardtop, Convertible, 4-door Station Wagon. *Falcon Bus.* Station Bus, Standard and De Luxe Club Wagons. *Fairlane.* 2- and 4-door Sedans, Station Wagon. *Fairlane 500.* 2- and 4-door Sedans, 2-door Hardtop, Sports Coupé, Station Wagon. *Custom.* 2- and 4-door Sedans. *Custom 500.* 2- and 4-door Sedans. *Galaxie 500.* 4-door Sedan, 2- and 4-door Hardtops, Convertible. *Galaxie 500 XL.* 2-door Hardtop, Convertible. *Galaxie 500 LTD.* 2- and 4-door Hardtops. *Station Wagons.* 4-door Ranch Wagon, 4-door Country Sedan (6–10-passenger), 4-door Country Squire (6–10-passenger). *Mustang.* Convertible, Hardtop, Fastback 2 + 2 Coupé. *Thunderbird.* Convertible, Hardtop, Landau Hardtop.

Ford Falcon Futura Hardtop: Number of cylinders 6 (6 and V8 optional). Cubic capacity 170 cu. in. (200 cu. in. (6), 289 cu. in. (V8) optional). Compression ratio 9·1 : 1 (9·2 : 1 (6), 9·3 : 1 (V8) optional). B.H.P. 105 (120 and 200 optional). Overall length 15 ft. 1⅗ in. Overall width 5 ft. 11⅜ in. Height 4 ft. 5⅛ in. Turning circle 38·8 ft. Wheel-base 9 ft. 1½ in. Track 4 ft. 7 in. (4 ft. 7⅜ in. V8) (front), 4 ft. 8 in. (rear). Fuel tank capacity 14 U.S. gals. Kerb weight 2495 lb. (6), 2706 lb. (V8).

Appearance: Full-width radiator air-intake has slightly undercurving grille of thin bars and incorporates headlamps. Leading edges of wings are pointed, straight-through wing line to squared-off tail having large, circular tail-lamps. Plain bumpers front and rear. Flat bonnet and rear deck. Well-raked, curved windscreen; long side windows. Note tapering, sculptured body panels. Wheel discs may be imitation " wire wheels ".

Ford Fairlane 500 Sports Coupé: Number of cylinders 6 (V8 optional). Cubic capacity 200 cu. in. (289 cu. in. V8 optional). Compression ratio 9·2 : 1 (9·3 : 1, 10 : 1 and 10·5 : 1 V8 optional). B.H.P. 120 (200, 225 and 271, V8 optional). Overall length 16 ft. 6⅘ in. Overall width 6 ft. 1⅘ in. Height 4 ft. 6·9/10 in. Turning circle 40·2 ft. Wheel-base 9 ft. 8 in. Track 4 ft. 9 in. (front), 4 ft. 8 in. (rear). Fuel tank capacity 16 U.S. gals. Kerb weight 3005 lb. (6), 3197 lb. and 3203 lb. (V8).

Appearance: Rather angular frontal styling. Small, oblong radiator air-intake with horizontally barred grille is flanked by paired headlamps. Vertical leading edges to wings; straight-through line to almost vertical wing trailing edges and tail-panel having large, oblong tail-lamps. Note broad, flat bonnets and tail-decks on Fords. Small passenger area and large rear window. Wheels have prominent, conical centres.

Ford Fairlane 500 Station Wagon: Number of cylinders 6

(V8 optional). Cubic capacity 200 cu. in. (289 cu. in. V8 optional). Compression ratio 9·2 : 1 (9·3 : 1 and 10 : 1 V8 optional). B.H.P. 120 (200 and 225 optional). Overall length 16 ft. 11 in. Overall width 6 ft. 1⅜ in. Height 4 ft. 8⅜ in. Turning circle 40·2 ft. Wheel-base 9 ft. 8 in. Track 4 ft. 9 in. (front), 4 ft. 8 in. (rear). Fuel tank capacity 20 U.S. gals. Kerb weight 3337 lb. (6), 3529 lb. and 3535 lb. (V8).

Appearance: Frontal styling as for Fairlane Coupé but note rather severe styling of utility type body. Sloping tail-panel slightly inset between rear wing trailing edges. Small, square tail-lamps flank tail-gate. Slight sculptured effect to body sides, narrow full-length trim strips.

Ford Galaxie 500 LTD 4-door Hardtop: Number of cylinders V8. Cubic capacity 289 cu. in. (352 cu. in., 390 cu. in. and 427 cu. in. optional). Compression ratio 9·3 : 1 (9·3 : 1, 10·1 : 1 and 11·1 : 1 optional). B.H.P. 200 (250, 300, 330 and 425 optional). Overall length 17 ft. 6 in. Overall width 6 ft. 5 9/16 in. Height 4 ft. 6 7/16 in. Turning circle 41 ft. Wheel-base 9 ft. 11 in. Track 5 ft. 2 in. (front and rear). Fuel tank capacity 20 U.S. gals. Kerb weight 3736 lb. (3938 lb., 3945 lb. and 3994 lb. optional V8s).

Appearance: Note changed styling this year with vertically mounted, paired headlamps flanking full-width radiator air-intake. Grille of thin, horizontal bars. Headlamps are hooded, straight-through wings to large, oblong tail-lamps which fill depth of tail-panel. Plain bumpers front and rear. Well-raked windscreen, angular passenger area—may be seen with vinyl-covered roof. Four-spoked effect to wheel discs.

Ford Mustang Convertible: Number of cylinders 6 (V8 optional). Cubic capacity 200 cu. in. (289 cu. in. V8 optional). Compression ratio 9·2 : 1 (9·3 : 1, 10 : 1 and 10·5 : 1 V8 optional). B.H.P. 120 (200, 225 and 271 V8 optional). Overall length 15 ft. 1⅜ in. Overall width 5 ft. 8⅛ in. Height 4 ft. 3 in. Turning circle 38 ft. 9 in. Wheel-base 9 ft. Track 4 ft. 7⅝ in. (4 ft. 8 in. V8) (front), 4 ft. 8 in. (rear). Fuel tank capacity 16 U.S. gals. Kerb weight 2755 lb. (6), 3025 lb., 3065 lb. and 3116 lb. (V8).

Appearance: Narrow, oblong radiator air-intake with inset grille and "Mustang" motif is thrust forward and flanked by high-set headlamps. Straight-through wing line rises slightly at rear wheels to merge into slightly inset rear panel bearing square tail-lamps. Plain bumpers front and rear. Note inset side body panels—may be seen with dummy intake forward of rear wheels. Deep, curved windscreen is well raked. Wheels have spoked effect or dummy "wire wheels".

GILBERN

GREAT BRITAIN

Gilbern Sports Car (Components) Ltd.,

Pentwyn Works,

Llantwit,

Near Pontypridd,

Glamorgan,

South Wales.

Current Model: *G.T. 1800.* 2-door Sports Saloon.

Gilbern G.T. 1800 Sports Saloon: Number of cylinders 4 (MGB). Cubic capacity 1798 c.c. Compression ratio 8·8 : 1 (10 : 1 optional). B.H.P. 96 (112). Max. m.p.h. 120. Overall length 12 ft. 6 in. Overall width 5 ft. Height 4 ft. 2½ in. Turning circle 30 ft. Wheel-base 7 ft. 7¾ in. Track 4 ft. 2 in. (front and rear). Fuel tank capacity 9½ Imp. gals. Kerb weight 16¼ cwt.

Appearance: Squarish frontal contours. Small radiator air-intake has horizontal bars; plain bumper and high-set head-lamps. Straight-through wing line to vertical tail-lamp clusters. Curved windscreen and well-rounded rear body with large rear window. Wire wheels with " knock-off " hub-caps.

GLAS

GERMANY

Hans Glas Isaria-Vertriebs-Kg.,
Dingolfing,
Bayern,
Western Germany.

Current Models: *Glas-Goggomobil T 250, T 300* and *T 400*. 2-door Saloon. *Glas-Goggomobil TS 250, TS 300* and *TS 400*. Coupé. *Glas-Isar 600* and *700*. 2-door Saloon. *Glas-Isar K 600* and *K 700*. Estate Car. *Glas S 1004*. 2-door Coupé, Cabriolet. *Glas S 1204*. 2-door Coupé, Cabriolet. *Glas 1300 GT*. 2-door Coupé. *Glas 1700*. 4-door Saloon.

Glas-Goggomobil T 250/300/400 Saloon: Number of cylinders 2. Cubic capacity 247 c.c., 296 c.c. or 395 c.c. Compression ratio 6 : 1. B.H.P. 13·6, 15 or 18·5. Overall length 9 ft. 6½ in. Overall width 4 ft. 2⅝ in. Height 4 ft. 3½ in. Turning circle 24 ft. Wheel-base 5 ft. 10⅘ in. Track 3 ft. 6⁹⁄₁₀ in. (front and rear). Fuel tank capacity 5½ Imp. gals. Weight 1584 lb.

Appearance: Small car with prominent, centrally placed passenger area. Rounded " bonnet "—note lack of frontal air-intake due to rear mounted engine—and inset headlamps. Flat windscreen, small side windows and curved rear window. Square styled wheel arches and " suggested " wings. Plain bumpers front and rear. Tiny wheels with domed hub-caps.

Glas 1300 GT Coupé: Number of cylinders 4. Cubic capacity 1290 c.c. Compression ratio 9·2 : 1. B.H.P. 75. Max. m.p.h. 105. Overall length 13 ft. 3½ in. Overall width 5 ft. 1 in. Height 4 ft. 2⅔ in. Turning circle 32 ft. 9 in. Wheel-base 7 ft. 7³⁄₁₀ in. Track 4 ft. 1⅝ in. (front), 3 ft. 11¼ in. (rear). Fuel tank capacity 9·85 Imp. gals. Weight 2640 lb.

Appearance: Sleek, graceful design. Narrow, full-width radiator air-intake with inset mesh grille flanked by thrust-forward headlamps. High-set, plain bumper has side/direction lamps below. Broad, flat bonnet; deep, well-raked windscreen and curved roof line. Straight-through wings to slightly cut-away tail. Wheel discs have oblong perforations.

GORDON-KEEBLE

GREAT BRITAIN

Gordon-Keeble Ltd.,
  The Airport,
    Southampton,
Hampshire, England.

Current Model: *GK 1*. 2-door Saloon.

Gordon-Keeble GK 1 Saloon: Number of cylinders V8
(Chevrolet Corvette). Cubic capacity 5355 c.c. Compression
ratio 10·5 : 1. B.H.P. 300. Max. m.p.h. 145. Overall length
15 ft. 4½ in. Overall width 5 ft. 8 in. Height 4 ft. 5 in.
Turning circle 32 ft. 6 in. Wheel-base 8 ft. 6 in. Track
4 ft. 7 in. (front and rear). Fuel tank(s) capacity 22 Imp. gals.
Weight (laden) 3486 lb.

Appearance: Shapely saloon design by Bertone. Simple
oblong radiator air-intake flanked by paired headlamps.
Straight-through wings to vertical tail-lamp clusters. Small
intake on broad, flat bonnet. Perforated disc wheels have
triple-eared " knock-off " hub-caps.

HILLMAN

GREAT BRITAIN

Hillman Motor Co., Ltd.,
Ryton-on-Dunsmore,
Coventry, England.

History: The Hillman Motor Car Company was established in 1907 by William Hillman, a famous British motorist of that time, who in collaboration with Louis Coatelen produced a car for participation in the T.T. race of that year.

The firm subsequently turned to the family car type on which its fame has been founded ever since they introduced a 9 h.p. model in 1912. In 1928 the Hillman Company was linked with Humbers in being distributed and sold overseas by the same organization. In 1932 both companies became a division of the Rootes Group. In the same year, after re-organization, the first Hillman Minx was offered to the public.

Hillmans produced many models of different size and power, but by 1952 all resources were concentrated on the production of a new Minx. It was completely re-styled to celebrate the 21st anniversary of the model. The four-cylinder engine of 1265 c.c. with an aluminium head developed 35·5 b.h.p.

In 1953, in addition to offering the saloon, convertible and estate car, the Californian Hardtop was introduced. This model, constructed by Thrupp & Maberly, incorporated a wide wrap-around rear window and narrow door pillars. These models were continued in 1954 with only minor modifications being made to the luggage boot and the tail-lights, although in 1955 the air-intake grille was re-styled.

May, 1956, saw the introduction of an entirely re-styled Minx, similar in general outline to the Sunbeam Rapier and the Singer Gazelle. The compression ratio was increased to 8 : 1 and b.h.p. to 51. For 1957 the "Jubilee" Minx had its grille re-designed and Manumatic transmission with two-pedal control was made available on the De Luxe Saloon, Convertible and Estate Car. "Easidrive" fully automatic transmission became available for these three models in 1960.

Current Models: *Imp.* Standard and De Luxe 2-door Saloons. *Super Minx (Mk. III).* 4-door Saloon, Estate Car. *Minx 1600 De Luxe (Series V).* 4-door Saloon. *Husky (Series III).* Estate Car.

Hillman Imp Saloon: Number of cylinders 4. Cubic capacity 875 c.c. Compression ratio 10 : 1. B.H.P. 39. Overall length 11 ft. 7 in. Overall width 5 ft. ¼ in. Height 4 ft. 6½ in. Turning circle 30 ft. 6 in. Wheel-base 6 ft. 10 in. Track 4 ft. 1 in. (front), 4 ft. (rear). Fuel tank capacity 6 Imp. gals. Dry weight 1446 lb. (Standard), 1486 lb. (De Luxe).

Appearance: Small car with large, prominent passenger **area.** Flat-fronted body; high-set bumper with grille and side/direction lamps below. Note large windscreen, side windows and rear window. Fluted body sides; vertical, paired tail-lamps. Squarish tail. Disc wheels have rounded hub-caps.

Hillman Super Minx Saloon: Number of cylinders 4. Cubic capacity 1592 c.c. Compression ratio 8·3 : 1. B.H.P. 62. Overall length 13 ft. 10¼ in. Overall width 5 ft. 3¾ in. Height 4 ft. 10 in. Turning circle 36 ft. Wheel-base 8 ft. 5 in. Track 4 ft. 3¾ in. (front), 4 ft. ½ in. (rear). Fuel tank capacity 10½ Imp. gals. Dry weight 2252 lb.

Appearance: Headlamps at ends of full-width radiator air-intake; " eyebrow " side/indicator lamps above headlamps. Deep, curved windscreen, almost flat roof line, curved rear window with " lip " over. Note flattened " fin " treatment at rear and vertical tail-lamp clusters. Wheel-discs have radial slots.

Hillman Super Minx Estate Car: Number of cylinders 4.

Cubic capacity 1592 c.c. Compression ratio 8·3 : 1. B.H.P. 62. Overall length 13 ft. 10¼ in. Overall width 5 ft. 3¾ in. Height 4 ft. 10 in. Turning circle 36 ft. Wheel-base 8 ft. 5 in. Track 4 ft. 3¾ in. (front), 4 ft. ½ in. (rear). Fuel tank capacity 10 Imp. gals. Dry weight 2358 lb.

Appearance: Frontal details as for Saloon but note rather attractive, severely lined utility type body. Flattened " fin " effect is maintained on this model. Plain bumpers front and rear have rubber-tipped overriders. Different side trim on Estate Car.

Hillman Minx 1600 De Luxe Saloon: Number of cylinders 4. Cubic capacity 1592 c.c. Compression ratio 8·3 : 1. B.H.P. 56·5. Overall length 13 ft. 5½ in. Overall width 5 ft. ¾ in. Height 4 ft. 10 in. Turning circle 36 ft. Wheel-base 8 ft. Track 4 ft. 3¾ in. (front), 4 ft. ⅞ in. (rear). Fuel tank capacity 10 Imp. gals. Dry weight 2095 lb.

Appearance: Narrow, full-width radiator air-intake, with side/direction lamps at ends, projects from body front. Slightly hooded headlamps; straight-through wing line to vertical tail-lamps. Note squarish styling to passenger area. Plain bumpers have rubber-tipped overriders. Disc wheels.

HINO

JAPAN

Hino Motors Limited,
Hino Building,
No. 4, Tori 2-Chome,
Nihonbashi,
Chuo-Ku,
Tokyo, Japan.

Hino

Current Model: *Contessa 1300*. 4-door Saloon, Coupé.

Hino Contessa 1300 Saloon: Number of cylinders 4. Cubic capacity 1251 c.c. Compression ratio 8·5 : 1. B.H.P. 55. Max. m.p.h. 81. Overall length 13 ft. 7⅞ in. Overall width 5 ft. ¼ in. Height 4 ft. 6¾ in. Turning circle 30·2 ft. Wheelbase 7 ft. 5¾ in. Fuel tank capacity 7·19 Imp. gals.

Appearance: Small car with body styling by Michelotti. Paired headlamps with small grilles beneath and side/indicator lamps on body "corners". Flat bonnet slopes gently down to front panel; deep curved windscreen; narrow roof line forms prominent peak over rear window. Full-width, horizontally barred grille forms rear panel with oblong tail-lamps high-set. Angular bumpers wrap-around. Disc wheels with simple hub-caps.

126

Current Models: *Sceptre*. 4-door Sports Saloon. ***Hawk (Series IV).*** 4-door Saloon, Limousine, Estate Car. ***Super Snipe (Series V).*** 4-door Saloon, Limousine, Estate Car. ***Imperial.*** 4-door Saloon, Limousine.

Humber Sceptre Sports Saloon: Number of cylinders 4. Cubic capacity 1592 c.c. Compression ratio 9·1 : 1. B.H.P. 84. Overall length 13 ft. 11 in. Overall width 5 ft. 3¼ in. Height 4 ft. 9 in. Turning circle 36 ft. Wheel-base 8 ft. 5 in. Track 4 ft. 3¾ in. (front), 4 ft. ½ in. (rear). Fuel tank capacity 10½ Imp. gals. Dry weight 2325 lb.

Appearance: Generally similar to Hillman Super Minx and Singer Vogue but roof line is sleeker. Paired, hooded head-lamps flank small, vertically barred radiator air-intake. Small intakes below headlamps incorporate side/direction lamps and wrap-around front body " corners ". Curved windscreen extends into rounded roof line; wrap-around, well-raked rear window. Flattened " fins "; the line of which encloses large, vertical tail-lamp clusters. Wheel discs have radial slots.

Humber Hawk Saloon: Number of cylinders 4. Cubic capacity 2267 c.c. Compression ratio 7·5 : 1. B.H.P. 78. Overall length 15 ft. 4 in. Overall width 5 ft. 10 in. Height 4 ft. 11¼ in. Turning circle 38 ft. Wheel-base 9 ft. 2 in. Track 4 ft. 8⅞ in. (front), 4 ft. 7½ in. (rear). Fuel tank capacity 16 Imp. gals. Dry weight 3080 lb.

Appearance: Oblong radiator air-intake has horizontal slats. Headlamps are slightly hooded; side/direction lamps below. Straight-through wing—note notch at rear window to suggest rear wings—to vertical triple tail-lamp cluster. Deep windscreen, narrow roof line and slight lip over rear window. Wrap-around bumpers. Disc wheels have large, domed hub-caps.

Humber Super Snipe Saloon: Number of cylinders 6. Cubic capacity 2965 c.c. Compression ratio 8 : 1. B.H.P. 137·5. Overall length 15 ft. 7½ in. Overall width 5 ft. 10 in. Height 4 ft. 11¾ in. Turning circle 38 ft. Wheel-base 9 ft. 2 in. Track 4 ft. 8⅝ in. (front), 4 ft. 7½ in. (rear). Fuel tank capacity 16 Imp. gals. Dry weight 3425 lb.

Appearance: Generally as for Humber Hawk but note differing frontal treatment. Wrap-around radiator air-intake grille consists of thin horizontal bars and includes side/direction lamps. Paired headlamps have slightly hooded effect. Deep wind-screen and rear window. Rounded bonnet line. Wheel discs have radial slots.

Humber Imperial Saloon: Number of cylinders 6. Cubic capacity 2965 c.c. Compression ratio 8 : 1. B.H.P. 137·5. Overall length 15 ft. 7½ in. Overall width 5 ft. 10 in. Height 4 ft. 11¾ in. Turning circle 38 ft. Wheel-base 9 ft. 2 in. Track 4 ft. 8⅞ in. (front), 4 ft. 7½ in. (rear). Fuel tank capacity 16 Imp. gals. Dry weight 3425 lb.

Appearance: Coachwork by Thrupp and Maberly. Generally similar lines to Super Snipe but more luxuriously finished. Note black leather finish to roof.

IMPERIAL

UNITED STATES OF AMERICA

Chrysler Division,
Chrysler Corporation,
Detroit, Michigan, U.S.A.

Current Models: *Crown.* 2- and 4-door Hardtops, Convertible Coupé. *Le Baron.* 4-door Hardtop.

Imperial Crown 2-door Hardtop: Number of cylinders V8. Cubic capacity 413 cu. in. Compression ratio 10 : 1 (8 : 1 available). B.H.P. 340. Overall length 18 ft. 11⅘ in. Overall width 6 ft. 8 in. Height 4 ft. 9½ in. Turning circle 47·6 ft. Wheel-base 10 ft. 9 in. Track 5 ft. 1⅘ in. (front), 5 ft. 1⁷⁄₁₀ in. (rear). Fuel tank capacity 25 U.S. gals.

Appearance: Divided, full-width radiator air-intake having paired headlamps behind glass panels set into grille of thin bars. Bumper end plates form lower edges of wings, those at rear mounting tail-lamps. Rather angular styling generally with broad, flat bonnet and rear deck. Well-raked, shallowish wrap-around windscreen. Wheel discs are polished, dished and have prominent centre portion.

INNOCENTI

ITALY

Soc. Generale per L'Industria Metallurgica e Meccanico,
Via Piterri 81,
Milan,
Italy.

Current Models: *A.40/S.* 2-door Saloon. *1100 Spider.*
2-seater Sports. *I.M.3.* 4-door Saloon. *J.4.* 4-door Saloon.

Innocenti I.M.3 Saloon: Number of cylinders 4. Cubic
capacity 1098 c.c. Compression ratio 8·9 : 1. B.H.P. 58.
Overall length 12 ft. 2¾ in. Overall width 5 ft. ½ in. Height
4 ft. 5 in. Turning circle 34 ft. 9 in. Wheel-base 7 ft. 9½ in.
Track 4 ft. 3½ in. (front), 4 ft. 2⅘ in. (rear). Fuel tank capacity
8½ Imp. gals. Weight 17 cwt.

Appearance: Generally similar to B.M.C. models but note
differing frontal treatment. Head and side lamps are mounted
as units and flank grille of thick horizontal bars. Windscreen
is deep and passenger area prominent. Perforated disc wheels
have large hub caps.

ISO

ITALY

Iso S.p.A. Automotoveicoli,
Bresso,
Milan,
Italy.

Current Model: *Rivolta.* 2-door Coupé.

Iso Rivolta Coupé: Number of cylinders V8 (Chevrolet).
Cubic capacity 5359 c.c. Compression ratio 10·5 : 1 or
11·25 : 1. B.H.P. 300, 340 or 400. Max. m.p.h. 150 plus.
Overall length 15 ft. 7 in. Overall width 5 ft. 8½ in. Height
4 ft. 4½ in. Turning circle 40 ft. Wheel-base 8 ft. 10 in.
Track 4 ft. 7 in. (front and rear). Fuel tank capacity 21 Imp.
gals. Kerb weight 26½ cwt.

Appearance: Graceful coachwork by Bertone. Oblong radiator air-intake with inset grille of horizontal bars and prominent
" lip " over. Headlamps are hooded and the line of the hoods
is carried back over wheel arches. Faired intake on bonnet
top. Rounded windscreen, narrow roof line and large well-
raked rear window. Rear aspect is squarish and tail-lamps
high-set on rear body " corners "; bumper wraps well round
to wheel arches. Perforated disc wheels or Borrani wire wheels
with triple-eared " knock-off " hub-caps.

JAGUAR

GREAT BRITAIN

Jaguar Cars Ltd.,
    Coventry,
    England.

History: The "Jaguar" concern began in a very modest way as a small coachbuilding shop in Blackpool, Lancs., where sidecars for motor cycles were made. That was in 1923, and five years later, the proprietor William Lyons, who had also been making special "Swallow" bodies for Austin Sevens, moved his firm to Coventry, where by 1931 as the Swallow Sidecar and Coachbuilding Co. they were building bodies on Standard car chassis.

The first car produced by the company—known as the "S.S.1" (Swallow Sports, 1)—was a very rakish two-seater coupé mounted on a chassis which used a 16 h.p. Standard side-valve engine and other Standard components, but its good finish and smart lines gave it immediate success from which the firm has never looked back.

Just before the war, the cars now fitted with overhead-valve engines were known as "S.S. Jaguars", but after the war the prefix was dropped and the name "Jaguar" used alone.

The company's world-wide fame dates from the appearance of the "XK.120" two-seater, in which an entirely new twin overhead-camshaft engine was embodied which immediately showed itself to be the fastest production car in the world.

This superb effort was followed by the Mark VII saloon with the same engine, and the range of models was still further increased by the introduction of a fixed-head coupé, and then a drop-head coupé on the XK.120 chassis; whilst the XK.120C, a very fast racing model, won the Le Mans 24-Hour Race for Britain in 1951. In all, Jaguars have won this gruelling event five times, the last occasion being in 1957.

Current Models: *Mark II.* 2·4 litre, 3·4 litre and 3·8 litre 4-door Saloons. *"S" Type.* 3·4 litre and 3·8 litre 4-door Saloons. *Mark X.* 3·8-litre and 4·2-litre 4-door Saloons. *"E" Type.* 3·8-litre and 4·2-litre open 2-seater, Fixed-head Coupé.

Jaguar Mark II Saloon: Number of cylinders 6. Cubic capacity 2483 c.c., 3442 c.c. or 3781 c.c. Compression ratio 8 : 1 (7 : 1 optional), 8 : 1 (7 : 1 or 9 : 1 optional on 3·4 and 3·8 litre engines). B.H.P. 120, 210 or 220. Overall length 15 ft. ¾ in. Overal width 5 ft. 6¾ in. Height 4 ft. 9½ in. Turning circle 33 ft. 6 in. Wheel-base 8 ft. 11⅜ in. Track 4 ft. 7 in. (4 ft. 7½ in. wire wheels) (front), 4 ft. 5⅜ in. (4 ft. 6½ in. wire wheels) (rear). Fuel tank capacity 12 Imp. gals. Kerb weight 28¼ cwt. or 29 cwt.

Appearance: Rounded car with small, oval, thrust-forward radiator air-intake. Headlamps faired into body; straight-through wing line to rounded tail. Massive, fluted bumpers have vertical over-riders. Rear wheels partially enclosed. Perforated disc wheels standard, wire wheels with "knock-off" hub-caps optional.

Jaguar ".S." Type Saloon: Number of cylinders 6. Cubic capacity 3442 c.c. or 3781 c.c. Compression ratio 8 : 1 (7 : 1 or 9 : 1 optional). B.H.P. 210 or 220. Overall length 15 ft.

7$\frac{13}{16}$ in. Overall width 5 ft. 6$\frac{3}{4}$ in. Height 4 ft. 6$\frac{1}{2}$ in. Turning circle 33 ft. 6 in. Wheel-base 8 ft. 11$\frac{3}{8}$ in. Track 4 ft. 7$\frac{1}{4}$ in. (front), 4 ft. 6$\frac{1}{4}$ in. (rear). Fuel tank(s) capacity 14 Imp. gals. Kerb weight 30$\frac{3}{4}$ cwt.

Appearance: Frontal details similar to Mk. II but note slightly hooded head and fog lamps, narrow bumpers and combined side/direction lamps. Note also long boot similar to Mk. X and wrap-around bumpers. Curved windscreen and rounded roof line. Rear wheels partially enclosed. Perforated disc wheels standard, wire wheels with " knock-off " hub-caps optional.

Jaguar Mark X Saloon: Number of cylinders 6. Cubic capacity 3781 c.c. or 4235 c.c. Compression ratio 8 : 1 (7 : 1 or 9 : 1 optional). B.H.P. 255 or 265. Overall length 16 ft. 10 in. Overall width 6 ft. 4 in. Height 4 ft. 6 in. Turning circle 37 ft. Wheel-base 10 ft. Track 4 ft. 10 in. (front and rear). Fuel tank(s) capacity 20 Imp. gals. Kerb weight 35$\frac{3}{4}$ cwt.

Appearance: Striking raked-forward frontal treatment. Squarish radiator air-intake with vertically barred grille. Slightly hooded, paired headlamps; straight-through wings to vertical tail-lamp clusters in trailing edges. Rounded passenger area; large boot with rear bumpers wrapping well around. Wheels have polished discs.

Jaguar " E " Type Fixed Head Coupé: Number of cylinders 6. Cubic capacity 3781 c.c. or 4235 c.c. Compression ratio 9 : 1 (8 : 1 optional). B.H.P. 265. Max. m.p.h. 150 plus. Overall length 14 ft. 7$\frac{5}{16}$ in. Overall width 5 ft. 5$\frac{1}{4}$ in. Height 4 ft. $\frac{1}{8}$ in. Turning circle 37 ft. Wheel-base 8 ft. Track 4 ft. 2 in. (front and rear). Fuel tank capacity 14 Imp. gals. Kerb weight 24 cwt.

Appearance: Aerodynamic lined body. Small, oval radiator air-intake flanked by divided bumpers. Wing line rises slightly over rear wheels to merge into sloping roof line. Note upswept tail-line; rear bumpers are high set and wrap around to wheel-arches. Large, tapering fairing on bonnet top. Wire wheels have " knock-off " hub-caps.

JENSEN

GREAT BRITAIN

Jensen Motors Ltd.,
Carter's Green, West Bromwich,
Staffordshire, England.

History: Alan and Dick Jensen constructed their first
" special " from an Austin Seven before they were twenty
years of age. The performance of the new version was
outstanding and the bodywork low and sleek. The car
came to the attention of the Chief Engineer of the Standard
company who agreed to supply chassis to the brothers for
the fitting of special bodies. The resulting models were
called the Avon Standard two-seater and, later, the coupé
of 1930.

By an arrangement with Wolseleys, the Patrick-Jensen
appeared soon after this, using the Hornet chassis. In
1936 the first standard model was put into production.
Powered by a modified Ford V8 engine it was capable of
90 m.p.h. and had a very low body. Also, it was the
first car in the world to fit overdrive as a standard feature.

As an indication of the adventurous experimenting
indulged in by the two brothers, it might be interesting
to note that in 1937 a truck was successfully produced,
having a tubular alloy chassis and underframe, which gave
the largest loading space of any commercial vehicle under
three tons.

Unfortunately at this time, World War II brought to
a halt any further pioneering and the company went over
to the production of war materials, but after hostilities
ceased, the Jensen Interceptor Coupé was introduced.

The 1954 model was powered by the Austin 125,
4-litre, six-cylinder engine, and new in 1954 and con-
tinuing through 1955, was the 541 saloon with the same
power unit but having a low two-door body of new design
constructed of reinforced glass fibre. This material is
becoming more widely used for car bodies, and is remark-
able for its lightness and resistance to accidental damage.

Disc brakes were made available on the De Luxe version of the 541 for 1957.

Current Model: *C-V8.* 2-door G.T. Saloon.

Jensen C-V8 G.T. Saloon: Number of cylinders V8 (Chrysler). Cubic capacity 6276 c.c. Compression ratio 10 : 1. Max. m.p.h. 130 plus. Overall length 15 ft. 4½ in. Overall width 5 ft. 7½ in. Height 4 ft. 7 in. Turning circle 38 ft. Wheelbase 8 ft. 9 in. Track 4 ft. 7¹³⁄₁₆ in. (front), 4 ft. 8⅛ in. (rear). Fuel tank capacity 16 Imp. gals. Weight 30 cwt.

Appearance: Distinctive frontal styling—low-set, divided radiator air-intake, paired headlamps mounted at an angle with direction indicators below. Small air-intake in rounded bonnet nose. Rounded tail features horizontal, triple rear-lamp clusters and wrap-around bumper. Smallish passenger area with well-raked windscreen and wrap-around rear window. Perforated disc wheels with large, rounded hub-caps.

LANCIA

ITALY

Lancia & Co.,

via Vincenzo Lancia, 27,

Turin, Italy.

Current Models: *Fulvia.* 4-door Saloon. *Fulvia 2C.* 4-door Saloon. *Flavia.* 4-door Saloon, Pininfarina Coupé, Zagato Sport Coupé, Vignale Convertible. *Flaminia.* 4-door Saloon, Pininfarina 3B Coupé, Touring 3C 2 + 2 G.T. Coupé, Touring 3C G.T. Coupé, Touring 3C Convertible, Zagato 3C Sport Coupé.

Lancia Fulvia Saloon: Number of cylinders V4. Cubic capacity 1091 c.c. Compression ratio 7·8 : 1 (9 : 1 2C). B.H.P. 60 (71). Max. m.p.h. 86. Overall length 13 ft. 7 in. Overall width 5 ft. 1½ in. Height 4 ft. 7 10/16 in. Turning circle 34 ft. Wheel-base 8 ft. 1½ in. Track 4 ft. 3½ in. (front), 4 ft. 2⅖ in. (rear). Fuel tank capacity 8·4 Imp. gals. Dry weight 19½ cwt.

Appearance: Rather angular styling. Oblong radiator air-intake with horizontally barred grille and framing which is carried around paired headlamps. Broad, flat bonnet, curved, rather upright windscreen, thin roof line and large rear window. Squared-off rear contours feature high-set, oblong rear lamps. Perforated disc wheels have large, plain hub-caps.

143

Appearance: Oblong radiator air-intake, small, shallow air-intake on bonnet top. Wrap-around front bumper with wide, under-curved overriders. Straight-through wing line. Perforated disc wheels. Rear passenger area line flows down to form shallow " fins ".

Lancia Flaminia Touring 3C G.T. Coupé: Number of cylinders V6. Cubic capacity 2775 c.c. Compression ratio 9 : 1. B.H.P. 150. Max. m.p.h. 120. Overall length 14 ft. $9\frac{1}{2}$ in. Overall width 5 ft. $5\frac{5}{8}$ in. Height 4 ft. $3\frac{2}{8}$ in. Turning circle 36 ft. Wheel-base 8 ft. $3\frac{1}{2}$ in. Track 4 ft. 6 in. (front and rear). Fuel tank capacity $12\frac{1}{2}$ Imp. gals. Kerb weight 27 cwt.

Appearance: Body by Touring of Milan. Large, oblong radiator air-intake with inset grille. Paired headlamps with oblong side-lamps below. Simple, wrap-around bumpers have vestigial overriders. Straight-through wing line to large, oddly shaped rear-lamp clusters. Deep wrap-around windscreen and rear window. Disc wheels have large perforations and hub-caps with prominent rims.

LINCOLN

UNITED STATES OF AMERICA

Lincoln Mercury Division,
    Ford Motor Co.,
      Detroit, Michigan,
        U.S.A.

History: In 1917 Henry Leland
founded the Lincoln company and
presented its first model in 1921.
This was a car of 90 b.h.p. and
a V8, but the Ford company
bought the new concern in the following year. Ford
continued to produce the engine without change until
1932, except in 1928 when an increase of $\frac{1}{8}$ in. was
made to the bore, during which time it produced 125
b.h.p.

From 1932 to 1940, a twelve-cylinder model was made,
the bore being reduced by $\frac{1}{8}$ in. in 1934. Also in 1932,
the Lincoln Continental was presented.

The frameless-bodied 110 b.h.p. Zephyr V12 was made
in 1936 and was produced until 1949. Two major
changes were made to the engine in that time. The first
occurred in 1940, when the bore was increased by $\frac{1}{8}$ in.,
and then in 1942 when it was increased again by $\frac{1}{16}$ in.
In 1941 the Continental was unusual in carrying the
spare wheel externally in a vertical position at the back.

A completely re-designed car was produced in 1949.
It was a V8 developing 152 b.h.p., and hydromatic drive
was optional.

A 160 b.h.p. overhead valve V8 engine was introduced
in 1952 and in the following year the power output was
increased to 205 b.h.p. In 1953 power-assisted brakes
and steering were offered as optional equipment. 1954
models continued with only minor modifications but
in the following year the power was raised to 225
b.h.p.

147

In 1956 the power of the V8 engine was raised again to 285 b.h.p., and the whole car drastically re-styled. A striking feature was the massive overriders incorporating very wide striplights, housing side and direction lights.

Current Models: *Continental*. 4-door Sedan, 4-door Convertible.

Lincoln Continental Sedan: Number of cylinders V8. Cubic capacity 430 cu. in. Compression ratio 10·1 : 1. B.H.P. 320. Overall length 18 ft. $\frac{3}{10}$ in. Overall width 6 ft. $6\frac{2}{3}$ in. Height 4 ft. $6\frac{1}{5}$ in. Turning circle 45·7 ft. Wheel-base 10 ft. 6 in. Track 5 ft. $2\frac{1}{10}$ in. (front), 5 ft. 1 in. (rear). Fuel tank capacity $23\frac{1}{2}$ U.S. gals. Kerb weight 5272 lb.

Appearance: Large car with distinctive styling—note rather "slab-sided" appearance and angular contours of wings. Full-width radiator air-intake with inset paired headlamps. Side/direction lamps in leading edges of wings. Wide, flat bonnet, well-raked windscreen and narrow roof line. Rather angular styling to passenger area. Rear tail-lamp and bumper treatment echo frontal styling. Large, dished hub-caps.

LOTUS

Lotus Engineering Co., Ltd.,
Delamare Road,
Cheshunt,
Hertfordshire,
England.

History: The extremely successful series of Lotus sports/racing cars had its beginnings in 1947 when Colin Chapman built a special based on an ancient Austin 7 saloon which, after suitable tuning, took part in races and trials. Mks. II and III followed, also based on Austin 7 components, and at the end of 1951 the Lotus Engineering Company was formed to cope with requests from the many people who were asking for replicas of the successful little Lotus.

The first car built by the new company was the Mk. IV, a trials special. A projected 100 m.p.h. unsupercharged Austin 7 powered car, to be designated Mk. V, has not been built.

However, the car which really set the small firm on the way to success was the Mk. VI, over 100 of which have been built and which, it was intended, should be constructed by amateur enthusiasts from various proprietary components, using as a basis a strong, light, multi-tubular frame. Powered mainly by Ford and M.G. engines, these cars served their owners as ordinary day-to-day transportation and enabled them to take part in sports car racing.

For 1954 the famous Mk. VIII was built, with a beautiful streamlined body which, with its twin tail fins, set a fashion for sports/racing cars. Following numerous competition successes with these cars, driven by Chapman himself and many private owners, 1955 saw the appearance of the Mk. IX, which continued the twin-finned streamlined body in modified form. Fitted with the 1097 c.c. Coventry Climax engine this model has also been very successful in competitions.

The "Eleven" was successful, in 1956, in winning the 1100 c.c. class at Le Mans. In the 1957 event, a 750 c.c. version won the Index of Performance and a 100 c.c. version finished second in the Index of Performance and also won its class.

Current Models: *Seven*. 2-seater Sports. ***Super Seven 1500*.** 2-seater Sports. ***Super Seven 1500 Cosworth*.** 2-seater Sports. ***Elan Series Two*.** 2-seater Sports. **Lotus/Ford Cortina.** 2-door Sports/Racing Saloon.

Lotus Super Seven 1500 Sports: Number of cylinders 4 (Ford). Cubic capacity 1498 c.c. Compression ratio 8·3 : 1 (9·5 : 1 on Cosworth model). B.H.P. 75 (95). Max. m.p.h. 100 (105). Overall length 12 ft. Overall width 4 ft. 8 in. Height (to top of scuttle) 2 ft. 4 in., (to top of hood) 3 ft. 7½ in. Turning circle 28 ft. Wheel-base 7 ft. 4 in. Track 3 ft. 11 in. (front and rear). Fuel tank capacity 8 Imp. gals. Weight 9¼ cwt.

Appearance: Small, stark 2-seater of very low build. Thrust-forward radiator air-intake has simple grille. Front suspension is fully exposed; headlamps small, high set. Long, flowing front wings; rear wings integrated with body. Note body sides cut away at cockpit. Flat tail with externally mounted spare wheel. Disc wheels with simple hub-caps.

Lotus Elan S2 Sports: Number of cylinders 4 (Ford with Lotus twin overhead camshaft cylinder head). Cubic **capacity** 1558 c.c. Compression ratio 9·5 : 1. B.H.P. 105. Max m.p.h. 115. Overall length 12 ft. 1½ in. Overall width 4 ft. 8 in. Height (to top of scuttle) 2 ft. 6 in., (to top of hood) 3 ft. 5 in. Turning circle 29 ft. 3 in. Wheel-base 7 ft. Track 3 ft. 11½ in. (front and rear). Fuel tank capacity 10 Imp. gals. Kerb weight 13¼ cwt.

Appearance: Sleek, smoothly lined bodywork with absence of projections. Note retractable headlamps. Low-set, slot radiator air-intake beneath novel foam-filled bumpers which merge with body. Straight-through wings to squared off tail having slightly inset rear panel mounting tail-lamp units. Well-raked windscreen has heavy framing. Perforated disc wheels standard, wire wheels with " knock-off " hub-caps optional.

Lotus/Ford Cortina Saloon. Number of cylinders 4 (Ford with Lotus twin overhead camshaft cylinder head). Cubic capacity 1558 c.c. Compression ratio 9·5 : 1 (10 : 1 Special Equipment model). B.H.P. 105 (115). Max. m.p.h. 108 (117). Overall length 14 ft. 3/10 in. Overall width 5 ft. 2½ in. Height 4 ft. 5 9/10 in. Turning circle 37 ft. Wheel-base 8 ft. 2 8/9 in. Track 4 ft. 3 3/5 in. (front), 4 ft. 2 1/8 in. (rear). Fuel tank capacity 8 Imp. gals. Kerb weight 16½ cwt.

Appearance: Generally as for standard Cortina model but note lower look. Front bumper is divided and wheels are wider. Lotus badge appears on radiator air-intake grille. Standard finish is white with green " flash " on body sides.

MARCOS
GREAT BRITAIN

Marcos Cars Limited,
  Greenland Mills,
  Bradford-on-Avon,
  Wiltshire, England.

Current Model: *1800 G.T.* 2-door Sports/Racing Coupé.

Marcos 1800 G.T. Coupé: Number of cylinders 4 (Volvo). Cubic capacity 1783 c.c. Compression ratio 10 : 1. B.H.P. 114. Max. m.p.h. 115 plus. Overall length 13 ft. 3 in. Overall width 5 ft. 2½ in. Height 3 ft. 5½ in. Turning circle 30 ft. Wheel-base 7 ft. 5 in. Track 4 ft. 1 in. (front), 4 ft. 1½ in. (rear). Fuel tank capacity 12 Imp. gals. Weight 11¾ cwt. (approx.).

Appearance: Very low and sleek. Long nose is rounded and tapering; low placed radiator air-intake is flanked by side/indicator lamps in tunnels. Paired headlamps beneath transparent fairings. Windscreen is well raked and curved; roof line thin. Gently sloping rear window extends down to rear wings and tail-panel is flat and slightly inset. Disc wheels with large hub-caps standard, fitted with spoked cast magnesium elektron wheels.

153

MASERATI

ITALY

Officine Alfieri Maserati S.p.A.,

via Ciro Menotti 322,

Modena, Italy.

Current Models: *3700 " Mistrale "*. G. T. Coupé, Convertible Coupé. ***3700 ' Sebring "***. G.T.I. Coupé. ***4100 " Quattro Porte "***. Sports Touring Saloon.

Maserati 3700 " Mistrale " G.T. Coupé: Number of cylinders 6. Cubic capacity 3692 c.c. Compression ratio 8·6 : 1. B.H.P. 245. Max. m.p.h. 154. Overall length 14 ft. 9 in. Overall width 5 ft. 4 in. Height 4 ft. 3 in. Wheel-base 7 ft. 10 in. Track 4 ft. 6$\frac{7}{10}$ in. (front), 4 ft. 5$\frac{1}{2}$ in. (rear). Fuel tank capacity 15·4 Imp. gals.

Appearance: Bonnet featuring three small intakes, flows down between slightly inset headlamps to high-set bumper with divided radiator air-intake below. Deep, curved windscreen; narrow roof iine and very large rear window. High-set, horizontal tail-lamp clusters and squared-off rear line. Wire wheels have triple-eared " knock-off " hub-caps.

Maserati 3700 " Mistrale " Convertible Coupé: Number of cylinders 6. Cubic capacity 3692 c.c. Compression ratio 8·6 : 1. B.H.P. 245. Max. m.p.h. 150 plus. Overall length

154

14 ft. 9 in.   Overall width 5 ft. 4 in.   Height 4 ft. 2 in.   Wheelbase 7 ft. 10 in.   Track 4 ft. $6\frac{7}{10}$ in. (front), 4 ft. $5\frac{1}{2}$ in. (rear). Fuel tank capacity 15·4 Imp. gals.

Appearance: Generally as for Coupé but note convertible fabric top.   Radiator air-intake has inset grille and side/indicator lamps below bumper on body " corners ".   Rear panel is flat and horizontal tail-lamps project.

Maserati 4100 " Quattro Porte " Sports Touring Saloon: Number of cylinders V8.   Cubic capacity 4136 c.c.   Compression ratio 8·5 : 1.   B.H.P. 260.   Max. m.p.h. 145.   Overall length 16 ft. $4\frac{9}{16}$ in.   Overall width 5 ft. $6\frac{1}{2}$ in.   Height 4 ft. $5\frac{1}{2}$ in.   Wheel-base 9 ft. $\frac{1}{4}$ in.   Track 4 ft. 7 in. (front and rear).   Fuel tank(s) capacity 23 Imp. gals.

Appearance: Striking frontal treatment consists of five oblongs—radiator air-intake with Trident motif and inset mesh grille, headlamps and side/indicator lamps.   Large passenger area.   Deep, curved windscreen, narrow roof line and curved rear window.   Borrani perforated disc wheels have large hubcaps.

MAZDA

JAPAN

Toyo Kogyo Co. Ltd.,
6047, Fuchu-Machi,
Aki-Gun,
Hiroshima,
Japan.

Current Models: *360*. 2- and 4-door Saloons. ***R.360*.**
Coupé. ***800*.** 4-door Saloon.

Mazda 800 Saloon: Number of cylinders 4. Cubic capacity
782 c.c. Compression ratio 8·5 : 1. B.H.P. 42. Overall
length 12 ft. $1\frac{7}{10}$ in. Overall width 4 ft. $5\frac{3}{4}$ in. Height 4 ft.
$6\frac{1}{2}$ in. Turning circle 29 ft. Wheel-base 7 ft. $2\frac{1}{5}$ in. Track
3 ft. $11\frac{1}{4}$ in. (front), 3 ft. $10\frac{27}{32}$ in. (rear). Fuel tank capacity
8·8 Imp. gals. Kerb weight 1606 lb.

Appearance: Full-width radiator air-intake with grille of thin
bars and incorporating headlamps; small lamps set into grille.
Bonnet has prominent leading edge and ridge is continued
around bodywork. Deep, slightly curved windscreen, narrow
roof line and large side and rear windows. Simple bumpers
with rubber-tipped overriders; tail-lamps on rear body corners.
Disc wheels have plain hub-caps.

MERCEDES-BENZ

GERMANY

Daimler-Benz A.G.,

Stuttgart-Unterturkheim,

Germany.

Current Models: *190* and *190D.* 4-door Saloons. *220*, *220S* and *220SE.* 4-door Saloons. *220SE.* Coupé, Convertible. *230SL.* Roadster, Coupé. *300SE.* 4-door Saloon, Long-wheel-base 4-door Saloon, Coupé, Convertible. *600.* 4-door Saloon, Pullman Limousine.

Mercedes-Benz 190 and 190D Saloon: Number of cylinders 4 (petrol or diesel). Cubic capacity 1897 c.c. or 1988 c.c. Compression ratio 8·7 : 1 or 21 : 1. B.H.P. 90 or 60. Overall length 15 ft. 6½ in. Overall width 5 ft. 10 7/10 in. Height 4 ft. 10 4/5 in. Turning circle 37·4 ft. Wheel-base 8 ft. 10 3/10 in. Track 4 ft. 10 3/10 in. (front), 4 ft. 10½ in. (rear). Fuel tank capacity 11·2 Imp. gals. Kerb weight 2755 lb. or 2865 lb.

Appearance: Rather severely lined car with absence of frills. Body style is standard on 190, 220 and 300 SE Series. Radiator shell thrust forward between high-set headlamps. Straight-through wings to squared-off rear line. Deep, curved windscreen and rear window, angular side windows. Simple bumpers front and rear. Disc wheels with domed hub-caps.

Mercedes-Benz 220 Saloon: Number of cylinders 6. Cubic capacity 2195 c.c. Compression ratio 8·7 : 1. B.H.P. 105, 124 (S), 134 (SE fuel injection). Overall length 16 ft. $\frac{1}{5}$ in. Overall width 5 ft. $10\frac{7}{10}$ in. Height 4 ft. 11 in. Turning circle 37·7 ft. Wheel-base 9 ft. $\frac{1}{5}$ in. Track 4 ft. $10\frac{3}{10}$ in. (front), 4 ft. $10\frac{2}{5}$ in. (rear). Fuel tank capacity 14·3 Imp. gals. Kerb weight 2910 lb., 2965 lb. (S), 3031 lb. (SE).

Appearance: Similar to 190 Saloon but note that head/side/direction lamps are all beneath large, transparent fairings. Plain bumpers; additional bars above on S and SE models. Wing line rises slightly at rear to give impression of " fins ". Squared-off rear line with horizontal tail-lamp clusters. Perforated disc wheels.

Mercedes-Benz 220SE Coupé: Number of cylinders 6 (fuel injection). Cubic capacity 2195 c.c. Compression ratio 8·7 : 1. B.H.P. 134. Max. m.p.h. 106. Overall length

16 ft.   Overall width 6 ft. $\frac{7}{10}$ in.   Height 4 ft. 7$\frac{9}{10}$ in.   Turning circle 37·7 ft.   Wheel-base 9 ft. $\frac{1}{4}$ in.   Track 4 ft. 10$\frac{3}{10}$ in. (front), 4 ft. 10$\frac{2}{5}$ in. (rear).   Fuel tank capacity 14·3 Imp. gals.   Kerb weight 3109 lb.

Appearance: Frontal details as for 220 Saloon but note sleek, two-door Coupé body.   Long side windows, deep windscreen and rear window.   Straight-through wing line; flanged wheel arches.   Deep bright trim strip along lower edges of body.

Mercedes-Benz 230SL: Number of cylinders 6 (fuel injection).   Cubic capacity 2306 c.c.   Compression ratio 9·3 : 1. B.H.P. 170.   Max. m.p.h. 124 (121 with automatic transmission).   Overall length 14 ft. 1$\frac{3}{8}$ in.   Overall width 5 ft. 9$\frac{1}{2}$ in. Height 4 ft. 3$\frac{2}{5}$ in. (Roadster), 4 ft. 2$\frac{4}{5}$ in. (Coupé).   Turning circle 32·8 ft.   Wheel-base 7 ft. 10 in.   Track 4 ft. 10$\frac{1}{2}$ in. (front and rear).   Fuel tank capacity 14·3 Imp. gals.   Kerb weight 2855 lb.

Appearance: Oblong radiator air-intake with Mercedes star in centre is flanked by vertical lamp fairings.   Straight-through wing line to squarish tail contours and horizontal tail-lamp clusters.   Prominent flanges over wheel arches.   Deep, well-raked windscreen; Coupé has extremely thin roof line.   Disc wheels.

Mercedes-Benz 300SE Convertible: Number of cylinders 6 (fuel injection).   Cubic capacity 2996 c.c.   Compression ratio 8·8 : 1.   B.H.P. 195.   Max. m.p.h. 115 (112 with automatic transmission).   Overall length 16 ft.   Overall width 6 ft. $\frac{3}{8}$ in. Height 4 ft. 7$\frac{1}{10}$ in.   Turning circle 38·4 ft.   Wheel-base 9 ft.

$\frac{3}{10}$ in.   Track 4 ft. 10$\frac{3}{10}$ in. (front), 4 ft. 10$\frac{3}{10}$ in. (rear). Fuel tank capacity 18 Imp. gals.   Kerb weight 3527 lb.

Appearance: Generally as for 220SE Coupé but note attractive convertible body with two large doors.   Trim strip runs full length of body and bright trim is carried over wheel arches.   Windscreen pillars are quite thick.   Bumpers wrap well round on 220 and 300 Mercedes.   Perforated disc wheels.

Mercedes Benz 600: Number of cylinders V8 (fuel injection)˙ Cubic capacity 6329 c.c.   Compression ratio 9 : 1.   B.H.P. 300.   Max. m.p.h. 127 (approx.).   Overall length 18 ft. 2 in. (Saloon), 20 ft. 6 in. (Limousine).   Overall width 6 ft. 4$\frac{4}{5}$ in. Height 4 ft. 11$\frac{2}{5}$ in.   Turning circle 40·7 ft. or 47·8 ft.   Wheelbase 10 ft. 6 in. or 12 ft. 9$\frac{1}{2}$ in.   Track 5 ft. 2$\frac{1}{2}$ in. (front), 5 ft. 2 in. (rear).   Fuel tank capacity 24·6 Imp. gals.   Kerb weight 5380 lb. or 5800 lb.

Appearance: Frontal styling similar to other Mercedes models but car is massive.   Note lack of depth over wheel arches.   Passenger area is large and angular (Pullman model has additional window between doors).   Large boot has squarish rear line and features horizontal tail-lamp clusters. Lavish use of bright trim.   Perforated wheel discs.

MERCURY

UNITED STATES OF AMERICA

Lincoln-Mercury Division,
    Ford Motor Co.,
      Detroit, Michigan,
        U.S.A.

History: Mercury was formed as a subsidiary to the Ford Motor Company in 1939. In that year the first model, with styling not unlike the bodies on the cars of the parent company, made its entry into the American market. But though the Ford car was furnished with an engine of 87 b.h.p. the Mercury was powered by one which produced 95 b.h.p.

Ten years later, in 1949, when Mercury became a part of Ford's Lincoln Division, the brake horse power of the V8 was increased to 110 obtained at 3600 r.p.m., and this was achieved, in part, by increasing the cubic capacity to 255·4 cubic inches. Also by this time Mercury styling had undergone a considerable change. Wings had now been extended until they faired into one another instead of being square in contour and separate. Front-end grilles, too, had followed the trend of becoming merely wide air-intakes protected by large bumpers. Overdrive in 1949 was optional and the power was delivered through an orthodox 3-speed gearbox. In that year the conventional layout for suspension was adopted by employing coil springs in the front and semi-elliptic leaf springs at the rear. 1950 saw the introduction of an automatic torque-converter transmission. Some models were designed with the one-piece wrap-around rear window in 1953 and a new V8 engine developing 161 b.h.p. was offered. By 1955 this output had been raised to 185 and 195 b.h.p.

Current Models: *Comet 202.* 2- and 4-door Sedans, Station Wagon. *Comet 404.* 2- and 4-door Sedans,

Station Wagon, Villager Station Wagon. **Comet Caliente.** 4-door Sedan, 2-door Hardtop, Convertible. **Comet Cyclone.** 2-door Hardtop. **Monterey.** 2- and 4-door Sedans. 4-door Breezeaway Sedan, 2- and 4-door Hardtops, Convertible. **Montclair.** 4-door Breezeaway Sedan, 2- and 4-door Hardtops. **Park Lane.** 4-door Breezeaway Sedan, 2- and 4-door Hardtops, Convertible. **Station Wagons.** Commuter (6- and 9-passenger), Colony Park (6- and 9-passenger).

Mercury Comet Caliente Hardtop: Number of cylinders 6 or V8. Cubic capacity 200 cu. in. (6), 289 cu. in. (V8). Compression ratio 9·2 : 1 (6), 9·3 : 1, 10 : 1 and 10·5 : 1 (V8). B.H.P. 120 (6), 200, 225 and 271 (V8). Overall length 16 ft. 3 3/16 in. Overall width 6 ft. 9/10 in. Height 4 ft. 7 1/10 in. Turning circle 40 ft. Wheel-base 9 ft. 6 in. Track 4 ft. 7 in. (6), 4 ft. 7 3/8 in. (V8) (front), 4 ft. 8 in. (rear). Fuel tank capacity 20 U.S. gals. Kerb weight 3073 lb. (V8).

Appearance: Angular styling with sculptured body side panels. Full-width, oblong radiator air-intake with grille of thin horizontal bars is flanked by vertically mounted, paired headlamps. Long flat bonnet and rear deck. Angular rear styling with tail-lamps concealed behind full-width horizontal grille bars. "Wire-wheel" discs and dummy "knock-off" hub-caps.

Mercury Park Lane Breezeaway Sedan: Number of cylinders V8. Cubic capacity 390 cu. in. (390 cu. in. and 427 cu. in. optional). Compression ratio 10 : 1 (10 : 1 and 11·2 : 1 optional). B.H.P. 300 (330 and 425 optional). Overall length 18 ft. 2 5/8 in. Overall width 6 ft. 7 5/8 in. Height 4 ft. 8 in. Turning circle 44 ft. 6 in. Wheel-base 10 ft. 3 in. Track 5 ft. 2 in. (front and rear). Fuel tank capacity 21 U.S. gals. Kerb weight 4024 lb.

Appearance: Vertical side/indicator lamps flanking full-width radiator air-intake. Straight-through wing line to large, divided vertical tail-lamps. Heavy-looking bumpers front and rear. Note reverse slope rear window. Wheels have spoked effect and prominent centres.

Mercury Park Lane 4-door Hardtop: Number of cylinders V8. Cubic capacity 390 cu. in. (390 cu. in. and 427 cu. in. optional). Compression ratio 10 : 1 (10 : 1 and 11.2 : 1 optional). B.H.P. 300 (330 and 425 optional). Overall length 18 ft. 2⅝ in. Overall width 6 ft. 7⅞ in. Height 4 ft. 7 10⁄10 in. Turning circle 44 ft. 6 in. Wheel-base 10 ft. 3 in. Track 5 ft. 2 in. (front and rear). Fuel tank capacity 21 U.S. gals. Kerb weight 4000 lb.

Appearance: Note vertical leading edges of wings formed by side/indicator lamps. Rather angular styling generally, long side windows, well-raked windscreen and rear window. Full-width " grille " forms rear panel. Spoked effect to wheel discs.

METEOR

CANADA

Ford Motor Company of Canada Ltd.,
The Canadian Road,
Oakville,
Ontario,
Canada.

Current Models: *Rideau.* 2- and 4-door Sedans, Station Wagon. *Rideau 500.* 2- and 4-door Sedans. *Montcalm.* 4-door Sedan, 2- and 4-door Hardtops, Convertible, Station Wagon (6- and 9-passenger).

Meteor Montcalm 2-door Hardtop: Number of cylinders 6 (V8 optional). Cubic capacity 240 cu. in. (352 cu. in. and 390 cu. in. optional). Compression ratio 9·2 : 1 (8·9 : 1 and 10·1 : 1 optional). B.H.P. 150 (220 and 300 optional). Overall length 18 ft. 2⅝ in. Overall width 6 ft. 7⅘ in. Height 4 ft. 8 in. Turning circle 44 ft. 6 in. Wheel-base 10 ft. 3 in. Track 5 ft. 2 in. (front and rear). Fuel tank capacity 21 U.S. gals. Kerb weight 4000 lb.

Appearance: Styling very similar to U.S. Mercury, but note differing radiator air-intake grille. Rather angular styling generally. Broad, flat bonnet and long flat rear deck. Curved windscreen and large rear window raked sharply forward. Massive bumpers front and rear; large rear lamps. Wheel discs give four-spoked effect.

M.G.

GREAT BRITAIN

M.G. Car Co., Ltd.,

Abingdon-on-Thames,

Berkshire, England.

History: M.G. Number One was built in 1923 and consisted of a Morris " Oxford " chassis fitted with an overhead valve Hotchkiss engine.   It was capable of 82 m.p.h. and was successful in winning a Gold Medal in the London to Land's End Trial.   Later, the M.G. Car Company was formed to produce a line of cars which today has become synonymous with motor sport in all its aspects. The initials " M.G." stood for Morris Garages where the first M.G. was built.

One of the first models produced was the Mark IV fitted with a 4-cylinder engine developing 35 b.h.p., and in April 1929 the famous " M " Type Midget was introduced.   The " M " Type was powered by an engine of 847 c.c. based on that of the Morris Minor.   Many racing successes fell to the Midget and a special car—EX.120—having an engine of only 743 c.c. achieved a speed of over 100 m.p.h. in 1931.   The Midget continued through the " J " Series to the " PA " and " PB " Series, production of which ceased in 1936.   The " TA " was the first of the Midgets to have an engine of over 1000 c.c.

The year 1933 saw the introduction of the " K " Series Magnette and in that year Tazio Nuvolari won the R.A.C. Ulster Tourist Trophy driving one of these models.   In addition to producing stark sports and racing cars, several shapely saloon models were made including the " SA " 2-litre and the " WA " 2·6-litre model of 1938.

The latest in the long line of records taken by M.G.s fell to the streamlined EX.181 in August 1947 when, driven by Stirling Moss, it broke the 1 kilometre record at 245·64 m.p.h. In 1958 the " Twin Cam " MGA was announced, remaining in production until 1960. The year 1961 saw the introduction of a new " Midget " based on the Austin Healey Sprite.

Current Models: *Midget Mk. II.* 2-seater Sports. *1100.* 2- and 4-door Saloons. *MGB.* 2-seater Sports. *Magnette Mk. IV.* 4-door Saloon.

M.G. Midget Mk. II Sports: Number of cylinders 4. Cubic capacity 1098 c.c. Compression ratio 8·9 : 1 (8·1 : 1 available). B.H.P. 59. Max. m.p.h. 90 plus. Overall length 11 ft. 5⅜ in. Overall width 4 ft. 6 9/10 in. Height 3 ft. 7 in. (to top of screen), 4 ft. 1¾ in. (to top of hood). Turning circle 31 ft. 2 in. Wheelbase 6 ft. 8 in. Track 3 ft. 9¾ in. (front), 3 ft. 8¾ in. (rear). Fuel tank capacity 6 Imp. gals. Weight (unladen) 14 cwt. (approx.).

Appearance: Generally similar to Austin Healey Sprite. Radiator air-intake grille of vertical slats with central bar. Straight-through wing line; trim strip runs full length of car. Bumpers front and rear. Perforated disc wheels standard, may be seen with wire wheels and " knock off " hub-caps.

M.G. 1100 Saloon: Number of cylinders 4. Cubic capacity 1098 c.c. Compression ratio 8·9 : 1 (8·1 : 1 available). B.H.P. 55. Overall length 12 ft. 2¾ in. Overall width 5 ft. ⅜ in. Height 4 ft. 5 in. Turning circle 34 ft. 9 in. Wheel-base 7 ft. 9½ in. Track 4 ft. 3½ in. (front), 4 ft. 2⁹⁄₁₀ in. (rear). Fuel tank capacity 8½ Imp. gals. Weight (unladen) 16½ cwt. (approx.).

Appearance: Comparatively large passenger area with lack of luggage boot giving van-like appearance. Broad, dummy radiator shell with grille of vertical slats. High-set headlamps, straight-through wing line to vertical tail-lamp clusters. Short, flat bonnet; deep windscreen and rear window. Small disc wheels.

M.G. MGB Sports: Number of cylinders 4. Cubic capacity 1798 c.c. Compression ratio 8·8 : 1 (8 : 1 available). B.H.P.

95. Max. m.p.h. 100 plus. Overall length 12 ft. 9⅘ in. Overall width 4 ft. 11⁹⁄₁₀ in. Height 4 ft. 1¾ in. (to top of hood). Turning circle 32 ft. Wheel-base 7 ft. 7 in. Track 4 ft. 1 in. (front), 4 ft. 1¼ in. (rear). Fuel tank capacity 10 Imp. gals. Weight (unladen) 18½ cwt. (approx.).

Appearance: Narrow radiator air-intake with famous octagon badge thrust well forward. Headlamps inset into wings, straight-through wing line to large, vertical tail-lamps. Simple bumpers front and rear wrap around. Bonnet is gently rounded; rather shallow, rounded windscreen. Perforated disc wheels standard; wire wheels with " knock-off " hub-caps optional.

M.G. Magnette Mk. IV Saloon: Number of cylinders 4. Cubic capacity 1622 c.c. Compression ratio 8·3 : 1. B.H.P. 68. Overall length 14 ft. 10¼ in. Overall width 5 ft. 3½ in. Height 4 ft. 11 in. Turning circle 37 ft. Wheel-base 8 ft. 4¼ in. Track 4 ft. 2⅜ in. (front), 4 ft. 3⅘ in. (rear). Fuel tank capacity 10 Imp. gals. Weight (unladen) 22½ cwt. (approx.).

Appearance: Traditional M.G. radiator shell blended into Farina designed coachwork. High-set headlamps; straight-through wings to vertical, pointed tail-lamps. "Fin" effect of rear wings is accentuated by styling line sloping gently down at rear. Disc wheels.

MORGAN

GREAT BRITAIN

Morgan Motor Co., Ltd.,
Pickersleigh Road,
Malvern Link, Worcester,
England.

History: The Morgan company commenced in 1909, when H. F. S. Morgan designed and built his own three-wheeler runabout with simple sliding pillar front-wheel suspension.

The first four-wheeled model, the 4/4, was produced in 1936, and its chassis design very closely resembled that of the modern Morgan "Plus-Four". This had been greatly improved by 1952, and in order to meet the increasing demand for a higher performance, the company decided to fit a Standard Vanguard power unit. The chassis was completely re-designed to accommodate the new engine, and featured larger front springs with hydraulic shock absorbers and automatic lubrication, a more rigid frame and larger tyres on wider base rims. Also the coachwork, which is hand-built on all models, had increased width and leg room. Improved protection from the weather was provided on the open models.

By 1955 Morgan cars featured modified front-ends, the radiator becoming rounded and longer with wings sweeping further down in front.

Current Models: *Plus 4.* 2-seater Tourer, 2-seater Super Sports, 4-seater Tourer, Drop-head Coupé. *Plus 4 Plus.* G.T. Coupé. *4/4 Series V.* 2-seater Tourer, 2-seater Competition Model.

Morgan Plus 4 2-seater Tourer: Number of cylinders 4 (Triumph). Cubic capacity 2138 c.c. Compression ratio 9 : 1. B.H.P. 105 (120 Super Sports). Max. m.p.h. 120 (Super Sports). Overall length 12 ft. Overall width 4 ft. 8 in. Height 4 ft. 4 in. Turning circle 32 ft. Wheel-base

8 ft.   Track 3 ft. 11 in. (front), 4 ft. 1 in. (rear).   Fuel tank capacity 12 Imp. gals.   Dry weight 16½ cwt. (15 cwt. Super Sports).

Appearance: Traditional "sports-car" appearance. Radiator grille of thin bars; exposed headlamps and separate front and rear wings.   Cut-away cockpit sides; spare wheel recessed into rear panel which follows line of rear wings. Super Sports model has bonnet bulge over Weber carburettors.   Perforated disc wheels or wire wheels with "knock-off" hub-caps.

Morgan Plus 4 Plus G.T. Coupé: Number of cylinders 4

Triumph). Cubic capacity 2138 c.c. Compression ratio 9 : 1. B.H.P. 105. Max. m.p.h. 110. Overall length 12 ft. 5 in. Overall width 5 ft. 3 in. Height 4 ft. 3 in. Turning circle 32 ft. Wheel-base 8 ft. Track 3 ft. 11 in. (front), 4 ft. 1 in. (rear). Fuel tank capacity 10 Imp. gals. Weight 16¾ cwt.

Appearance: Sleek, well streamlined design with small, prominent passenger area. Small, vertical radiator air-intake flanked by low-set horizontal intakes. Straight-through wing line to vertically mounted tail-lamp clusters. Long, rounded bonnet, large doors. Curved, well-raked wind-screen and small side windows. Squared-off tail panel. Wire wheels with " knock-off " hub-caps.

Morgan 4/4 Series V 2-seater Tourer: Number of cylinders 4 (Ford). Cubic capacity 1498 c.c. Compression ratio 8·3 : 1 (9 : 1 Competition Model). B.H.P. 59·5 (78). Max. m.p.h. 85/95. Overall length 12 ft. Overall width 4 ft. 8 in. Height 4 ft. 3 in. Turning circle 32 ft. Wheel-base 8 ft. Track 3 ft. 11 in. (front), 4 ft. 1 in. (rear). Fuel tank capacity 8½ Imp. gals. Weight 13 cwt.

Appearance: General outline similar to Plus 4 2-seater Tourer, but bonnet line is noticeably lower and has no louvres on top, only eight louvres on each side. Shallow, flat windscreen. Perforated disc wheels standard, wire wheels available.

MORRIS

AUSTRALIA

British Motor Corporation (Aus.) Pty. Ltd.,
Joynton Avenue,
Zetland,
Sydney, N.S.W., Australia.

Current Models: *Major "Élite".* 4-door Saloon.
Oxford Series VI. 4-door Saloon.

Morris Major "Élite" Saloon: Number of cylinders 4.
Cubic capacity 1622 c.c. Compression ratio 7·7 : 1. B.H.P.
58. Overall length 13 ft. 5 in. Overall width 5 ft. 1 in.
Height 4 ft. 11 in. Turning circle 35 ft. 11 in. Wheel-base
7 ft. 8 in. Max. track 4 ft. 3½ in. Fuel tank capacity 9 Imp.
gals. Kerb weight 2130 lb. (approx.).

Appearance: Wide radiator air-intake with grille of horizontal
slats flanked by high-set headlamps and side/indicator lamps
mounted as units. Straight-through wing line giving "fin"
effect at rear. Windscreen is rather shallow and only slightly
curved. Simple wrap-around bumpers front and rear. Disc
wheels have plain hub-caps.

173

MORRIS

GREAT BRITAIN

Morris Motors Limited,
Cowley, Oxford,
England.

History: William Morris, Viscount Nuffield, produced his first motor-car at Cowley in 1912, although ten years earlier he had marketed a motor-cycle. World War I frustrated his first attempts to develop an economical passenger car, but after the war, despite the depression, a new effort was made.

At the 1921 London Motor Show the prices of all Morris cars were cut by £100. This led to a huge demand so that a few years later 65,000 cars were produced in twelve months. The Hotchkiss company, who had made the Morris engines, was bought in 1923. Also Hillock and Pratt bodies were acquired and now form the Bodies Branch. In 1925 the M.G. Car Company was started and two years later Wolseley Motors Ltd. was taken over. S.U. Carburettors sold out to Morris in 1926 and the Osberton company became responsible for all Morris radiators. In 1938 Riley cars became part of the Morris group. In 1951 Morris—by then the Nuffield Organization—merged with the Austin company to form the British Motor Corporation.

By the end of 1954 production was concentrated on the " Minor " Series II, the " Cowley " and the " Oxford " Series II. The " Isis " was added during 1955 but was dropped from the range during 1958.

Current Models: *Mini-Minor.* Standard and Super De Luxe 2-door Saloons, Traveller. *Mini-Cooper.* 2-door Saloon. *Mini-Cooper " S " 1000.* 2-door Saloon. *Mini-Cooper " S " 1275.* 2-door Saloon. *Minor 1000.* Standard and De Luxe 2- and 4-door Saloons, Standard and De Luxe Convertible, Traveller and Traveller De Luxe. *1100.* Standard and De Luxe 2- and 4-door Saloons. *Oxford (Series VI).* Standard and De Luxe 4-door Saloons, Traveller.

174

Morris Mini-Minor Saloon: Number of cylinders 4. Cubic capacity 848 c.c. (998 c.c. Cooper, 970 c.c. and 1275 c.c. " S "). Compression ratio 8·3 : 1 (9 : 1 Cooper, 10 : 1 and 9·75 : 1 " S "). B.H.P. 34 (55, 65 and 76). Max. m.p.h. 73 (87, 92 and 100). Overall length 10 ft. ¼ in. Overall width 4 ft. 7½ in. Height 4 ft. 5 in. Turning circle 31 ft. 7 in. Wheelbase 6 ft. 8 in. Track 3 ft. 11½ in. (front), 3 ft. 9⅘ in. (rear), (3 ft. 10¾₀ in. (rear) Cooper). Fuel tank capacity 5½ Imp. gals. Weight (unladen) 11½ cwt. (12½ cwt. Cooper).

Appearance: Small car generally similar in appearance to Austin Mini. Note, however, different radiator grille consisting of the thin horizontal and vertical slats. Line of windscreen is carried down to front wheel arch, large doors have prominent hinges. Almost straight down back panel is flanked by projecting tail-lamps. Car has tiny disc wheels. Photograph depicts Mini-Cooper.

Morris Minor 1000 2-door Saloon: Number of cylinders 4. Cubic capacity 1098 c.c. Compression ratio 8·5 : 1 (7·5 : 1

available). B.H.P. 48 (45). Overall length 12 ft. 4 in. Overall width 4 ft. 11⅞ in. Height 5 ft. Turning circle 33 ft. Wheel-base 7 ft. 2 in. Track 4 ft. 2³⁄₁₀ in. (front and rear). Fuel tank capacity 6½ Imp. gals. Weight (unladen) 14¾ cwt. (approx.).

Appearance: Small, compact looking car with rounded contours. Oblong radiator air-intake has five horizontal slats. Headlamps faired into front wings which merge into doors. Prominent rear wings; simple bumpers front and rear. Rounded bonnet and tail. Disc wheels with plain hub-caps.

Morris 1100 Saloon: Number of cylinders 4. Cubic capacity 1098 c.c. Compression ratio 8·5 : 1 (7·5 : 1 available). B.H.P. 48. Overall length 12 ft. 2¾ in. Overall width 5 ft. ⅖ in. Height 4 ft. 5 in. Turning circle 34 ft. 9 in. Wheel-base 7 ft. 9½ in. Track 4 ft. 3½ in. (front), 4 ft. 2⁹⁄₁₀ in. (rear). Fuel tank capacity 8½ Imp. gals. Weight (unladen) 16¼ cwt. (approx.).

Appearance: Car has rather long appearance due to wheels being placed at extremities of bodywork. Oblong air-intake with horizontally slatted grille; largish, high-set headlamps. Broad, flat bonnet; straight-through wing line to pointed, vertical tail-lamp clusters. Large passenger area gives car a van-like appearance accentuated by lack of tail. Disc wheels have plain, flat hubcaps.

Morris Oxford (Series VI) Saloon: Number of cylinders 4. (petrol or diesel). Cubic capacity 1622 c.c. or 1489 c.c. Compression ratio 8·3 : 1 (7·2 : 1 available) or 23 : 1. B.H.P. 61 or 40. Overall length 14 ft. 6½ in. Overall width 5 ft. 3½ in. Height 4 ft. 10 9/10 in. Turning circle 37 ft. Wheelbase 8 ft. 4¼ in. Track 4 ft. 2⅗ in. (front), 4 ft. 3⅗ in. (rear). Fuel tank capacity 10 Imp. gals. Weight (unladen) 22¼ cwt. (approx.).

Appearance: Generally similar to other Farina styled B.M.C. models. Full-width radiator air-intake with horizontally slatted grille incorporates side/direction lamps. Broad, flat bonnet flows down between head-lamps, straight-through wing line to pointed, vertical tail-lamp clusters. Rear over-riders form lower extremities of these units. Boot-line is squared off. Bumpers have tiny overriders at front. Rather angular passenger area. Disc wheels.

Morris Oxford (Series VI) Traveller: Number of cylinders 4. Cubic capacity 1622 c.c. Compression ratio 8·3 : 1 (7·2 : 1 available). B.H.P. 61. Overall length 14 ft. 9 in. Overall width 5 ft. 3½ in. Height 5 ft. Turning circle 37 ft. 5 in. Wheel-base 8 ft. 4¼ in. Track 4 ft. 2⅝ in. (front), 4 ft. 3⅝ in. (rear). Fuel tank capacity 10 Imp. gals. Weight (unladen) 23¼ cwt.

Appearance: Frontal details as for Saloon but note utility type body with long, flat roof. One-piece, curved windscreen, smallish side windows and sharply raked rear panel inset between vertical tail-lamp clusters. Thin, full-length styling line runs along body sides. Squarish styled wheel arches.

MOSKVITCH

U.S.S.R.

MZMZ Light Car Works
Moscow,
U.S.S.R.

Current Models: *M-408*. 4-door Saloon. ***M-426*.** 4-door Utility.

Moskvitch M-408 Saloon: Number of cylinders 4. Cubic capacity 1360 c.c. Compression ratio 7 : 1. B.H.P. 60·5. Overall length 13 ft. 5 in. Overall width 5 ft. 1 in. Height 4 ft. 10¼ in. Turning circle 33 ft. Wheel-base 7 ft. 10½ in. Track 4 ft. ¾ in. (front), 4 ft. ⅜ in. (rear). Fuel tank capacity 10 Imp. gals. Dry weight 17¾ cwt.

Appearance: Handsome saloon with crisp styling. Full-width radiator air-intake with paired headlamps at ends. (May be seen with single headlamps.) Deep windscreen and rear window wrap-around slightly. Side/indicator lamps just above plain bumpers on front body " corners ". Vertical tail-lamp clusters; flat bonnet and rear deck. Disc wheels have large, plain hub-caps.

NISSAN

JAPAN

Nissan Motor Co., Ltd.,

4, 1-Chome,

Otemachi, Tokyo, Japan.

Current Models: ***Datsun Bluebird***. 4-door Saloon, Station Wagon. ***Datsun 1500 "Fairlady"***. 2-seater Sports. ***Nissan Cedric***. Standard and De Luxe 4-door Saloons, Station Wagon.

Datsun Bluebird Saloon: Number of cylinders 4. Cubic capacity 1189 c.c. Compression ratio 8·2 : 1. B.H.P. 60. Overall length 13 ft. 1⅖ in. Overall width 4 ft. 10⁷⁄₁₀ in. Height 4 ft. 8³⁄₁₀ in. Turning circle 32 ft. Wheel-base 7 ft. 9⅘ in. Track 3 ft. 11½ in. (front), 3 ft. 11⅕ in. (rear). Fuel tank capacity 9 Imp. gals. Weight 1947 lb.

Appearance: Large radiator air-intake with thinly barred, inwardly curved grille and paired headlamps. Rather bulky looking front end to car. Well-raked, almost flat windscreen, thin roof line forms peak over rear window. Horizontal tail-lamp clusters project from rear body "corners". Plain bumpers have rubber-tipped overriders. Perforated wheel discs and domed hub-caps.

Datsun 1500 "Fairlady" Sports: Number of cylinders 4. Cubic capacity 1488 c.c. Compression ratio 9 : 1. B.H.P. 85. Max. m.p.h. 96. Overall length 12 ft. 11⅝ in. Overall

width 4 ft. 10$\frac{9}{10}$ in.   Height 4 ft. 3$\frac{2}{5}$ in.   Turning circle 32 ft.
Wheel-base 7 ft. 5$\frac{4}{5}$ in.   Track 3 ft. 11$\frac{4}{5}$ in. (front), 3 ft. 11$\frac{7}{10}$ in.
(rear).   Fuel tank capacity 9$\frac{1}{2}$ Imp. gals.   Weight 2006 lb.

Appearance: Low, sporting. Smallish, oblong radiator air-intake has grille of narrow bars and is flanked by slightly inset headlamps. Rather angular frontal bonnet line; wide air-intake on bonnet top. Straight-through wings to vertical, triple tail-lamp clusters. Well curved windscreen has narrow framing. Narrow bumpers have large, vertical overriders. Perforated wheel discs and plain hub-caps.

Nissan Cedric Saloon: Number of cylinders 4. Cubic capacity 1883 c.c. Compression ratio 8·5 : 1. B.H.P. 95.

Overall length 15 ft. $\frac{7}{10}$ in.   Overall width 5 ft. 6½ in.   Height 4 ft. 11$\frac{3}{10}$ in.   Turning circle 36·6 ft.   Wheel-base 8 ft. 7½ in. Track 4 ft. 4$\frac{7}{10}$ in. (front), 4 ft. 6$\frac{1}{10}$ in. (rear).   Fuel tank capacity 9·7 Imp. gals.   Weight 2670 lb. (Standard), 2740 lb. (De Luxe).

Appearance: Full-width radiator air-intake with paired head-lamps slightly inset at ends: large, oblong side/indicator lamps below.   Grille consists of narrow, horizontal bars.   Straight-through wing line to vertical tail-lamps in wing trailing edges. Wrap-around windscreen and rear window; rather square rear contours.   Perforated wheel discs and plain hub-caps.

N.S.U.

GERMANY

 N.S.U. Motorenwerke Aktiengesellschaft,
Neckarsulm,
Germany.

Current Models: *Prinz 4.* 2-door Sports Saloon (Fixed and Sliding Roof). *Prinz 1000.* 2-door Saloon. *Sport Prinz.* Coupé. *Spider (Wankel engine).* Open 2-seater.

N.S.U. Prinz 1000 Saloon: Number of cylinders 4. Cubic capacity 996 c.c. Compression ratio 8 : 1. B.H.P. 51. Overall length 12 ft. 5½ in. Overall width 4 ft. 10½ in. Height 4 ft. 5½ in. Turning circle 31 ft. Wheel-base 7 ft. 4 in. Track 4 ft. 2 in. (front), 4 ft. (rear). Fuel tank capacity 8 Imp. gals. Weight (unladen) 1367 lb.

Appearance: Note rather unusual styling with body appearing to "sit on" the small wheels. Prominent flange running around top of body. Passenger area almost centrally placed with curved windscreen and rear window, large side windows and narrow roof line. Large oval headlamps, horizontally mounted triple rear-lamp clusters. Cooling air grilles above rear wheels for rear mounted engine. Large, plain hub-caps.

N.S.U. Wankel Spider: Water-cooled N.S.U./Wankel rotary piston engine. Chamber volume 500 c.c. B.H.P. 64. Max. m.p.h. 95 plus. Overall length 11 ft. 9 in. Overall width 5 ft. Height (to top of hood) 4 ft. 1 in. Turning circle 30 ft. Wheel-base 6 ft. 7½ in. Track 4 ft. 2 in. (front), 4 ft. (rear). Fuel tank capacity 7½ Imp. gals. Kerb weight 1510 lb.

Appearance: Shapely open 2-seater with full-width, divided air-intake with narrow intake below bumper. "Bonnet" slopes gently down between high-set headlamps; straight-through wing line to slightly hooded, vertical tail-lamps. Slightly inset, flat tail panel; mesh grilles below bumper for air exit. Deep, well raked windscreen and almost flat rear deck. Disc wheels have very large hub-caps.

OLDSMOBILE

Oldsmobile Division,

General Motors Corpn.,

Lansing 21,

Michigan,

U.S.A.

History: In 1897, Ransom Olds began producing a single-cylinder machine with " tiller " steering and continued to do so for ten years. In 1905 a two-cylinder car was marketed, and a year later production began on a four-cylinder model which developed 26–28 b.h.p.

In 1908 Oldsmobile became a division of General Motors and produced a larger four-cylinder car and a Six. 1909 saw the introduction of a small four-cylinder model. In the following year, a large Four and Six were produced.

From 1916 to 1920 a V8 engine was manufactured. In 1917 a Six was introduced and continued until 1920. In 1929 the V8 Viking appeared and in 1931 down-draught carburettors and synchro-mesh gears were offered. A semi-automatic transmission was followed in 1940 by the first use of hydromatic drive, re-designed in 1946.

A 135 b.h.p. V8 engine was adopted in 1949 for the Futuramic " 88 " and the " 98 " as well as a Six for the " 76 ". The power was raised to 160 b.h.p. in 1952, and increased to 165 b.h.p. in 1953.

The Autronic Eye was adopted in 1952 for automatically controlling the headlight beams and the following year air-conditioning and power-assisted braking were offered. Ten models in three series were offered in 1954 and 1955: the Eighty-Eight, Super Eighty-Eight and Ninety-

Eight. In 1956 the power of the V8 engine was raised to a maximum of 240 b.h.p. and the compression ratio to 9·25 : 1.

Current Models: *F-85*. Standard and De Luxe 4-door Sedans, Club Coupé, V6 Sports Coupé, Cutlass Sports Coupé, Cutlass Holiday Coupé, Cutlass Convertible, Standard and De Luxe 6-seat Station Wagons, Standard and Custom 6- and 9-seat Vista-Cruisers. ***Jetstar 88*.** 4-door Celebrity Sedan, 4-door Holiday Sedan, Holiday Coupé, Convertible. ***Jetstar I*.** Sports Coupé. ***Dynamic 88*.** 4-door Celebrity Sedan, 4-door Holiday Sedan, Holiday Coupé, Convertible. ***Delta 88*.** 4-door Celebrity Sedan, 4-door Holiday Sedan, Holiday Coupé. ***Starfire*.** Coupé, Convertible. ***98*.** 4-door Town Sedan, 4-door Luxury Sedan, 4-door Holiday Sports Sedan, Holiday Sports Coupé, Convertible.

Oldsmobile F-85 Cutlass Holiday Coupé: Number of cylinders V8. Cubic capacity 330 cu. in. (400 cu. in. optional). Compression ratio 10·25 : 1. B.H.P. 315 (345 optional). Overall length 17 ft. $\frac{2}{5}$ in. Overall width 6 ft. 1$\frac{1}{5}$ in. Height 4 ft. 5$\frac{7}{10}$ in. Turning circle 41 ft. Wheel-base 9 ft. 7 in. Track 4 ft. 10 in. (front and rear). Fuel tank capacity 20 U.S. gals. Kerb weight 3472 lb.

Appearance: Rather angular styling generally. Narrow full-width radiator air-intake opens out at ends to include paired headlamps. Broad, flat bonnet and rear deck. Note full-length flutes running along top line of wings. Bumper end plates form lower edges of wings. Slightly curved windscreen and narrow roof line. Wheels may be fitted with dummy " wire wheel " discs.

Oldsmobile Jetstar 88 Holiday Sedan: Number of cylinders V8. Cubic capacity 330 cu. in. Compression ratio 10·25 : 1 (8·3 : 1 available). B.H.P. 260 (250 and 315 optional, 235 and 260 available). Overall length 18 ft. $\frac{9}{10}$ in. Overall width 6 ft. 8 in. Height 4 ft. 7$\frac{1}{2}$ in. Turning circle 43·6 ft. Wheelbase 10 ft. 3 in. Track 5 ft. 2$\frac{1}{2}$ in. (front), 5 ft. 3 in. (rear). Fuel tank capacity 25 U.S. gals. Kerb weight 3965 lb.

Appearance: Generally similar to F-85. Note clean styling of these cars and noticeable overhang at rear. Rather shallow passenger area with long side windows. Windscreen and rear window curved and well raked. Tail-lamps inset into flat rear panel. Deep body sides. Wheels have narrow row of spokes and conical centres.

Oldsmobile Delta 88 Holiday Coupé: Number of cylinders V8. Cubic capacity 425 cu. in. Compression ratio 10·25 : 1 (9 : 1, 10·25 : 1 and 10·5 : 1 optional, 8·3 : 1 available). B.H.P. 310 (300, 360 and 370 optional, 285 available). Overall length 18 ft. $\frac{9}{10}$ in. Overall width 6 ft. 8 in. Height 4 ft. 7$\frac{1}{2}$ in. Turning circle 43·6 ft. Wheel-base 10 ft. 3 in.

Track 5 ft. 2½ in. (front), 5 ft. 3 in. (rear).   Fuel tank capacity 25 U.S. gals.   Kerb weight 4085 lb.

Appearance: Radiator air-intake has double-barred grille and massive under-bumper.   Note broad, flat bonnet on these cars.   Sharply sloped rear roof line features large window. Abrupt rise of wing line over rear wheels.   Full-width rear bumper moulds in with bodywork.   Generally sporting look. Slotted wheel discs, flattish hub-caps.

Oldsmobile Starfire Convertible: Number of cylinders V8. Cubic capacity 425 cu. in.   Compression ratio 10·5 : 1.   B.H.P. 370.   Overall length 18 ft. $\frac{9}{10}$ in.   Overall width 6 ft. 8 in. Height 4 ft. 5$\frac{3}{10}$ in.   Turning circle 43·6 ft.   Wheel-base 10 ft. 3 in.   Track 5 ft. 2½ in. (front), 5 ft. 3 in. (rear).   Fuel tank capacity 25 U.S. gals.   Kerb weight 4303 lb.

Appearance: Styling generally as for other Oldsmobile models but note convertible fabric top. Radiator air-intake is divided vertically and horizontally. Rear panel has concave panel flanked by large, square tail-lamps. Massive front and rear bumpers. Exhaust outlets just ahead of rear bumper. More lavish use of bright trim. Dummy wire wheels and " knock-off " hub-caps.

Oldsmobile 98 Luxury Sedan: Number of cylinders V8. Cubic capacity 425 cu. in. Compression ratio 10·25 : 1 (10·5 : 1 optional, 8·3 : 1 available). B.H.P. 360 (370 optional, 320 available). Overall length 18 ft. 6$\frac{9}{10}$ in. Overall width 6 ft. 8 in. Height 4 ft. 7$\frac{4}{5}$ in. Turning circle 44 ft. 6 in. Wheel-base 10 ft. 6 in. Track 5 ft. 2$\frac{1}{2}$ in. (front), 5 ft. 3 in. (rear). Fuel tank capacity 25 U.S. gals. Kerb weight 4446 lb.

Appearance: Top model in Oldsmobile range. May be seen with vinyl-covered roof. Radiator air-intake grille is thinly barred. Broad band of bright trim along body sides accentuates length of car and rear overhang. Rear wheels partially concealed. Large oblong tail-lamps mounted vertically in almost flat rear panel. Spoked wheel discs and conical hub-caps.

OPEL

GERMANY

Adam Opel A.G. (General Motors), Russelsheim Am Main, Germany.

Current Models: *Kadett.* 2-door Saloon Coupé. *Kadett "L".* 2-door Saloon. *"Car-A-Van" 1000.* Station Wagon. *Rekord.* 2-door Coach, 4-door Saloon, Coupé. *"Car-A-Van"* Station Wagon. *Rekord "L".* 4-door Saloon. *Kapitan.* 4-door Saloon. *Admiral.* 4-door Saloon. *Diplomat.* 4-door Saloon.

Opel Kadett "L" Saloon: Number of cylinders 4. Cubic capacity 993 c.c. Compression ratio 7·8 : 1. B.H.P. 40. Overall length 12 ft. 10½ in. Overall width 4 ft. 9 9/10 in. Height 4 ft. 7½ in. Turning circle 32·2 ft. Wheel-base 7 ft. 7½ in. Track 3 ft. 11½ in. (front), 3 ft. 11⅔ in. (rear). Fuel tank capacity 8·7 U.S. gals. Kerb weight 1477 lb.

Appearance: Full-width radiator air-intake with grill of horizontal slats and indicator lamps on body "corners". Squarish styling, large windows, curved windscreen and rear window. Horizontal tail-lamps set just above bumper. Perforated disc wheels, large, plain hub-caps.

Opel Rekord Coupé: Number of cylinders 4 or 6. Cubic capacity 1680 c.c. or 2605 c.c. Compression ratio 8 : 1 or 8·2 : 1. B.H.P. 67 or 100. Overall length 14 ft. 9 7/10 in. Overall width 5 ft. 6⅘ in. Height 4 ft. 7¾ in. Turning circle 35·4 ft. Wheel base 8 ft. 7 9/10 in. Track 4 ft. 4 in. (front),

4 ft. $2\frac{2}{5}$ in. (rear) (4), 4 ft. $4\frac{1}{5}$ in. (front), 4 ft. $2\frac{2}{5}$ in. (rear) (6). Fuel tank capacity $11\cdot9$ U.S. gals. Kerb weight 2127 lb. (4), 2403 lb. (6).

Appearance: Full-width radiator air-intake has grille of outwardly "veed" bars and incorporates headlamps. Deep windscreen; narrow roof line and large rear window. Cutback wheel arches. Perforated wheel discs.

Opel Diplomat Saloon: Number of cylinders V8 (Chevrolet). Cubic capacity 4638 c.c. Compression ratio $9\cdot25:1$. B.H.P. 220. Overall length 16 ft. $2\frac{4}{5}$ in. Overall width 6 ft. $2\frac{9}{10}$ in. Height 4 ft. $8\frac{9}{10}$ in. Turning circle $35\cdot4$ ft. Wheel-base 9 ft. 4 in. Track 4 ft. $10\frac{4}{5}$ in. (front), 4 ft. $11\frac{3}{5}$ in. (rear). Fuel tank capacity $18\cdot5$ U.S. gals. Kerb weight 3351 lb.

Appearance: Angular styling. Full-width radiator air-intake has oblong headlamps at ends. Broad, flat bonnet, well-raked windscreen, narrow roof line and concave rear window. Oblong tail-lamps in rear panel and small lamps on rear body "corners". Wheel discs have projecting centres and oblong slots.

O.S.C.A.

ITALY

Automobili O.S.C.A. S.p.A.,
San Lazzaro di Savena,
Via Emilia 243,
Bologna,
Italy.

Current Models: *1050.* Coupé, Spyder. *1600 TC.* Coupé.

O.S.C.A. 1600 TC Coupé: Number of cylinders 4. Cubic capacity 1568 c.c. Compression ratio 9 : 1. B.H.P. 125. Max. m.p.h. 125. Overall length 14 ft. 3½ in. Overall width 5 ft. 2⅜ in. Height 4 ft. Wheel-base 7 ft. 10½ in. Track 4 ft. 5 in. (front), 4 ft. 4 in. (rear). Fuel tank capacity 11 Imp. gals. Weight 1852 lb.

Appearance: Unusual combination of flowing curves and razor-edged styling. Small, oblong radiator air-intake with horizontal barred grille is flanked by paired headlamps and side/indicator lamps. Note flowing wing line and flat bonnet running down to prominent " lip " around front of car. Narrow, divided bumpers front and rear. Rear wing line is squared-off and of triangular section; paired tail-lamps. Angular passenger area with well-raked and curved windscreen and rear window. Perforated disc wheels have very large, domed hub-caps.

PANHARD
FRANCE

S. A. Panhard and Levassor,

19, Avenue d'Ivry,

Paris, France.

Current Models: 17. Luxe, Superluxe, Relmax and Relmax Tigre 4-door Saloons, Break Station Wagon. **24BT.** 2-door Sports Saloon. **24CT.** 2-door Sports Coupé 2 + 2. **24CD.** Grand Tourisme Coupé, Rallye Coupé.

Panhard 24CT Sports Coupé: Number of cylinders Flat-2. Cubic capacity 848 c.c.   Compression ratio 7·2 : 1.   B.H.P. 60. Max. m.p.h. 90 plus.   Overall length 14 ft.   Overall width 5 ft. 4 in.   Height 4 ft.   Turning circle 30 ft.   Wheel-base 7 ft. 6 in.   Track 4 ft. 3 in. (front and rear).   Fuel tank capacity 9¼ Imp. gals.   Kerb weight 14 cwt.

Appearance: Striking blend of rounded body contours and angular passenger area styling.   Tiny, narrow slot air-intake between rubber overriders on bumper which sweeps around to front wheel arches.   Paired headlamps inset into rounded bonnet.   Rear deck forms "brow" over rounded tail panel. Long rear-lamp clusters are high set and massive rear bumper wraps around to wheel arches.   Passenger area with narrow pillars has similar front and rear contours; narrow roof line. Wheel centres are ribbed.

PEUGEOT

FRANCE

S. A. Automobiles Peugeot,

29, Rue de Berri,

Paris 8, France.

Current Models: *403 Sept.* 4-door Saloon. *403.* Confort 4-door Saloon, De Luxe 4-door Saloon. *404.* 4-door Grand Tourisme Saloon, 4-door Grand Tourisme Saloon De Luxe, De Luxe Convertible, De Luxe Coupé, De Luxe Family Limousine (Station Wagon), De Luxe Break (Station Wagon).

Peugeot 403 Sept Saloon: Number of cylinders 4 (petrol or diesel). Cubic capacity 1290 c.c. or 1816 c.c. Compression ratio 7·3 : 1 or 21 : 1. B.H.P. 54 or 55. Overall length 14 ft. 7⅕ in. Overall width 5 ft. 5¾ in. Height 4 ft. 11 in. (petrol), 4 ft. 11½ in. (diesel). Turning circle 31 ft. Wheelbase 8 ft. 8¾ in. Track 4 ft. 5½ in. (front), 4 ft. 4½ in. (rear). Fuel tank capacity 11 Imp. gals. Kerb weight 2147 lb. or 2424 lb.

Appearance: Rather severe styling with simple oval radiator air-intake having mesh grille. High-set headlamps with side/indicator lamps below. Note crease line along top line of wings. Vertical tail-lamps; rounded luggage boot. Curved windscreen and rear window. Prominent flanges over wheel arches; simple bumpers. Disc wheels with plain hub-caps.

Peugeot 404 Grand Tourisme Saloon: Number of cylinders 4 (carburettor or fuel injection, or diesel). Cubic capacity 1618 c.c. (petrol) or 1948 c.c. (diesel). Compression ratio 7·4 : 1, 8·8 : 1 or 21 : 1. B.H.P. 72, 85 or 68. Overall length 14 ft. 6¼ in. Overall width 5 ft. 3⅘ in. Height 4 ft. 9¼ in. Turning circle 32 ft. Wheel-base 8 ft. 8³⁄₁₀ in. Track 4 ft. 4¾ in. (front), 4 ft. 2¼ in. (rear). Fuel tank capacity 11 Imp. gals. Kerb weight 2354 lb.

Appearance: Flat bonnet slopes gently down between high-set headlamps with pointed rims. Full-width, oblong radiator air-intake having deeply inset grille of mesh and four thin horizontal bars. Large, oblong side-lamps just above plain bumper having vertical overriders. Straight-through wings to vertical tail-lamp clusters. Squarish rear contours. Smallish passenger area, deep windscreen, rear window has slight " lip " over. Disc wheels have large, plain hub-caps.

Peugeot 404 De Luxe Coupé: Number of cylinders 4 (carburettor or fuel injection). Cubic capacity 1618 c.c. Compression ratio 7·4 : 1 or 8·8 : 1. B.H.P. 72 or 85. Overall length 14 ft. 8⅘ in. Overall width 5 ft. 6¹⁄₁₀ in. Height 4 ft. 6⁸⁄₁₀ in. Turning circle 32 ft. Wheel-base 8 ft. 8³⁄₁₀ in. Track 4 ft. 4¾ in. (front), 4 ft. 2¼ in. (rear). Fuel tank capacity 11 Imp. gals. Kerb weight 2376 lb.

Appearance: Wide, oblong radiator air-intake with horizontally barred grille. Note how wing line rises slightly over rear wheels. Deep, curved windscreen and large rear window.

Large, vertical tail-lamps; plain bumpers front and rear. Narrow roof line and large side windows. Wheel discs have long slots.

Peugeot 404 De Luxe Family Limousine: Number of cylinders 4 (petrol or diesel). Cubic capacity 1618 c.c. or 1816 c.c. Compression ratio 7·4 : 1 or 21 : 1. B.H.P. 72 or 55. Overall length 15 ft. $\frac{2}{8}$ in. Overall width 5 ft. 4 in. Height 4 ft. 10$\frac{4}{5}$ in. Turning circle 35 ft. Wheel-base 9 ft. 3$\frac{4}{5}$ in. Track 4 ft. 4$\frac{3}{4}$ in. (front), 4 ft. 2$\frac{1}{4}$ in. (rear). Fuel tank capacity 11 Imp. gals. Kerb weight 2585 lb. or 2750 lb.

Appearance: Frontal details as for Grand Tourisme Saloon but note van-like utility body. Straight-through wing line to long, vertical tail-lamp clusters forming trailing edges of wings. Note lack of rear bumper—twin narrow bars run full width of body with end plates forming lower edges of rear wings. Disc wheels.

PLYMOUTH

UNITED STATES OF AMERICA

Plymouth Division,
Chrysler Corp.,
Detroit, Michigan,
U.S.A.

History: The history of the Plymouth began with the Maxwell cars in 1904. In 1923 the Maxwell company was bought by the Chrysler Corporation of which Plymouth is now a subsidiary.

Both the first two Maxwells had two cylinders horizontally opposed with a 3-speed, sliding-gear transmission. The multiple-disc clutch disengaged when the hand brake was applied. Two-cylinder models were discontinued in 1912.

Four- and six-cylinder models of varying prices were made prior to 1914 but in that year production began on a low-priced four-cylinder model which had a cubic capacity of 185·8 cu. in., and developed 25 b.h.p. It had a cone clutch with a 3-speed sliding-gear transmission and remained on the market until 1926. In the same year the name of the model was changed to Chrysler 58 and in 1927 it was re-named the Chrysler 50.

The word " Plymouth " was seen in 1929 on the model just described. In the next year, a Four was manufactured with a bore and stroke of 3⅝ in. × 4¾ in. and was continued until 1933 when a 189·9 cubic inch Six superseded it. This capacity was raised to 201·3 cubic inches a year later and in 1942 again increased to 217·8 cubic inches. In 1952 Plymouth introduced overdrive and, in 1953, offered a torque converter with a clutch and 3-speed gearbox. 1954 models continued with only minor modifications. Two series of models were offered in 1955: the " Plaza " and the " Belvedere ". 1956 saw the introduction of the Savoy series and the Fury Coupé.

198

Current Models: *Valiant V-100*. 2- and 4-door Sedans, Station Wagon. ***Valiant V-200*.** 2- and 4-door Sedans, Convertible, Station Wagon. ***Valiant Signet*.** 2-door Hardtop, Convertible. ***Valiant Barracuda*.** 2-door Sport Coupé. ***Belvedere I*.** 2- and 4-door Sedans, Station Wagon. ***Belvedere II*.** 4-door Sedan, 2-door Hardtop, Convertible, Station Wagon (6- and 9-passenger). ***Satellite*.** 2-door Hardtop, Convertible. ***Fury I*.** 2- and 4-door Sedans, Station Wagon. ***Fury II*.** 2- and 4-door Sedans, Station Wagon (6- and 9-passenger). ***Fury III*.** 4-door Sedan, 2- and 4-door Hardtops, Convertible, Station Wagon (6- and 9-passenger). ***Sport Fury*.** 2-door Hardtop, Convertible.

Plymouth Valiant V-200 4-door Sedan: Number of cylinders 6 or V8. Cubic capacity 170 cu. in. (6), 273 cu. in. (V8), (225 cu. in. (6) optional). Compression ratio 8·5 : 1 (7·1 : 1 available) (6), 8·8 : 1 (7·5 : 1 available) (V8), (8·4 : 1 (7·3 : 1 available) (6) optional, 10·5 : 1 (V8) optional). B.H.P. 101 (6), 180 (V8), (145 (6), 235 (V8) optional). Overall length 15 ft. 8¼ in. Overall width 5 ft. 10 1/10 in. Height 4 ft. 6⅔ in. Turning circle 37·1 ft. Wheel-base 8 ft. 10 in. Track 4 ft. 7 9/10 in. (front), 4 ft. 7⅗ in. (rear). Fuel tank capacity 18 U.S. gals.

Appearance: Full-width radiator air-intake has grille of thin horizontal bars and thrust-forward central portion. High-set bumper has slot intake beneath; side/indicator lamps at ends of slot. Tail-lamp units at ends of rear panel. Narrow roof line. Flat wheel discs have thinly spoked effect.

Plymouth Valiant Barracuda Sport Coupé: Number of cylinders 6 or V8. Cubic capacity 170 cu. in. (6), 273 cu. in. (V8) (225 cu. in. (6) optional). Compression ratio 8·5 : 1 (7·1 : 1 available) (6), 8·8 : 1 (7·5 : 1 available) (V8), (8·4 : 1 (7·3 : 1 available) (6) optional, 10·5 : 1 (V8) optional). B.H.P. 101 (6), 180 (V8), (145 (6), 235 (V8) optional). Overall length 15 ft. $8\frac{1}{5}$ in. Overall width 5 ft. $10\frac{1}{10}$ in. Height 4 ft. $6\frac{2}{5}$ in. Turning circle 37·1 ft. Wheel-base 8 ft. 10 in. Track 4 ft. $7\frac{9}{10}$ in. (front), 4 ft. $7\frac{3}{5}$ in. (rear). Fuel tank capacity 18 U.S. gals.

Appearance: Frontal styling similar to Valiant V-200 but note additional lamps mounted in intake. "Fast-back" body styling has extremely large rear window. Straight-through wing line to vertical tail-lamp clusters in trailing edges of wings. Long side windows and rounded roof line. Wheel discs have oblong perforations and no hub-caps.

Plymouth Belvedere II 4-door Sedan: Number of cylinders V8. Cubic capacity 273 cu. in. (318 cu. in., 361 cu. in., 383 cu. in. and 426 cu. in. optional). Compression ratio 8·8 : 1 (7·5 : 1 available), (9 : 1 (7·5 : 1 available), 9 : 1, 10 : 1 and 10·3 : 1 optional). B.H.P. 180 (230, 265, 330 and 480 optional). Overall length 16 ft. $11\frac{2}{5}$ in. Overall width 6 ft. $3\frac{3}{5}$ in. Height 4 ft. $7\frac{4}{5}$ in. Wheel-base 9 ft. 8 in. Track 4 ft. $11\frac{1}{2}$ in (front), 4 ft. $10\frac{1}{2}$ in. (rear). Fuel tank capacity 19 U.S. gals.

Appearance: Full-width, oblong radiator air-intake with narrow mesh grille opens out at the ends to accommodate headlamps beneath squarish styled hoods. Plain bumpers with rubber-tipped overriders front and rear. Note prominent "fluting" of straight-through wing line. Oblong tail-lamps on squared-off tail-panel. Angular passenger area with narrow roof line. Bonnet is flat. Wheel discs have row of narrow slots.

PMC

JAPAN

Prince Motors Ltd.,
88, Shuku-machi,
Suginami-ku,
Tokyo, Japan.

Current Models: *Skyline 1500*. Standard and De Luxe 4-door Saloons. ***Gloria 6*.** Standard and De Luxe 4-door Saloons, Estate Car.

PMC Skyline 1500 Saloon: Number of cylinders 4. Cubic capacity 1484 c.c. Compression ratio 8·3 : 1. B.H.P. 73. Overall length 13 ft. 1 in. Overall width 4 ft. 10$\frac{9}{10}$ in. Height 4 ft. 8$\frac{2}{5}$ in. Turning circle 31 ft. 6 in. Wheel-base 7 ft. 10$\frac{1}{10}$ in. Track 4 ft. 1$\frac{2}{5}$ in. (front), 4 ft. $\frac{3}{5}$ in. (rear). Fuel tank capacity 8·8 Imp. gals. Weight 2060 lb.

Appearance: Rather angular styling. Full-width radiator air-intake has grille of horizontal bars and incorporates paired head-lamps. Oblong side/indicator lamps above high-set, plain bumper. Straight-through wings to flat rear panel mounting large, circular tail-lamps. Slight razor edge styling to passenger area which has large glass area. Perforated wheel discs.

PMC Gloria 6 Saloon: Number of cylinders 6. Cubic capacity 1988 c.c. Compression ratio 8·8 : 1. B.H.P. 106.

Overall length 15 ft. 3$\frac{1}{10}$ in. Overall width 5 ft. 6$\frac{7}{10}$ in.
Height 4 ft. 10$\frac{3}{10}$ in. Turning circle 34·8 ft. Wheel-base
8 ft. 9$\frac{1}{2}$ in. Track 4 ft. 6$\frac{3}{10}$ in. (front), 4 ft. 7$\frac{1}{10}$ in. (rear).
Fuel tank capacity 11 Imp. gals. Weight 2865 lb.

Appearance: Attractive modern styling. Slightly inset
grille of fine mesh to radiator air-intake and paired headlamps. Massive plain bumpers, those at front have cut-aways
for side/indicator lamps. Heavy bright trim line runs completely around car. Sloping, flat bonnet; deep windscreen
and wrap-around rear window. Large, oval tail-lamp clusters.
Perforated wheel discs, large, rounded hub-caps.

PMC Gloria 6 Estate Car: Number of cylinders 6. Cubic
capacity 1988 c.c. Compression ratio 8·8 : 1. B.H.P. 106.
Overall length 15 ft. 4$\frac{3}{10}$ in. Overall width 5 ft. 6$\frac{7}{10}$ in.
Height 4 ft. 10$\frac{1}{10}$ in. Turning circle 34·8 ft. Wheel-base
8 ft. 9$\frac{1}{2}$ in. Track 4 ft. 6$\frac{3}{10}$ in. (front), 4 ft. 7$\frac{1}{10}$ in. (rear).
Fuel tank capacity 9·7 Imp. gals. Weight 3186 lb.

Appearance: Generally as for Saloon but angularly styled,
rather heavy-looking utility type body. Large rear side windows
and longish overhang at rear.

PONTIAC

CANADA

General Motors of Canada,
Oshawa,
Ontario,
Canada.

Current Models: *Strato Chief Series*. 2- and 4-door Sedans, Safari Station Wagon. ***Laurentian*.** 2- and 4-door Sedans, Safari Station Wagon (6- and 9-passenger). ***Parisienne*.** 4-door Sedan, 4-door Sport Sedan, Sport Coupé, Convertible, Safari Station Wagon. ***Parisienne Custom Sport*.** Coupé, Convertible.

Pontiac Parisienne Custom Sport Coupé: Number of cylinders 6 (V8 optional). Cubic capacity 230 cu. in. (283 cu. in., 327 cu. in. and 409 cu. in. optional). Compression ratio 8·5 : 1 (9·25 : 1, 10·5 : 1, 10 : 1 and 11 : 1 optional). B.H.P. 140 (195, 250, 300, 340 and 400 optional). Overall length 17 ft. 10$\frac{3}{5}$ in. Overall width 6 ft. 7$\frac{3}{5}$ in. Height 4 ft. 6$\frac{1}{10}$ in. Turning circle 40·8 ft. Wheel-base 9 ft. 11 in. Track 5 ft. 2$\frac{1}{2}$ in. (front), 5 ft. 2$\frac{2}{5}$ in. (rear). Fuel tank capacity 16$\frac{1}{2}$ Imp. gals.

Appearance: Characteristic Pontiac divided radiator air-intake but note two additional vertical bars; paired, vertically mounted headlamps are hooded. Straight-through, flowing wing line; massive bumpers front and rear. Horizontal tail-lamps follow contours of rear panel which curves out at ends to meet wing trailing edges. Shapely passenger area with sloping "fast-back" styling. Wheels have triple-eared "hub caps".

PONTIAC

UNITED STATES OF AMERICA

Pontiac Motor Division,
General Motors Corpn.,
Pontiac, Michigan,
U.S.A.

History: In 1908 the company became a division of
General Motors, and adopted the name Pontiac in 1932.
The first model developed 20 b.h.p. 1909 saw the
first four-cylinder model, and 1913 the first Six. By
1914 four new Fours and two more Sixes had appeared.
A six-cylinder was the only model produced from 1918
to 1923. In 1916 and 1917 a V8 was used, and another
V8 developing 85 b.h.p. was manufactured from 1930
to 1932. A new Six was brought out in 1926.
An entirely new Eight was created in 1933, developing
75 b.h.p., and re-appeared in 1942, delivering 103 b.h.p.
A Six of similar design, delivering 80 b.h.p., came on
the market in 1935, and by 1953 it delivered 90 b.h.p.
In 1938 Pontiac re-introduced the steering column gear
change and in 1948 hydromatic drive. The 1949 range
of models was named " Silver Streak ". Power-assisted
steering came in 1953 and the " Star Chief " in 1954.

Current Models: *Tempest Series.* 4-door Sedan, Sports
Coupé, Safari Station Wagon. *Tempest Custom Series.*
4-door Sedan, Hardtop Coupé, Sports Coupé, Convertible,
Safari Station Wagon. *Tempest Le Mans Series.* 4-
door Sedan, Hardtop Coupé, Sports Coupé, Convertible.
Catalina Series. 2- and 4-door Sedans, 4-door Vista
Hardtop, Sports Coupé, Convertible, Safari Station Wagon
(6- and 9-passenger). *Star Chief Series.* 4-door Sedan,
4-door Vista Hardtop. *Bonneville Series.* 4-door Vista
Hardtop, Sports Coupé, Convertible, Safari Station Wagon
(6-passenger). *Grand Prix Series.* Sports Coupé.

Pontiac Tempest Custom Hardtop Coupé: Number of cylinders 6 (V8 optional). Cubic capacity 215 cu. in. (326 cu. in. optional). Compression ratio 8·6 : 1 (9·2 : 1 and 10·5 : 1 optional, 7·2 : 1 available for 6 cylinder engine). B.H.P. 140 (250 and 285 optional, 125 available). Overall length 17 ft. 2$\frac{3}{10}$ in. Overall width 6 ft. 1$\frac{7}{10}$ in. Height 4 ft. 6 in. Turning circle 40·9 ft. Wheel-base 9 ft. 7 in. Track 4 ft. 10 in. (front and rear). Fuel tank capacity 21$\frac{1}{2}$ U.S. gals. Kerb weight 3140 lb.

Appearance: Vertically mounted paired headlamps flank full-width oblong radiator air-intake; slot intake in under-bumper. Broad, flat bonnet, well-raked windscreen with thin pillars. Note angular styling of passenger area, thin roof line and long side windows. Long rear deck, horizontal tail-lamp clusters. Massive bumpers front and rear. Slightly dished wheels have oblong perforations and " knock-off " hub-caps.

Pontiac Catalina Sports Coupé: Number of cylinders V8. Cubic capacity 389 cu. in. (389 cu. in. and 421 cu. in. optional). Compression ratio 8·6 : 1 (8·6 : 1, 10·5 : 1 and 10·75 : 1 optional, 7·9 : 1 available). B.H.P. 256 (256, 290, 325, 333, 338, 356 and 376 optional). Overall length 17 ft. 10$\frac{3}{5}$ in. Overall width 6 ft. 7$\frac{3}{5}$ in. Height 4 ft. 7$\frac{1}{5}$ in. Turning circle 42·8 ft. Wheel-base 10 ft. 1 in. Track 5 ft. 3 in. (front), 5 ft. 4 in.

(rear). Fuel tank capacity 26½ U.S. gals. Kerb weight 3949 lb.

Appearance: " Divided " oblong radiator air-intake with central horizontal bar is flanked by vertically mounted paired headlamps. Well-rounded passenger area, sharply raked, curved windscreen and large rear window. Note how prominent side body moulding " flares out " at rear wheel arches. Long side windows. Oblong tail-lamps in rear panel. Wheels have spoked effect.

Pontiac Bonneville Convertible: Number of cylinders V8. Cubic capacity 389 cu. in. (389 cu. in. and 421 cu. in. optional). Compression ratio 10·5 : 1 (8·6 : 1, 10·5 : 1 and 10·75 : 1 optional, 7·9 : 1 available). B.H.P. 333 (256, 325, 338, 356 and 376 optional). Overall length 18 ft. 5 $\frac{1}{10}$ in. Overall width 6 ft. 7 $\frac{3}{8}$ in. Height 4 ft. 6 $\frac{9}{10}$ in. Turning circle 43·7 ft. Wheel-base 10 ft. 4 in. Track 5 ft. 3 in. (front), 5 ft. 4 in. (rear). Fuel tank capacity 26½ U.S. gals. Kerb weight 4136 lb.

rounded tail having air-outlets. Perforated disc wheels have large, plain hub-caps.

Porsche Type 901 Coupé: Number of cylinders Flat-6. Cubic capacity 1991 c.c. Compression ratio 9 : 1. B.H.P. 130. Max. m.p.h. 130. Overall length 13 ft. 6⅖ in. Overall width 5 ft. 3 in. Height 4 ft. 2²⁄₁₀ in. Turning circle 32·8 ft. Wheel-base 7 ft. 2¾ in. Track 4 ft. 4⅖ in. (front), 4 ft 3⁷⁄₁₀ in. (rear). Fuel tank capacity 15 Imp. gals.

Appearance: Typically Porsche, but sleeker in line. Large headlamps with side/direction lamps below on body " corners ". Note tiny grilles below headlamps. Windscreen is large and well-raked; rear window in gently sloping rear panel is almost flat. Air-outlet grille below rear window runs full width of car. Horizontal tail-lamp clusters. Perforated disc wheels.

Porsche Type 904 Carrera GTS Coupé: Number of cylinders Flat-4. Cubic capacity 1966 c.c. Compression ratio 9·8 : 1. B.H.P. 180. Max. m.p.h. 150 (approx.). Overall length 13 ft. 5 in. Overall width 5 ft. ⅜ in. Height 3 ft. 5⁹⁄₁₀ in. Turning circle 42 ft. (approx.). Wheel-base 7 ft. 6½ in. Track 4 ft. 3⁷⁄₁₀ in. (front and rear). Fuel tank capacity 24 Imp. gals.

Appearance: " Bonnet " runs down between front wheel fairings to narrow, slot intake flanked by driving lamps and side/indicator lamps. Headlamps covered by long, transparent fairings. Wrap-around windscreen is well raked and flat rear window is deeply inset into body. Outlet for cooling air runs across rear deck. Tail panel is flat and slightly inset. Perforated disc wheels.

RAMBLER

UNITED STATES OF AMERICA

American Motors Corporation,
14250, Plymouth Road,
Detroit 32,
Michigan,
United States of America.

Rambler

Current Models: *American 220.* 2- and 4-door Sedans, Station Wagon. *American 330.* 2- and 4-door Sedans, Station Wagon. *American 440.* 4-door Sedan, 2-door Hardtop, Convertible. *American 440-H.* 2-door Hardtop. *Classic 550.* 2- and 4-door Sedans, Station Wagon. *Classic 660.* 2- and 4-door Sedans, Station Wagon. *Classic 770.* 4-door Sedan, 2-door Hardtop, Convertible, Station Wagon. *Classic 770-H.* 2-door Hardtop. *Ambassador 880.* 2- and 4-door Sedans, 2-door Hardtop, Station Wagon. *Ambassador 990.* 4-door Sedan, 2-door Hardtop, Convertible, Station Wagon. *Ambassador 990-H.* 2-door Hardtop. *Marlin.* 2-door Fastback Coupé.

Rambler American 2-door Hardtop: Number of cylinders 6. Cubic capacity 3206 c.c. (3802 c.c. optional). Compression ratio 8·7 : 1 (8·5 : 1). B.H.P. 125 (155). Overall length 14 ft. 9¼ in. Overall width 5 ft. 8⅗ in. Height 4 ft. 6½ in. Turning circle 36 ft. Wheel-base 8 ft. 10 in. Track 4 ft. 8 in. (front), 4 ft. 7 in. (rear). Fuel tank capacity 13⅜ Imp. gals.

Appearance: Narrow, full-width radiator air-intake flanked by inset headlamps; narrow slot intake below. Simple bumpers, broad, flat bonnet and deep, curved windscreen. Note lack of central door pillars and curved rear window. Wheel discs are rimmed.

Rambler Classic 770 Station Wagon: Number of cylinders 6 (6 and V8 optional). Cubic capacity 3802 c.c. (3802 c.c. (6), 4704 c.c. or 5360 c.c. (V8) optional). Compression ratio 8·5 : 1 (8·5 : 1, 8·7 : 1 or 9·7 : 1). B.H.P. 145 (155, 198 or 270). Overall length 16 ft. 1 in. Overall width 6 ft. 2½ in. Height 4 ft. 6⅝ in. Turning circle 37 ft. Wheel-base 9 ft. 4 in. Track 4 ft. 10½ in. (front), 4 ft. 9⅖ in. (rear). Fuel tank capacity 14⅕ Imp. gals.

Appearance: Narrow radiator air-intake with outwardly "veed" grille and paired headlamps at ends. Straight-through wing line to vertical rear wing line and "wrap-around" tail-lamps. Plain, heavy-looking bumpers. Note how rear of body gives impression of being "added on" to Sedan body. Wheel discs have thinly spoked effect.

Rambler Ambassador 990 4-door Sedan: Number of cylinders 6 (V8 optional). Cubic capacity 3802 c.c. (4704 c.c. or 5360 c.c.). Compression ratio 8·5 : 1 (8·7 : 1 or 9·7 : 1). B.H.P. 155 (198 or 270). Overall length 16 ft. 8 in. Overall width 6 ft. 2½ in. Height 4 ft. 7 in. Turning circle 39 ft.

2 in. Wheel-base 9 ft. 8 in. Track 4 ft. 10⅗ in. (front), 4 ft. 9½ in. (rear). Fuel tank capacity 15⅕ Imp. gals.

Appearance: Shapely, well-balanced car. Outwardly " veed " styling of radiator air-intake grille is carried out to vertical headlamp mountings. Straight-through wings to vertical tail-lamps. Broad, flat bonnet and rear deck; rather angular passenger area with deep windscreen and narrow roof line. Wheel discs have thin, radial spokes.

RELIANT
GREAT BRITAIN
Reliant Motor Company Ltd.,
Watling Street, Twogates,
Tamworth, Staffordshire, England.

Current Models: *Rebel.* 2-door Saloon. *Sabre Six.* 2-seater Sports (Soft and Hard Top), Gran Turismo Coupé. *Scimitar GT.* 2-door Coupé.

Reliant Scimitar GT Coupé: Number of cylinders 6 (Ford). Cubic capacity 2553 c.c. Compression ratio 8·3 : 1. B.H.P. 120. Max. m.p.h. 120 (approx.) Overall length 14 ft. Overall width 5 ft. 2¾ in. Height 4 ft. 2½ in. Turning circle 35 ft. Wheel-base 7 ft. 8 in. Track 4 ft. 2 in. (front and rear). Fuel tank capacity 20 Imp. gals. Kerb weight 19¾ cwt.

Appearance: Body design by DavidOgle Associates Ltd. Paired headlamps set into outwardly "veed" bonnet front. Radiator air-intake of narrow bars in lower part of "vee". Flat bonnet, slightly curved windscreen, well-raked rear window to flat deck and almost flat rear panel. Plain bumpers front and rear—those at rear are high-set; paired tail-lamps. Wire wheels with "knock-off" hub-caps.

RENAULT

FRANCE

S.A. des Usines Renault,
Régie Nationale, Avenue E. Zola, *also*
Billancourt,
France.

Renault Ltd.,
Western Avenue,
London, W.3,
England.

Current Models: *R3*, *R4* and ***R4L*.** 4-door Saloons, Estate Car. ***Dauphine Gordini*.** 4-door Saloon. ***R8*.** Standard and De Luxe 4-door Saloons. ***R8 " 1100 "*.** 4-door Saloon. ***Caravelle*.** Fixed Head Coupé, Convertible. ***R16*.** 4-door Saloon.

Renault R4L Saloon: Number of cylinders 4. Cubic capacity 845 c.c. Compression ratio 8 : 1. B.H.P. 28. Overall length 12 ft. Overall width 4 ft. 10½ in. Height 5 ft. Turning circle 28 ft. 6 in. Wheel-base (right) 8 ft., (left) 7 ft. 10½ in. Track 4 ft. 1¼ in. (front), 4 ft. ¾ in. (rear). Fuel tank capacity 5¾ Imp. gals. Kerb weight 1324 lb.

Appearance: Utilitarian, van-like body with six windows. Smallish radiator air-intake with vertically barred grille flanked by headlamps inset into bonnet front. Simple bumpers front and rear. Shallow, flat windscreen, one-piece rear window in panel which lifts up for access. Disc wheels with simple hub-caps.

Renault R8 Saloon: Number of cylinders 4. Cubic capacity 956 c.c. (1108 c.c. " 1100 "). Compression ratio 8·5 : 1. B.H.P. 42 (44·5). Overall length 13 ft. 1 in. Overall width 4 ft. 10½ in. Height 4 ft. 7½ in. Turning circle 30 ft. 6 in. Wheel-base 7 ft. 5¼ in. Track 4 ft. 1¼ in. (front), 4 ft. (rear). Fuel tank capacity 8½ Imp. gals. Kerb weight 1676 lb.

Appearance: Unusual square styling; note lack of frontal air intake and slightly inset headlamps. Almost similar front and rear contours; simple bumpers with vertical overriders. Large, high-set rear-lamp clusters. Air-outlet grille runs full width of tail. Large windscreen and rear window. Perforated disc wheels with large plain hub-caps.

Renault Caravelle Convertible: Number of cylinders 4. Cubic capacity 1108 c.c. Compression ratio 8·5 : 1. B.H.P.

48. Overall length 14 ft. Overall width 5 ft. 2 in. Height 4 ft. 3⅞ in. Turning circle 31 ft. 6 in. Wheel-base 7 ft. 5¼ in. Track 4 ft. 1¼ in. (front), 4 ft. (rear). Fuel tank capacity 8½ Imp. gals. Kerb weight 1700 lb. (1775 lb. with hardtop).

Appearance: Plain flat front to body; note lack of frontal air-intake (rear engine). Headlamps are inset; straight-through wings to high-set, vertical tail-lamps. Front bumper has raised central portion, rear bumper is plain. Sculptured effect from inset side body panels. Curved windscreen and convertible fabric top. Perforated disc wheels with large hub-caps.

Renault R16 Saloon: Number of cylinders 4. Cubic capacity 1470 c.c. Compression ratio 8·5 : 1. B.H.P. 62·6. Overall length 13 ft. 10½ in. Overall width 5 ft. 4⅝ in. Height 4 ft. 1⅛ in. Turning circle 32·8 ft. Wheel-base 8 ft. 9½ in. Track 4 ft. 4⅜ in. (front), 4 ft. 2⅞ in. (rear). Fuel tank capacity 12 Imp. gals. Kerb weight 2160 lb.

Appearance: Unique and unusual styling. Narrow, full-width air intake has dip in centre which is carried up into bonnet top. Oblong headlamps and side/indicator lamps. Fluted bumpers front and rear widen out at ends. Note sharply raked forward rear body line with rear window inset. Tail-lamps mounted high. Perforated disc wheels with prominent, flat hub-caps.

RILEY

GREAT BRITAIN

Riley Motors Ltd.,

Abingdon-on-Thames,

Berkshire, England.

History: Rileys started business, originally as a family concern, in 1896, the first Riley car designed by Percy Riley appearing on the roads of Britain in 1898. Since then the various models produced by the company have gained a world-wide reputation. In high performance and in the average run of everyday motoring, the name Riley has achieved great renown.

In 1926 the famous Riley Nine was introduced to the public. In the hands of such drivers as Freddie Dixon, this model gained innumerable successes in the sporting field as well as a fine reputation in normal road use. It continued to be produced, virtually unchanged, for ten years. A 1½-litre model finally replaced the Nine and this was superseded by a 2½-litre car. These last two were the forerunners of the present-day products.

In 1938 Riley passed into the hands of the Nuffield group of companies and after the Second World War the Riley organization was moved from Coventry to Abingdon-on-Thames, alongside the M.G. works there.

The first engines of the E.R.A. cars, so successful in the immediate pre-war period, were originally developed from Riley power-units.

The Pathfinder was introduced in 1954, having a capacity of 2443 c.c. and developing 110 b.h.p. This was the last model to make use of the well-known Riley 2½-litre engine with its inclined overhead valves operated by short push-rods from two high-set camshafts, the design of which dates back to 1926.

For 1957 the Two-Point-Six saloon, powered by a modified B.M.C. " C " type engine, was introduced.

Current Models: *Elf Mk. II.* 2-door Saloon. *One-Point-Five.* 4-door Saloon. *4/Seventy-Two.* 4-door Saloon.

Riley Elf Mk. II Saloon: Number of cylinders 4. Cubic capacity 998 c.c. Compression ratio 8·3 : 1. B.H.P. 38. Overall length 10 ft. 10⅖ in. Overall width 4 ft. 7½ in. Height 4 ft. 5 in. Turning circle 31 ft. 7 in. Wheel-base 6 ft. 8 1/10 in. Track 3 ft. 11⅖ in. (front), 3 ft. 9 9/10 in. (rear). Fuel tank capacity 5½ Imp. gals. Weight (unladen) 13 cwt. (approx.).

Appearance: Familiar "Mini" basic shape to which a dummy radiator shell at the front and a luggage boot at the rear have been added. Radiator shell is flanked by twin horizontal intakes incorporating side/direction lamps. Simple bumpers, those at rear wrap around. Plated wheel discs have oblong perforations.

Riley One-Point-Five Saloon: Number of cylinders 4. Cubic capacity 1489 c.c. Compression ratio 8·3 : 1. B.H.P. 63·5. Overall length 12 ft. 9 in. Overall width 5 ft. 1 in. Height 4 ft. 11 in. Turning circle 34 ft. 3 in. Wheel-base 7 ft. 2 in. Track 4 ft. 2 9/10 in. (front), 4 ft. 2 3/10 in. (rear). Fuel tank capacity 7 Imp. gals. Weight (unladen) 18¾ cwt. (approx.).

Appearance: Compact looking car. Traditional Riley radiator shell flanked by low-set horizontal grilles incorporating side/indicator lamps. Slightly hooded headlamps, straight-through wing line, vertical tail-lamp units. Rounded bonnet, rather prominent passenger area. Heavily flanged wheel arches, flange is continued around lower edges of body. Disc wheels.

Riley 4/Seventy-Two Saloon: Number of cylinders 4. Cubic

capacity 1622 c.c. Compression ratio 8·3 : 1. B.H.P. 68. Overall length 14 ft. 10$\frac{1}{10}$ in. Overall width 5 ft. 3$\frac{1}{2}$ in. Height 4 ft. 11 in. Turning circle 37 ft. Wheel-base 8 ft. 4$\frac{1}{4}$ in. Track 4 ft. 2$\frac{3}{5}$ in. (front), 4 ft. 3$\frac{2}{5}$ in. (rear). Fuel tank capacity 10 Imp. gals. Weight (unladen) 22$\frac{1}{2}$ cwt. (approx.).

Appearance: Smallish, vertical "radiator" grille flanked by low-set wrap-around grilles incorporating side/direction lamps. Straight-through wings to raked-forward, vertical tail-lamp units. Note how rear bumper wraps right around to wheel-arches; overriders are vestigial. Sweeping styling line runs full length of body. Disc wheels have simple hub-caps.

ROLLS ROYCE
GREAT BRITAIN

Rolls Royce Ltd.,
(Motor Car Division),
14–15, Conduit Street,
London, W.1, England.

History: Although the Rolls Royce company was not registered until 1906, Frederick Henry Royce met the Hon. Charles Stewart Rolls two years earlier. Together they were for some years to produce cars which have been known all over the world for their supreme quality, but the partnership was unfortunately cut short by the untimely and tragic death of Rolls in 1910.

Royce had bought a French "Decauville" car which he set out to improve, towards the end of 1903, by constructing three two-cylinder 10 h.p. models of his own design. Rolls was impressed and undertook to sell all that Royce could produce. Four types of chassis were then made: a two-cylinder 10 R.A.C.h.p., a three-cylinder 15 R.A.C.h.p., a four-cylinder 20 R.A.C.h.p., and a six-cylinder 30 R.A.C.h.p. model, all with the same bore. From 1906 to 1925 the famous side-valve, 40–50 R.A.C.h.p. "Silver Ghost" was produced. In 1910 Rolls was tragically killed in a flying accident. Royce became ill, but throughout his illness he continued to design and direct. In 1922 the forerunner of the "Wraith" was offered and in 1925 the "Phantom" appeared, replacing the old "Ghost".

The firm had entered many sporting events with success prior to World War I and this interest was strengthened in 1931 by taking over the Bentley concern. At this time chassis only were offered—the task of building the coachwork being left to the specialist body-building companies. Cars were produced again after the war and though chassis alone were offered they became available complete with bodies.

Current Models: *Silver Cloud III.* 4-door Saloon, L.W.B. Saloon (with division), James Young L.W.B. Saloon, H. J. Mulliner Park Ward 2- and 4-door Saloons, Convertible Coupé and Drophead Coupé. ***Phantom V.*** James Young Touring Limousine and 7-passenger Limousine, Park Ward 7-passenger Limousine.

Rolls Royce Silver Cloud III Saloon: Number of cylinders V8. Cubic capacity 6230 c.c. Compression ratio 9 : 1 (8 : 1 available). B.H.P. not disclosed. Overall length 17 ft. 7¾ in. Overall width 6 ft. 2¾ in. Height 5 ft. 4 in. Turning circle 41 ft. 8 in. Wheel-base 10 ft. 3 in. Track 4 ft. 10½ in. (front), 5 ft. (rear). Fuel tank capacity 18 Imp. gals. Kerb weight 40¼ cwt.

Appearance: Traditional straight-lined radiator shell blending into modern, semi-razor-edged styling. Paired headlamps faired into body between radiator and large front wings, which sweep across doors to meet " separate " rear wings. Plain bumpers with vertical overriders; prominent flange along lower edges of body. Disc wheels with large-section tyres.

Rolls Royce Silver Cloud III 2-door Saloon: Number of cylinders V8. Cubic capacity 6230 c.c. Compression ratio 9 : 1 (8 : 1 available). B.H.P. not disclosed. Overall length

17 ft. 7¾ in.   Overall width 6 ft. ½ in.   Height 5 ft. 1 in.   Turning circle 41 ft. 8 in.   Wheel-base 10 ft. 3 in.   Track 4 ft. 10½ in. (front), 5 ft. (rear).   Fuel tank capacity 18 Imp. gals.

Appearance: Sleek bodywork by Mulliner Park Ward. High-set, paired headlamps, straight-through wings to vertical tail-lamp clusters.   Well-raked, curved windscreen; rather shallow passenger area.   Long rear deck.   Cut-back wheel-arches.

Rolls Royce Phantom V Park Ward Limousine: Number of cylinders V8.   Cubic capacity 6230 c.c.   Compression ratio 9 : 1 (8 : 1 available).   B.H.P. not disclosed.   Overall length 19 ft. 10 in.   Overall width 6 ft. 7 in.   Height 5 ft. 9 in. Turning circle 48 ft. 9 in.   Wheel-base 12 ft.   Track 5 ft. 1 in. (front), 5 ft. 4 in. (rear).   Fuel tank capacity 24 Imp. gals. Kerb weight 49½ cwt.

Appearance: Large car with famous radiator thrust forward. Note " Silver Lady " mascot on Rolls Royces.   Small, paired headlamps; large, domed wings sweep across body to meet slightly bulging rear wings.   Curved, one-piece windscreen, large passenger area.   Small disc wheels with large tyres.

ROVER
GREAT BRITAIN

The Rover Co., Ltd.,
Meteor Works,
Solihull, Birmingham,
England.

History: The Rover company's history goes back to 1877, when J. K. Starley and W. Sutton began building penny-farthing bicycles in Coventry, the original company being founded in 1896 as the Rover Cycle Company.

The first Rover motor cycle appeared in 1903, being followed by the first car—an 8 h.p. single cylinder—the following year.

One of the most famous Rovers ever produced was the twin-cylinder air-cooled model which became extremely popular in the 1920's, but of later years the company specialized in the construction of medium-sized cars with a high standard of finish and equipment.

The modern Rover engine has an unusual cylinder-head arrangement with overhead inlet and side exhaust valves, whilst the radiator grille is still recognizably derived from the radiators of earlier Rover cars.

"Roverdrive" automatic transmission was introduced in 1956 and was fitted to the new "105R" model which was announced at the same time.

In 1950 the Rover company made history by constructing the first car to be powered by a gas turbine, and the Rover company, by entering this field so early, has built up a great deal of practical experience in the new problems involved in this form of power application.

A further step towards the ideal of a practical gas-turbine-powered car was taken in 1956 when the Rover T.3 was revealed. This was the first car in Britain designed initially for gas-turbine propulsion and was equipped with four-wheel drive and a glass-fibre body.

The year 1961 saw the appearance of the T.4 gas-turbine-powered prototype. Fitted with a shapely body, the T.4 has been designed with future production in mind.

Current Models: *3-litre*. 4-door Saloon Mk. II, Coupé. **2000.** 4-door Saloon. **Land Rover.** Short and Long Wheel-base Station Wagons and Utilities.

Rover 3-litre Saloon Mk. II: Number of cylinders 6. Cubic capacity 2995 c.c. Compression ratio 8·75 : 1 (manual transmission), 8 : 1 (automatic transmission). B.H.P. 121 or 119. Overall length 15 ft. 6½ in. Overall width 5 ft. 10 in. Height 5 ft. ½ in. Turning circle 40 ft. Wheel-base 9 ft. 2½ in. Track 4 ft. 7 5/16 in. (front), 4 ft. 8 in. (rear). Fuel tank capacity 14 Imp. gals.

Appearance: Large radiator air-intake with central dividing bar. Headlamps set close to intake, high-set sidelamps and indicator lamps on front body " corners ". Straight-through wing line to vertical tail-lamps. Smallish passenger area with shallow windows. Perforated disc wheels have prominent hub-caps.

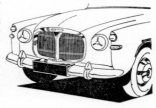

Rover 3-litre Coupé: Number of cylinders 6. Cubic capacity 2995 c.c. Compression ratio 8·75 : 1 (manual transmission), 8 : 1 (automatic transmission). B.H.P. 121 or 119. Overall length 15 ft. 6½ in. Overall width 5 ft. 10 in. Height 4 ft. 9½ in. Turning circle 40 ft. Wheel-base 9 ft. 2½ in. Track 4 ft. 7 5/16 in. (front), 4 ft. 8 in. (rear). Fuel tank capacity 14 Imp. gals.

Appearance: Generally as for Saloon, but note generally more rounded contours of passenger area; roof line is slimmer. Wrap-around windscreen and rear window. Deep body sides.

Rover 2000 Saloon: Number of cylinders 4. Cubic capacity 1978 c.c. Compression ratio 9 : 1. B.H.P. 90. Overall length 14 ft. 10½ in. Overall width 5 ft. 6 in. Height 4 ft. 6¾ in. Turning circle 31 ft. 6 in. Wheel-base 8 ft. 7¾ in. Track 4 ft. 5⅝ in. (front) 4 ft. 4½ in. (rear). Fuel tank capacity 12 Imp. gals.

Appearance: Full-width, narrow radiator air-intake incorporating paired headlamps. High-set bumper, broad, flat bonnet; deep, curved windscreen and narrow roof line. Straight-through wing line to vertical tail-lamps. Wheel discs have radial spoked effect.

SAAB
SWEDEN

Svenska Aeroplan Aktiebolaget,

Linköping,

Sweden.

Current Models: 96. 2-door Saloon. *96 Sport.* 2-door Saloon. **95.** Station Wagon.

SAAB 96 Saloon: Number of cylinders 3. Cubic capacity 841 c.c. Compression ratio 8·1 : 1. B.H.P. 40. Overall length 13 ft. 8 in. Overall width 5 ft. 2 in. Height 4 ft. 10 in. Turning circle 34 ft. 8 in. Wheel-base 8 ft. 2 3/10 in. Track 4 ft. (front and rear). Fuel tank capacity 8·8 Imp. gals. Kerb weight 1820 lb.

Appearance: Well-rounded, streamlined car with shallow, sharply raked windscreen and unbroken roof line. Full-width mesh grille incorporates headlamps and has narrow, central vertical " radiator " outline. Straight-through wing line to small, high-set tail-lamps. Curved side windows and wrap-around rear window. Perforated disc wheels have domed hub-caps.

SAAB 96 Sport Saloon: Number of cylinders 3. Cubic capacity 841 c.c. Compression ratio 9 : 1. B.H.P. 55. Overall length 13 ft. 8 in. Overall width 5 ft. 2 in. Height 4 ft. 10 in. Turning circle 34 ft. 8 in. Wheel-base 8 ft. 2 3/10 in. Track 4 ft. (front and rear). Fuel tank capacity 8·8 Imp. gals. Kerb weight 1960 lb.

Appearance: Generally similar to 96 Saloon but note differing side trim strips and wheel discs. SAAB models appear high off the ground and have well rounded roof line.

SAAB 95 Station Wagon: Number of cylinders 3. Cubic capacity 841 c.c. Compression ratio 8·1 : 1. B.H.P. 40. Overall length 14 ft. Overall width 5 ft. 3 in. Height 4 ft. 10 in. Turning circle 34 ft. 8 in. Wheel-base 8 ft. 2$\frac{3}{10}$ in. Track 4 ft. (front and rear). Fuel tank capacity 9½ Imp. gals. Kerb weight 1985 lb.

Appearance: Frontal details as for other models but note distinctive styling of utility type body. Roof line flows straight back to prominent peak over rear window. Sloping tail panel inset between trailing edges of rear wings. Paired, vertically mounted, twin tail lamps.

SIMCA

FRANCE

Soc. Anon. Simca,
45–61, Rue J. P. Timbaud,
Poissy (Seine-et-Oise),
France.

Current Models: *900* and *900C*. 4-door Saloons. *1000*. 4-door Saloon, Coupé. *1000 GL* and *1000 GLS*. De Luxe 4-door Saloons. *1300*. 4-door Saloon. *1300 GL*. De Luxe 4-door Saloon. *1500*. 4-door Saloon, Station Wagon. *1500 GL*. De Luxe 4-door Saloon, De Luxe Station Wagon.

Simca 1000 Saloon: Number of cylinders 4. Cubic capacity 944 c.c. Compression ratio 8·2 : 1 (9 : 1 GL and GLS). B.H.P. 50 (52). Overall length 12 ft. 5½ in. Overall width 4 ft. 10½ in. Height 4 ft. 6⅝ in. Turning circle 29 ft. 6 in. Wheel-base 7 ft. 3½ in. Track 4 ft. 1½ in. (front), 4 ft. ¾ in. (rear). Fuel tank capacity 7·9 Imp. gals. Kerb weight 14¼ cwt. (14¾ cwt.).

Appearance: Rather angular contours. Note lack of frontal air-intake (rear engine). Prominent, centrally placed passenger area with large curved windscreen and rear window. Large headlamps and oblong side/indicator lamps just above plain bumper. Flat " bonnet ". Disc wheels.

Simca 1000 Coupé: Number of cylinders 4. Cubic capacity 944 c.c. Compression ratio 9 : 1. B.H.P. 52. Overall length

231

12 ft. 10½ in. Overall width 5 ft. Height 4 ft. 1⅞ in. Turn-ing circle 30 ft. Wheel-base 7 ft. 3½ in. Track 4 ft. 1 1/10 in. (front), 4 ft. 1⅖ in. (rear). Fuel tank capacity 7·9 Imp. gals. Kerb weight 15·6 cwt.

Appearance: Headlamps rather thrust forward; straight-through wing line to squared-off rear panel with large circular tail-lamps. Deep, well-raked windscreen and extremely large rear window in sloping roof line. Note lack of frontal air-intake. Bumpers are plain and wrap-around. Perforated disc wheels with simple hub-caps.

Simca 1300 Saloon: Number of cylinders 4. Cubic capacity 1290 c.c. Compression ratio 8·3/8·5 : 1. B.H.P. 62. Overall length 13 ft. 11 3/10 in. (13 ft. 11⅞ in. GL). Overall width 5 ft. 2⅛ in. Height 4 ft. 7 7/10 in. Turning circle 32 ft. Wheel-base 8 ft. 3½ in. Track 4 ft. 4 in. (front), 4 ft. 3⅖ in. (rear). Fuel tank capacity 12 Imp. gals. Kerb weight 18·9 cwt.

Appearance: Neat, well-proportioned lines. Flat bonnet runs down between headlamps. Full-width radiator air-intake with slightly " veed " grille of thin horizontal bars. Prominent angular passenger area with large windows and deep windscreen. Perforated disc wheels have large, flat hub-caps.

Simca 1500 Station Wagon: Number of cylinders 4. Cubic capacity 1475 c.c. Compression ratio 9/9·3 : 1. B.H.P. 81. Overall length 13 ft. 11⅕ in. Overall width 5 ft. 2⅛ in. Height 4 ft. 7½ in. Turning circle 32 ft. 8 in. Wheel-base 8 ft. 3⅛ in. Track 4 ft. 4 in. (front), 4 ft. 3⅗ in. (rear). Fuel tank capacity 12 Imp. gals. Kerb weight 20½ cwt. (21 cwt. GL).

Appearance: Styling generally similar to 1300 model but note attractive utility type body which has angular windows. Wide radiator air-intake with grille of thin horizontal bars and head-lamps at ends. Straight-through wing line to vertical tail-lamps. Bumpers have rubber-tipped overriders and rear bumper wraps around to wheel arches. Perforated disc wheels with large, flat hub-caps.

SINGER

GREAT BRITAIN

Singer Motors Ltd.,
Coventry Road Works,
Birmingham, England.

History: In 1876 George Singer started his own company for the manufacture of bicycles. Five years later the Singer Cycle Co. Ltd., of Coventry, was exhibiting and selling motor cycles, and by 1902 three-wheeler motor "voiturettes" with seating for two or three passengers were being produced. In the same year the engine was fitted inside the wheel of the cycle, similar to ones seen to this day on auto-wheels.

The first four-wheeled cars were built in 1904 and sold the following year. By 1909 four models were being made from the 7·9 R.A.C.h.p. twin-cylinder. In this year the company name was changed to Singer and Co. Ltd., and the following year a Singer broke the 15 R.A.C.h.p. record at Brooklands with an average speed of 77·108 m.p.h. for ten laps.

The Singer 10 appeared in 1912 and many were used by the Army in World War I. 1933 saw the introduction of the famous Nine followed by a period of great success in sporting events. In 1934 Singers fitted independent front suspension and fluid-drive clutchless gear change—the first British manufacturers to offer these two advancements. In the same year the aerodynamic Airstream model was built.

Before World War II the company was the only automobile maker in the world to guarantee its engines against cylinder bore wear. In 1953 an all-plastic bodied car was produced, and in 1954 the new Hunter part-plastic saloon was put into production to replace the 1½-litre SM 1500.

At the end of 1955 the Singer company became a member of the Rootes Group and in September 1956

234

the new Gazelle, bearing a strong resemblance to the Hillman Minx but still using the Hunter overhead camshaft engine, was announced.

Current Models: *Chamois*. 2-door Saloon. ***Vogue (Mk. III).*** 4-door Saloon, Estate Car. ***Gazelle (Series V).*** 4-door Saloon.

Singer Chamois Saloon: Number of cylinders 4. Cubic capacity 875 c.c. Compression ratio 10 : 1 (8 : 1 available). B.H.P. 42. Overall length 11 ft. 7 in. Overall width 5 ft. ¼ in. Height 4 ft. 6½ in. Turning circle 30 ft. 6 in. Wheelbase 6 ft. 10 in. Track 4 ft. 1½ in. (front), 4 ft. ½ in. (rear). Fuel tank capacity 6 Imp. gals. Dry weight 1467 lb.

Appearance: As for Hillman Imp but note differing frontal treatment featuring dummy grille. Distinctive side "flash". Prominent "crease" line running all around body. Very large and deep passenger area with big windows. Wheel discs have radial slots and domed hub-caps.

Singer Vogue Saloon: Number of cylinders 4. Cubic capacity 1592 c.c. Compression ratio 9·1 : 1. B.H.P. 84.

235

Overall length 13 ft. 11 in.   Overall width 5 ft. 3 in.   Height
4 ft. 10 in.   Turning circle 36 ft.   Wheel-base 8 ft. 5 in.
Track 4 ft. 3¾ in. (front), 4 ft. ½ in. (rear).   Fuel tank capacity
10½ Imp. gals.   Dry weight 2291 lb.

Appearance: Paired,
hooded headlamps flanking
smallish radiator air-intake
with vertically barred grille
—slot   intakes   below.
Bumpers have widely spaced
rubber-tipped   overriders.
Body styling is generally
similar to Hillman Super
Minx but note triple tail-
lamp clusters.   Roof line is
thin and flattish, windscreen
deep.   Wheel   discs   have
radial slots.

Singer Vogue Estate Car: Number of cylinders 4.   Cubic
capacity 1592 c.c.   Compression ratio 9·1 : 1.   B.H.P. 84.
Overall length 13 ft. 11 in.   Overall width 5 ft. 3 in.   Height
4 ft. 10 in.   Turning circle 36 ft.   Wheel-base 8 ft. 5 in.
Track 4 ft. 3¾ in. (front), 4 ft. ½ in. (rear).   Fuel tank capacity
10 Imp. gals.   Dry weight 2384 lb.

Appearance: Frontal treatment as for Vogue saloon but note rather severely lined utility body. Rear side windows have rounded corners—the others are angular. Wheel centres are prominent.

Singer Gazelle Saloon: Number of cylinders 4. Cubic capacity 1592 c.c. Compression ratio 8·3 : 1. B.H.P. 56·5. Overall length 13 ft. 8½ in. Overall width 5 ft. ¾ in. Height 4 ft. 10 in. Turning circle 36 ft. Wheel-base 8 ft. Track 4 ft. 3¾ in. (front), 4 ft. ⅞ in. (rear). Fuel tank capacity 10 Imp. gals. Dry weight 2153 lb.

Appearance: Bodywork similar to Hillman Minx. Vertical, oval radiator grille flanked by slot intakes incorporating side/direction lamps. Hooded headlamps; straight-through wing line to vertical tail-lamps. Almost flat windscreen and curved rear window. Rather angular styling to passenger area. Note generally "low-slung" appearance. Disc wheels have large hub-caps.

SKODA

CZECHOSLOVAKIA

Skoda Automobilove,
29 Junmannova,
Prague 11,
Czechoslovakia.

Current Models: *1000 MB*. 4-door Saloon. ***Octavia Super*.** 2-door Saloon. ***Octavia Combi*.** Estate Car.

Skoda 1000 MB Saloon: Number of cylinders 4. Cubic capacity 988 c.c. Compression ratio 8·3 : 1. B.H.P. 45. Overall length 13 ft. 7½ in. Overall width 5 ft. 3⅘ in. Height 4 ft. 6⁷⁄₁₀ in. Turning circle 34 ft. Wheel-base 7 ft. 10⅞ in. Track 4 ft. 2⅖ in. (front), 4 ft. 1⅕ in. (rear). Fuel tank capacity 7 gals. Kerb weight 1665 lb.

Appearance: Generally similar front and rear contours. Note lack of frontal air-intake (rear engine). High-set headlamps, indicator lamps on front body " corners "; straight-through wing line to vertical tail-lamp clusters. Prominent air-intakes above rear wheels and full-width grille in tail panel for cooling air exit. Wrap-around windscreen and rear window. Disc wheels have large, domed hub-caps.

STUDEBAKER

UNITED STATES OF AMERICA

Studebaker Division,
Studebaker Corporation,
South Bend 27,
Indiana,
U.S.A.

History: Though the Studebaker Brothers began to make petrol-driven cars in 1904 the firm had been producing horse-drawn vehicles of quality since the middle of the previous century.

The first model had a two-cylinder horizontal petrol engine, but an electric machine was constructed in 1902. For the three years 1906, 1907 and 1908 four-cylinder models were on the market. The E.M.F. concern was bought in 1909 and Studebaker produced, until 1914, a number of very popular models bearing the name of the original company. Also, a four-cylinder model, named the " Flanders ", was produced in 1910, but this name was withdrawn in 1914. In 1911, the name of the company was changed to the Studebaker Corporation.

In the same year, two new cars were made, a Four and a Six. Studebaker produced the last Four in 1919. From 1927 to 1929 the " Erskine " was made and a small Six, named the " Rockne ", appeared in 1932. A free-wheeling device was available in 1930.

The " Champion " was presented in 1939, developing 78 b.h.p., and proved an economical car. In 1950 an automatic gearbox with a torque-converter was incorporated, and the following year a V8 with overhead valves producing 120 b.h.p. was manufactured. Raymond Loewy was responsible for post-war body styling and introduced the wrap-around rear window. All models continued with only minor improvements in 1954, and later in the year the company merged with Packard. Power outputs for 1955 ranged from 101 to 175 b.h.p.

For 1956, only the Hawk series bore any resemblance to the sleek Loewy designs, and the " Skypower V8 " engine used in the Golden Hawk developed 275 b.h.p.

Current Models: *Commander.* 2- and 4-door Sedans Wagonaire Station Wagon. *Daytona.* 2-door Sports Sedan, Wagonaire Station Wagon. *Cruiser.* 4-door Sedan.

Studebaker Daytona Sports Sedan: Number of cylinders V8. Cubic capacity 283 cu. in. Compression ratio 9·25 : 1. B.H.P. 195. Overall length 15 ft. 10 in. Overall width 5 ft. 11½ in. Height 4 ft. 6⅝ in. Turning circle 37 ft. 6 in. Wheelbase 9 ft. 1 in. Track 4 ft. 9⅜ in. (front), 4 ft. 8 9/16 in. (rear). Fuel tank capacity 15 Imp. gals. Weight (dry) 3006 lb.

Appearance: Radiator air-intake tapers towards the bottom and is flanked by headlamps in oblong " sockets ". Straight-through wing line to tail-lamp clusters set horizontally in prominent rear moulding. Squarish styling to passenger area; curved windscreen, thin roof line and large, almost flat rear window. Simple, sturdy bumpers. Wheel discs are polished and have spoke motif.

SUNBEAM

GREAT BRITAIN

Sunbeam-Talbot Ltd.,

  Ryton-on-Dunsmore,

nr. Coventry, England.

History: Although in 1938 the name Sunbeam-Talbot appeared on cars under the control of the Rootes Group, actually the Sunbeam Motor Car Company and Clement-Talbot Limited, acquired in 1935, had been producing passenger vehicles for some considerable time.

Sunbeam cars had many racing successes and gained various speed records from 1909 to 1927; in 1926 a Sunbeam achieved 150 m.p.h. Sunbeams achieved fame by the world speed attempts made by the late Sir Henry Segrave, and they were the first cars to exceed 200 m.p.h. (Talbots were the first cars to cover 100 miles in one hour.)

Talbot cars, and later the Sunbeam-Talbots, were originally manufactured in London, but with the re-organization that followed World War II the entire plant was moved to the present site.

In 1952 Sunbeam-Talbots did well as a team, gaining eleven prizes in the International Alpine Rally. In that same year, the " 90 " was introduced which had been developed from the experiences gained at sporting events.

The bodies of the " 90's " were coachbuilt by Thrupp and Maberly Limited, a company which, though now in the Rootes Group, began in 1907. The Sunbeam " Alpine " was introduced in 1953 for export only. It was a development of the " 90 " and appeared as a two-seater sports roadster. This car broke two records at Jabbeke, Belgium, in its first road test: the flying kilometer at 120·132 m.p.h. and the flying mile at 119·402 m.p.h.

The power of the Mark III four-cylinder engine was raised to 85·5 b.h.p. and this model was discontinued in 1958. The " Rapier " with its engine based on the well-tried Hillman unit was introduced in 1956.

Current Models: *Alpine (Series IV)*. Sports Tourer, Gran Turismo Hardtop. *Tiger*. Sports Tourer. *Rapier (Series IV)*. Sports Saloon.

Sunbeam Alpine Sports Tourer: Number of cylinders 4. Cubic capacity 1592 c.c. Compression ratio 9·1 : 1. B.H.P. 87·75. Max. m.p.h. 100. Overall length 13 ft. Overall width 5 ft. ½ in. Height 4 ft. 3½ in. (4 ft. 4½ in. G.T.). Turning circle 34 ft. Wheel-base 7 ft. 2 in. Track 4 ft. 3¾ in. (front), 4 ft. ½ in. (rear). Fuel tank capacity 11¼ Imp. gals. Dry weight 2083 lb.

Appearance: Broad, rounded bonnet curves down to narrow, low-set radiator air-intake having central bar bearing medallion. Slightly hooded headlamps; straight-through wing line to large, oval tail-lamps. Deep, curved windscreen and two large doors. May be seen with hard-top. Perforated disc wheels standard, centre-lock wire wheels optional.

Sunbeam Tiger Sports Tourer: Number of cylinders V8 (Ford). Cubic capacity 4261 c.c. Compression ratio 8·8 : 1. B.H.P. 164. Max. m.p.h. 125. Overall length 13 ft. Overall width 5 ft. ½ in. Height 4 ft. 3½ in. (4 ft. 4½ in. with hardtop). Turning circle 37·6 ft. Wheel-base 7 ft. 2 in. Track 4 ft. 3¾ in. (front), 4 ft. ½ in. (rear). Fuel tank(s) capacity 11¼ Imp. gals. Dry weight 2407 lb.

Appearance: Generally as for Alpine—note sleek, sporting lines of these cars. Perforated disc wheels only.

Sunbeam Rapier Sports Saloon: Number of cylinders 4. Cubic capacity 1592 c.c. Compression ratio 9 : 1. B.H.P. 84. Max. m.p.h. 90 plus. Overall length 13 ft. 7¼ in. Overall width 5 ft. ¾ in. Height 4 ft. 9½ in. Turning circle 36 ft. Wheel-base 8 ft. Track 4 ft. 3¾ in. (front), 4 ft. ½ in. (rear). Fuel tank capacity 10 Imp. gals. Dry weight 2231 lb.

Appearance: Small, vertical radiator air-intake is flanked by prominent horizontal intakes. Straight-through wing line to long, canted "fins". Note long side windows and wrap-around rear window. Wheel discs feature radial slots.

TATRA

CZECHOSLOVAKIA

Tatra,
Narodni Podnik,
Koprivnice,
Czechoslovakia.

Current Model: *2-603*. 4-door Saloon.

Tatra 2-603 Saloon: Number of cylinders V8 (air-cooled). Cubic capacity 2472 c.c. Compression ratio 8·2 : 1. B.H.P. 105. Max. m.p.h. 105. Overall length 16 ft. 7$\frac{2}{5}$ in. Overall width 6 ft. 3$\frac{1}{5}$ in. Height 5 ft. 1 in. Wheel-base 6 ft. 9$\frac{7}{10}$ in. Max. track 4 ft. 7 in. Fuel tank capacity 13·2 Imp. gals. Kerb weight 3240 lb.

Appearance: Well rounded, heavy-looking car. No fronta air-intake due to rear-mounted engine, but note paired headlamps set into front of car. " Bonnet " thrust-forward and rounded; " suggested " front wings with streamlined side/ indicator lamps. Heavy bumpers wrapped well round front and rear. Large rear window. Note air-intakes on body sides just behind rear wheels. Disc wheels have large hub-caps.

TOYOTA

JAPAN

Toyota Motor Co. Ltd.,
No. 1, Toyota-Cho,
Toyota-Shi, Aichi-Ken,
Japan.

Current Models: *700 Publica UP.10 and UP.10D.*
2-door Saloons. *700 Publica UP.10S.* Convertible. *Corona RT.40.* 4-door Saloon. *Corona De Luxe RT.40-DC.*
4-door Saloon. *Crown RS.40.* 4-door Saloon. *Crown De Luxe RS.41.* 4-door Saloon. *Crown Eight VG.10.*
4-door Saloon. *Custom RS.46G.* Station Wagon.

Toyota Corona De Luxe RT.40-DC Saloon: Number of cylinders 4. Cubic capacity 1490 c.c. Compression ratio 8 : 1. B.H.P. 70. Overall length 13 ft. $5\frac{4}{5}$ in. Overall width 5 ft. 1 in. Height 4 ft. 8 in. Turning circle 32 ft. 6 in. Wheel-base 7 ft. $11\frac{3}{10}$ in. Track 4 ft. 2 in. (front and rear). Fuel tank capacity 9.9 Imp. gals. Weight 2112 lb.

Appearance: Slightly raked flat front has small radiator air-intake flanked by paired headlamps. Slot intake below with side-lamps at ends. Flat bonnet and angular passenger area, large windscreen and rear window. Angular bumpers have rubber-tipped overriders. Perforated wheel discs, flat hub-caps.

Toyota Crown De Luxe RS.41 Saloon: Number of cylinders 4. Cubic capacity 1897 c.c. Compression ratio 8 : 1. B.H.P. 90. Overall length 15 ft. $1\frac{1}{2}$ in. Overall width 5 ft. $6\frac{7}{10}$ in. Height 4 ft. $9\frac{1}{2}$ in. Turning circle 36 ft. Wheel-base 8 ft.

9$\frac{9}{10}$ in.   Track 4 ft. 5$\frac{1}{2}$ in. (front), 4 ft. 6$\frac{3}{10}$ in. (rear).   Fuel tank capacity 11 Imp. gals.   Weight 2783 lb.

Appearance: Full-width radiator air-intake has slightly inset grille and incorporates paired headlamps.   Note side/indicator lamps mounted in external housings on front bumper.   Broad, flat bonnet to curved, well-raked windscreen.   Rather angular passenger area, narrow roof line and large rear window. Wedge-shaped tail line.   Wheel discs have radial perforations.

Toyota Crown Eight VG.10 Saloon: Number of cylinders V8. Cubic capacity 2599 c.c.   Compression ratio 9 : 1.   B.H.P. 115.   Overall length 15 ft. 5$\frac{4}{5}$ in.   Overall width 6 ft. 3$\frac{2}{5}$ in. Height 4 ft. 9$\frac{1}{2}$ in.   Turning circle 39 ft.   Wheel-base 8 ft. 11$\frac{7}{8}$ in.   Track 5 ft. (front), 5 ft. $\frac{2}{5}$ in. (rear).   Fuel tank capacity 11 Imp. gals.   Weight 3025 lb.

Appearance: Similar to Crown De Luxe but note differing radiator air-intake grille.   Simple bumpers front and rear.

TRABANT

GERMANY

V.E.B. Sachsenring Automobilwerke
Zwickau,

Zwickau (Sachs),

Germany.

Current Models: *600*.   2-door Saloon, Station Wagon.

Trabant 600 Saloon: Number of cylinders 2.   Cubic capacity
594 c.c. Compression ratio 7·6 : 1.   B.H.P. 26.   Overall
length 11 ft.   Overall width 4 ft. 10¾ in.   Height 4 ft. 9½ in.
Turning circle 32 ft.   Wheel-base 6 ft. 7½ in.   Max. track
4 ft. 1½ in.   Fuel tank capacity 5·3 Imp. gals.   Kerb weight
1370 lb.

Appearance: Neat, compact design. Rounded " bonnet "
between high-set headlamps; straight-through wings to high-set
tail-lamps.   Note lack of frontal air-intake due to rear engine.
Shallow windscreen and rear window.   Bumpers feature a
thin bright strip.   Disc wheels have large hub-caps.

TRIUMPH

GREAT BRITAIN

Triumph Motor Co. (1945) Ltd.,
Coventry,
England.

History: One of the old-established companies which traces its origin to the cycle business, having been established in Coventry in 1885. In pre-last-war days this company was famous for its high-quality small- and medium-sized cars with stylish coachwork and better-than-average finish. They achieved great success in British concours d'elégance.

After the war, in 1945, the Triumph Company was acquired by the Standard Motor Company and, in the capable hands of Sir John Black, the marque gained new successes. The " Vanguard " engine, made at the 103-acre plant at Canley, was fitted to the " Renown " saloon. This model retained the traditional British appearance by featuring a vertical, chromium radiator with razor-edge body styling and also had unusually large window areas with narrow pillars. Another model, the " Mayflower ", was introduced in 1949, and although adhering to a similar body treatment the wings were given a single contour that swept down and across the body sides. The power unit was smaller than that of the " Renown ", being of 1247 c.c. capacity and developing 38 b.h.p. However, this model was later discontinued.

By 1954 the range of Triumph cars comprised the " Renown " saloon and the T.R.2 sports two-seater model first introduced at the London Motor Show in 1952. Disc brakes on the front wheels of the T.R.3 were introduced for 1957.

Current Models: *Herald 1200*. 2-door Saloon, Coupé, Convertible, Estate Car. *Herald 12/50*. 2-door Sunshine

Roof Saloon. *Vitesse.* 2-door Saloon, Convertible. *2000.*
4-door Saloon. *Spitfire 4.* 2-seater Sports, Hardtop. *TR4.*
2-seater Sports, Hardtop.

Triumph Herald 1200 Saloon: Number of cylinders 4.
Cubic capacity 1147 c.c. Compression ratio 8 : 1 (7 : 1 available). B.H.P. 39. Overall length 12 ft. 9 in. Overall width
5 ft. Height 4 ft. 4 in. Turning circle 25 ft. Wheel-base
7 ft. 7½ in. Track 4 ft. (front and rear). Fuel tank capacity
6½ Imp. gals. Dry weight 15¼ cwt.

Appearance: Divided radiator air-intake with square
mesh grille. Headlamps have
heavy, hooded rims; straight-through wing line to peaked.
vertical rear lamp clusters,
Bumpers are of white rubber
—large vertical overriders at
front. Narrow roof line
Small disc wheels.

Triumph Vitesse Convertible: Number of cylinders 6.
Cubic capacity 1596 c.c. Compression ratio 8·75 : 1. B.H.P.
70. Overall length 12 ft. 9 in. Overall width 5 ft. Height
4 ft. 4½ in. (hood up), 4 ft. 1½ in. (hood down). Turning circle

25 ft. Wheel-base 7 ft. 7½ in. Track 4 ft. 1 in. (front), 4 ft. (rear). Fuel tank capacity 8¾ Imp. gals. Dry weight 17¼ cwt.

Appearance: Generally similar to Herald models but note differing frontal treatment. Small radiator air-intake with mesh grille flanked by paired headlamps with side/direction lamps below. Bumpers are of polished aluminium, have large overriders at front and wrap around to wheel-arches at rear. Wheel discs have small slots.

Triumph 2000 Saloon: Number of cylinders 6. Cubic capacity 1998 c.c. Compression ratio 8·5 : 1. B.H.P. 90. Overall length 14 ft. 5¾ in. Overall width 5 ft. 5 in. Height 4 ft. 8 in. Turning circle 32 ft. Wheel-base 8 ft. 10 in. Track 4 ft. 4 in. (front), 4 ft. 2⅜ in. (rear). Fuel tank capacity 14 Imp. gals. Dry weight 21¾ cwt.

Appearance: Flat bonnet with shallow air-intake has rounded leading edge and inset, paired headlamps. Narrow, full-width radiator air-intake has grille of thin bars and side/direction lamps at ends. Straight-through wing line to squared-off, slightly inset rear panel; vertical tail-lamps. Large passenger area. Disc wheels have oblong perforations.

Triumph Spitfire 4 Sports: Number of cylinders 4. Cubic capacity 1147 c.c. Compression ratio 9 : 1 (7·5 : 1 available). B.H.P. 63. Max. m.p.h. 92. Overall length 12 ft. 1 in. Overall width 4 ft. 9 in. Height 3 ft. 11½ in. (hood up),

3 ft. 8¼ in. (hood down). Turning circle 24 ft. Wheel-base 6 ft. 11 in. Track 4 ft. 1 in. (front), 4 ft. (rear). Fuel tank capacity 8¼ Imp. gals. Dry weight 13¾ cwt.

Appearance: Trim, sporting lines. Small, divided radiator air-intake having mesh grille is slightly inset into car front. Headlamps, also slightly inset, have paired side/direction lamps below. Wing line dips slighty at cockpit: tail-lamps small and high set. Rear bumpers with vertical over-riders are divided; windscreen has rather thick framing. Wheel discs have oblong slots.

Triumph TR4 Sports: Number of cylinders 4. Cubic capacity 2138 c.c. (1991 c.c. engine available). Compression ratio 9 : 1 (8·5 : 1). B.H.P. 100. Max. m.p.h. 110 (Touring trim). Overall length 13 ft. Overall width 4 ft. 10 in. Height 4 ft. 2 in. (hood up), 3 ft. 10 in. (hood down). Turning circle 34 ft. Wheel-base 7 ft. 4 in. Track 4 ft. 1 in. (front), 4 ft. (rear—disc wheels), 4 ft. 2 in. (front) 4 ft. 1 in. (rear—wire wheels). Fuel tank capacity 11¾ Imp. gals. Dry weight 18½ cwt.

Appearance: Narrow, full-width radiator air-intake incorporates head, side and indicator lamps. Note "power" bulge on bonnet. Wing line rises slightly at cockpit; tail-lamps are vertical and pointed, rear bumpers wrap around to wheel-arches. Prominent flanges over wheel-arches. Perforated disc or wire wheels with "knock-off" hub-caps.

TURNER

ALEXANDER TURNER

GREAT BRITAIN

Turner Sports Cars (Wolverhampton) Ltd.,
Municipal Aerodrome, Pendeford,
Wolverhampton, England.
Alexander Autos & Marine Ltd.,
Thame Road, Haddenham,
Buckinghamshire, England.

Current Model: *Mk. III.* 2-seater Sports.

Turner Mk. III Sports: Number of cylinders 4 (Ford). Cubic capacity 1498 c.c. Compression ratio 9·3 : 1. B.H.P. 85. Overall length 11 ft. 6 in. Overall width 4 ft. 6 in. Height (to top of screen) 3 ft. 11 in. Turning circle 32 ft. Wheelbase 6 ft. 9½ in. Track 3 ft. 9½ in. (front), 3 ft. 8¾ in. (rear). Fuel tank capacity 6 Imp. gals. Weight 10½ cwt.

Appearance: Wide radiator air-intake with grille of thin "rippled" bars. Rounded bonnet between largish head-lamps; straight-through wing line to vertical, triple tail-lamp clusters; rounded tail. Wire wheels with "knock-off" hub-caps.

T.V.R.

GREAT BRITAIN

Grantura Engineering Limited,
Hoo Hill Industrial Estate,
Blackpool, England.

Current Models: *Mark III 1800 G.T.* 2-seater Coupé.
Griffith 200 Series G.T. 2-seater Coupé. *Trident.*
2-seater Coupé.

T.V.R. Griffith 200 Series G.T. Coupé: Number of cylinders
V8 (Ford). Cubic capacity 4727 c.c. Compression ratio 9·1 : 1
(10·9 : 1 Special Equipment model). B.H.P. 195 (271).
Max. m.p.h. 140 (160). Overall length 11 ft. 6 in. Overall
width 5 ft. 4 in. Height 4 ft. 1½ in. Turning circle 32 ft.
Wheel-base 7 ft. 1½ in. Track 4 ft. 4½ in. (front), 4 ft. 5½ in.
(rear). Fuel tank capacity 17 Imp. gals. Kerb weight 17 cwt.

Appearance: Note lack of tail—body sweeps down between
projecting rear wings. Narrow " slot " radiator air-intake
projects forward of wheels; bumpers on front body " corners "
Headlamps slightly inset; bonnet has " power bulge " and
sweeps down to intake. Curved, well-raked windscreen, small
passenger area and wrap-around rear window. Wire wheels
have " knock-off " hub-caps.

VANDEN PLAS

GREAT BRITAIN

Vanden Plas (England) 1923 Ltd.,

Longbridge,

Birmingham,

England.

Current Models: *Princess 1100*. 4-door Saloon. ***Princess 4-litre R.*** 4-door Saloon. ***Princess 4-litre.*** 4-door Saloon, Limousine.

Vanden Plas Princess 1100 Saloon: Number of cylinders 4. Cubic capacity 1098 c.c. Compression ratio 8·9 : 1 (8·1 : 1 available). B.H.P. 55. Overall length 12 ft. 3¼ in. Overall width 5 ft. ⅔ in. Height 4 ft. 4¾ in. Turning circle 34 ft. 9 in. Wheel-base 7 ft. 9½ in. Track 4 ft. 3½ in. (front), 4 ft. 2⁹⁄₁₀ in. (rear). Fuel tank capacity 8½ Imp. gals. Weight (unladen) 1904 lb. (approx.).

Appearance: Striking blend of Princess styling with ADO 16 bodywork. Large, almost square air-intake with grille of vertical slats is flanked by spot-lamps inset into body front. Note how leading edges of bonnet form " lips " over these lamps. Large, high-set headlamps, straight-through wing line to vertical tail-lamps. Simple bumpers with vertical over-riders. Disc wheels have large, projecting centres. Rear panel is raked forward between trailing edges of wings.

Vanden Plas Princess 4-litre R Saloon: Number of cylinders 6 (Rolls-Royce). Cubic capacity 3909 c.c. Compression ratio 7·8 : 1. B.H.P. 175. Overall length 15 ft. 8 in. Overall width 5 ft. 8½ in. Height 4 ft. 11 in. Turning circle 41 ft. Wheel-base 9 ft. 2 in. Track 4 ft. 6$\frac{9}{10}$ in. (front), 4 ft. 5¼ in. (rear). Fuel tank capacity 16 Imp. gals. Weight (unladen) 32 cwt. (approx.).

Appearance: Low, broad radiator air-intake has thin framing and is thrust-forward; grille consists of vertical slats. Spot-lamps with prominent " lips " over flank intake and side/direction lamps are on body " corners ". Rounded bonnet, curved windscreen and rear window; narrow roof line. Straight-through wings. Wrap-around bumpers with vertical overriders. Disc wheels have large, plain hubcaps.

VAUXHALL

Vauxhall Motors Ltd.,
Luton, Bedfordshire,
England.

History: The first Vauxhall car was built in 1903 by a Company which took its name from the Vauxhall Iron-works which was making marine engines in 1857.

An improved 6 h.p. model, equipped with a reverse gear and wire wheels, was produced in 1904, and in 1905 the firm moved its works to Luton. Since that time the town has become as famous for cars as it had been for hats.

The legendary " 30/98 " made its appearance in 1913, remaining in production until 1927, the last model in the series, the " OE ", being fitted with a push-rod overhead valve engine and hydraulic brakes.

In 1926 General Motors took over control of the Company and the 20/60 model was produced from 1927 to 1929. The " Cadet ", the first British car with synchro-mesh, appeared in 1930 and was replaced by the low-priced Light Six. The year 1937 saw the introduction of the 10 R.A.C.h.p. model which featured torsion bar front suspension and an integral body and chassis. A 3·2 litre was offered in 1936, and in 1939 there were two 4-cylinder and two 6-cylinder models in production.

During the 1939–45 war large quantities of munitions were produced, including the " Churchill " tank which was powered by a 12-cylinder Bedford engine.

The " Victor " saloon was introduced in 1956 and was notable in the fact that it did not feature the famous tapered " flutes " on the bonnet.

Current Models: *Viva*. Standard and De Luxe 2-door Saloons. *Victor Series 101*. Standard, Super and De

Luxe 4-door Saloons, Standard and De Luxe Estate Cars.
VX 4/90. 4-door Sports Saloon. **Velox.** 4-door Saloon.
Cresta. 4-door Saloon.

Vauxhall Viva Saloon: Number of cylinders 4. Cubic
capacity 1057 c.c. Compression ratio 8·5 : 1 (7·3 : 1 available).
B.H.P. 44·2. Overall length 12 ft. 11$\frac{1}{10}$ in. Overall width
4 ft. 11$\frac{2}{5}$ in. Height 4 ft. 5$\frac{3}{10}$ in. Turning circle 29 ft.
Wheel-base 7 ft. 7$\frac{1}{2}$ in. Track 3 ft. 11$\frac{2}{5}$ in. (front), 4 ft. $\frac{1}{5}$ in.
(rear). Fuel tank capacity 7 Imp. gals. Kerb weight 1564 lb.
(Standard), 1575 lb. (De Luxe).

Appearance: Pleasing,
rather angular contours. Full-
width, oblong radiator air-
intake has grille of horizontal
bars and incorporates headlamps. Flat bonnet; well-
raked windscreen; narrow
roof line and large rear deck.
Large doors and deep body
sides. Small, perforated disc
wheels have large hub-caps.

Vauxhall Victor Series 101 Saloon: Number of cylinders 4.
Cubic capacity 1594 c.c. Compression ratio 9 : 1 (7 : 1 avail-
able). B.H.P. 70. Overall length 14 ft. 6$\frac{6}{10}$ in. Overall
width 5 ft. 4$\frac{7}{10}$ in. Height 4 ft. 7$\frac{1}{5}$ in. Turning circle 33 ft.
Wheel-base 8 ft. 4 in. Track 4 ft. 3 in. (front), 4 ft. 4$\frac{3}{5}$ in. (rear).
Fuel tank capacity 10 Imp. gals. Kerb weight 2150 lb.
(Standard), 2170 lb. (Super), 2212 lb. (De Luxe).

Appearance: Full-width radiator air-intake with grille of thickish bars and head-lamps at ends. Vertical leading edges of wings; straight-through wing line to horizontal tail-lamp clusters. Well-raked windscreen and rear window are both deep. Narrow roof line. Radially spoked wheel discs have large, flat centres.

Vauxhall Victor Series 101 Estate Car: Number of cylinders 4. Cubic capacity 1594 c.c. Compression ratio 9 : 1 (7 : 1 available). B.H.P. 70. Overall length 14 ft. 6$\frac{7}{10}$ in. Overall width 5 ft. 4$\frac{7}{10}$ in. Height 4 ft. 7$\frac{1}{8}$ in. Turning circle 33 ft. Wheel-base 8 ft. 4 in. Track 4 ft. 3 in. (front), 4 ft. 4$\frac{3}{8}$ in. (rear). Fuel tank capacity 10 Imp. gals. Kerb weight 2292 lb. (Standard), 2331 lb. (De Luxe).

Appearance: Generally similar to Saloon but note attractive utility type body the rear panel of which is raked sharply forward. Note fairing from rear wheel arches to bumper ends. Disc wheels have four long perforations and large, flat hubcaps.

Vauxhall VX 4/90 Sports Saloon: Number of cylinders 4. Cubic capacity 1594 c.c. Compression ratio 9·3 : 1. B.H.P. 85·5. Overall length 14 ft. 6 $\frac{7}{10}$ in. Overall width 5 ft. 4 $\frac{7}{10}$ in. Height 4 ft. 7 $\frac{1}{5}$ in. Turning circle 33 ft. Wheel-base 8 ft. 4 in. Track 4 ft. 3 in. (front), 4 ft. 4 $\frac{3}{5}$ in. (rear) Fuel tank capacity 10 Imp. gals. Kerb weight 2254 lb.

Appearance: As for Victor Saloon but note differing air-intake grille of thick horizontal bar and three vertical bars also distinctive " flash " on body sides. Wheel discs are perforated and have flat centres. Side/indicator lamps are in bumper ends on Victors and VX 4/90.

Vauxhall Cresta Saloon: Number of cylinders 6. Cubic

capacity 3293 c.c. Compression ratio 8·5 : 1 (7 : 1 available). B.H.P. 114·8. Overall length 15 ft. 1$\frac{4}{5}$ in. Overall width 5 ft. 10$\frac{3}{10}$ in. Height 4 ft. 8$\frac{3}{5}$ in. Turning circle 36 ft. 6 in. Wheel-base 8 ft. 11$\frac{1}{2}$ in. Track 4 ft. 6$\frac{4}{5}$ in. (front), 4 ft. 8$\frac{1}{5}$ in. (rear). Fuel tank capacity 10$\frac{3}{4}$ Imp. gals. Kerb weight 2700 lb.

Appearance: Broad, flat bonnet with full-width radiator air-intake grille of five bars. Headlamps at ends of grille and side/indicator lamps on front body " corners ". Straight-through wing line to slight " wedge " shaped rear styling. Windscreen is deep, well-raked and curved. Simple bumpers front and rear. Wheel discs have long perforations.

VOLGA

U.S.S.R.

Molotov Works,
Gorky 46,
U.S.S.R.

Current Models: *M-21P.* 4-door Saloon. *M-22.* Estate Car.

Volga M-21P Saloon: Number of cylinders 4. Cubic capacity 2445 c.c. Compression ratio 6·7, 7·15 or 7·65 : 1. B.H.P. 75, 80 or 85. Overall length 15 ft. 7¾ in. Overall width 5 ft. 10¾ in. Height 5 ft. 3¾ in. Turning circle 41·4 ft. Wheelbase 8 ft. 10¼ in. Track 4 ft. 7¼ in. (front), 4 ft. 7¾ in. (rear). Fuel tank capacity 13·2 Imp. gals. Dry weight 2999 lb.

Appearance: Bulky looking car. Oblong radiator air-intake with grille of thin, undercurving bars. Headlamps rather thrust forward; straight-through wing line to "suggested" rear wings, the leading edges of which are raked forward. Windscreen and rear window are rather shallow. Plain bumpers; vertical tail-lamps. Disc wheels with plain hubcaps.

VOLKSWAGEN

GERMANY

Volkswagenwerk Aktiengesellschaft,
Wolfsburg, Brunswick,
Germany.

Current Models: 1200. 2-door Saloon, De Luxe 2-door Saloon, Convertible. **1200 Karmann Ghia.** Coupé, Convertible. **1500 " N ".** 2-door Saloon, Variant (Station Wagon). **1500 " S ".** 2-door Saloon, Variant (Station Wagon). **1500 Karmann Ghia.** Coupé.

Volkswagen 1200 De Luxe Saloon: Number of cylinders Flat-4. Cubic capacity 1192 c.c. Compression ratio 7 : 1. B.H.P. 34. Overall length 13 ft. 5 in. Overall width 5 ft. ½ in. Height 4 ft. 11 in. Turning circle 36 ft. Wheel-base 7 ft. 10½ in. Track 4 ft. 3⅝ in. (front), 4 ft. 2 7/10 in. (rear). Fuel tank capacity 8·8 Imp. gals. Kerb weight 1675 lb.

Appearance: Well-known, functional " beetle " shape, but note small indicator lamps on latest versions. General appearance is rounded, " bonnet " slopes rather sharply down to front bumper. No frontal air-intake, large headlamps, separate wings and running-boards. Shallow, flat windscreen. Disc wheels have large, domed hub-caps.

Volkswagen 1500 Saloon: Number of cylinders Flat-4. Cubic capacity 1493 c.c. Compression ratio 7·8 : 1 (" N "), 8·5 : 1 (" S "). B.H.P. 45 or 54. Overall length 13 ft. 10$\frac{3}{10}$ in. Overall width 5 ft. 3$\frac{1}{5}$ in. Height 4 ft. 10$\frac{1}{10}$ in. Turning circle 36 ft. 6 in. (approx.). Wheel-base 7 ft. 10$\frac{1}{2}$ in. Track 4 ft. 3$\frac{3}{8}$ in. (front), 4 ft. 5 in. (rear). Fuel tank capacity 8·8 Imp. gals. Weight (unladen) 2006 lb.

Appearance: Simple, restrained styling. Rounded " bonnet " between prominent headlamps, large " VW " badge, straight-through wings to vertical tail-lamps in wing trailing edges. Passenger area has deep, curved windscreen and rear window. Large rear " boot "—note air louvres beneath rear window. Simple bumpers. Disc wheels have large hub-caps.

Volkswagen 1500 Variant: Number of cylinders Flat-4. Cubic capacity 1493 c.c. Compression ratio 7·8 : 1 (" N "), 8·5 : 1 (" S "). B.H.P. 45 or 54. Overall length 13 ft. 10$\frac{3}{10}$ in. Overall width 5 ft. 3$\frac{1}{5}$ in. Height 4 ft. 9$\frac{7}{10}$ in. Turning circle 36 ft. 6 in. (approx.). Wheel-base 7 ft. 10$\frac{1}{2}$ in. Track 4 ft. 3$\frac{3}{8}$ in. (front), 4 ft. 5 in. (rear). Fuel tank capacity 8·8 Imp. gals. Weight (unladen) 2260 lb.

Appearance: Generally similar to saloon but note utility type body. Note side/indicator lamps on front body " corners " (" S ") (" bullet " type on " N " model). Perforated wheel discs.

VOLVO

SWEDEN

Aktiebolaget Volvo,
  Gothenburg,
    Sweden.

Current Models: 544. 2-door Saloon. **210.** Utility. **121.** 2- and 4-door Saloons, Estate Car. **122S.** 2-door Saloon. **131.** 2-door Coupé. **P1800S.** 2-door Sports Coupé.

Volvo 131 Coupé: Number of cylinders 4. Cubic capacity 1778 c.c. Compression ratio 8·5 : 1. B.H.P. 75. Overall length 14 ft. 7 in. Overall width 5 ft. 3¾ in. Height 4 ft. 11¼ in. Turning circle 34 ft. Wheel-base 8 ft. 6½ in. Track 4 ft. 3¾ in. (front and rear). Fuel tank capacity 10 Imp. gals. Kerb weight 2296 lb.

Appearance: Divided, slightly " veed " radiator air-intake, high-set headlamps, straight-through wing line to small, high mounted tail-lamps. Note side/direction lamps on front body " corners ". Smallish passenger area; shallow windscreen is curved and rear window well raked. High waist line. Perforated wheels have large, prominent hub-caps.

Volvo 121 Estate Car: Number of cylinders 4. Cubic capacity 1778 c.c. Compression ratio 8·5 : 1. B.H.P. 75. Overall length 14 ft. 8½ in. Overall width 5 ft. 3¾ in. Height

5 ft. ¼ in. Turning circle 34 ft. 5 in. Wheel-base 8 ft. 6½ in. Track 4 ft. 3¾ in. (front and rear). Fuel tank capacity 10 Imp. gals. Kerb weight 2645 lb.

Appearance: Generally as for 131 Coupé but note rather severely lined utility type body with small, angular windows. Bumpers front and rear wrap-around and have vertical over-riders. Thin rubbing strip runs full length of car.

Volvo P1800S Sports Coupé: Number of cylinders 4. Cubic capacity 1778 c.c. Compression ratio 10 : 1. B.H.P. 108. Overall length 14 ft. 5¼ in. Overall width 5 ft. 7 in. Height 4 ft. 2½ in. Turning circle 31 ft. Wheel-base 8 ft. ½ in. Track 4 ft. 3¾ in. (front and rear). Fuel tank capacity 10 Imp. gals. Kerb weight 2640 lb.

Appearance: Flat bonnet slopes gently down to thrust-forward oval radiator air-intake having cellular grille. Straight-through wing line, note how rear wings form " fins "; horizontally mounted, paired tail-lamps. Curved windscreen is well raked and roof line falls away. Divided front bumper. Disc wheels have domed hub-caps.

WARTBURG

GERMANY

V E B Automobilwerk,
    Eisenach,
    Germany.

Current Models: Limousine, Limousine (Sliding Roof), Limousine De Luxe, Limousine De Luxe (Sliding Roof), Coupé, Camping Limousine, Kombiwagen (Utility).

Wartburg Camping Limousine: Number of cylinders 3. Cubic capacity 992 c.c. Compression ratio 7·3–7·5 : 1. B.H.P. 45. Overall length 13 ft. 5⅝ in. Overall width 5 ft. 1⅝ in. Height 4 ft. 9 7/10 in. Turning circle 36·1 ft. Wheelbase 8 ft. ½ in. Track 3 ft. 10¾ in. (front), 4 ft. 1⅗ in. (rear). Fuel tank capacity 8·8 Imp. gals.

Appearance: Wide radiator air-intake has inwardly " veed " square-mesh grille—note how bonnet line " tucks under " above intake. Large headlamps; straight-through wing line to " separate " rear wings which house oval tail-lamp clusters in trailing edges. Note rather unusual utility type body with rear windows extending up into roof line, also unusual two-tone colour scheme. Perforated disc wheels have large hub-caps.

WILLYS

BRAZIL

Willys-Overland do Brasil S.A.,
Sao Paulo,
Brazil.

Current Model: *Aero-Willys 2600*. 4-door Sedan.

Aero-Willys 2600 Sedan: Number of cylinders 6. Cubic capacity 161 cu. in. Compression ratio 7·6 : 1. B.H.P. 110. Overall length 15 ft. 4 in. Overall width 6 ft. ½ in. Height 5 ft. 2 in. Turning circle 39 ft. (left), 40 ft. (right). Wheelbase 9 ft. Max. track 4 ft. 10 in. Fuel tank capacity 19 gals. Kerb weight 3180 lb.

Appearance: Divided, full-width radiator air-intake with grille of horizontal bars and incorporating large side/indicator lamps. Grille projects from rounded bonnet front. Hooded headlamps; straight-through wing line to squared-off trailing edges containing vertical tail-lamps. Angular styling to passenger area and curved windscreen and rear window. Substantial front bumpers wrap around. Perforated disc wheels.

WILLYS

UNITED STATES OF AMERICA

Willys Motors, Inc.,
Toledo 1,
Ohio,
United States of America.

Current Model: "*Jeep*" *Wagoneer*. 2- and 4-door Standard and De Luxe Station Wagons.

Willys "Jeep" Wagoneer 4-door Station Wagon: Number of cylinders 6. Cubic capacity 230·5 cu. in. Compression ratio 8·5 : 1 (7·5 : 1 optional). B.H.P. 140 (133). Overall length 15 ft. 3⅜ in. Overall width 6 ft. 3⅜ in. Height 5 ft. 4 in. (5 ft. 4⅘ in. Four-wheel drive). Turning circle 41 ft. (44 ft. 6 in. Four-wheel drive). Wheel-base 9 ft. 2 in. Track 4 ft. 9 in. (front and rear). Fuel tank capacity 20 U.S. gals. Kerb weight 3615 lb. (3758 lb. Four-wheel drive).

Appearance: Angular styling giving utilitarian appearance. Flat front panel has small, almost square radiator air-intake with vertically barred grille flanked by circular ventilator ports and headlamps. Oblong side/indicator lamps just above simple, fluted bumpers. Note van-like body with angular windows and tail-lamps on rear body "corners". Rear bumpers echo frontal styling. Recessed wheel discs have spoked effect and rounded hub-caps.

Appearance: Strong resemblance to Riley 1·5. Vertical radiator air-intake flanked by five-barred grilles incorporating side/direction lamps. Headlamps rather high-set in squarish frontal contours; straight-through wings—note " suggestion " of rear wings indicated by pressing on rear doors; vertical tail-lamps. Heavily flanged wheel-arches. Full-length styling line hooks down at front. Simple bumpers, vertical overriders. Disc wheels.

Wolseley 16/60 Saloon: Number of cylinders 4. Cubic capacity 1622 c.c. Compression ratio 8·3 : 1 (7·2 : 1 available). B.H.P. 61. Overall length 14 ft. 6½ in. Overall width 5 ft. 3½ in. Height 4 ft. 10 9/10 in. Turning circle 37 ft. Wheelbase 8 ft. 4¼ in. Track 4 ft. 2⅜ in. (front), 4 ft. 3⅖ in. (rear). Fuel tank capacity 10 Imp. gals. Weight (unladen) 22 cwt. (approx.).

Appearance: Body, with design by Pinin Farina, has rather square contours. Thrust-forward radiator grille with vertical slats flanked by oblong intakes. Note how "thrust-forward" look is accentuated by side trim. Straight-through wings to upswept fins and vertical, pointed tail-lamps. Front and rear bumpers wrap right around to wheel-arches. Plain disc wheels.

Wolseley 6/110 Mk. II Saloon: Number of cylinders 6. Cubic capacity 2912 c.c. Compression ratio 8·3 : 1 (7·3 : 1 available). B.H.P. 120. Overall length 15 ft. 7¾ in. Overall width 5 ft. 8½ in. Height 4 ft. 10½ in. Turning circle 41 ft. Wheel-base 9 ft. 2 in. Track 4 ft. 7 in. (front), 4 ft. 5¼ in. (rear). Fuel tank capacity 16 Imp. gals. Weight (unladen) 30 cwt. (approx.).

Appearance: Generally similar to 16/60 but this car is larger. Also note spotlamps flanking radiator air-intake grille. Side/direction lamps beneath headlamps are circular. Straight-through wings rise sharply at rear window to form "fins". Sturdy front bumpers have dip in centre, those at rear wrap around to rear wheelarches. Well-raked windscreen; rear window wraps around and has "peak" over. Disc wheels.

ZAPOROGETS

U.S.S.R.

Komunard Factory,
Zaporozh,
U.S.S.R.

Current Model: *Zaporogets Model 3A3-965.* 2-door Saloon.

Zaporogets Saloon: Number of cylinders V4. Cubic capacity 748 c.c. Compression ratio 6·5 : 1. B.H.P. 23. Overall length 10 ft. 11 in. Overall width 4 ft. 7 in. Height 4 ft. 6½ in. Turning circle 31 ft. 4 in. Wheel-base 6 ft. 7½ in. Max. track 3 ft. 9½ in. Fuel tank capacity 6½ Imp. gals. Weight 11⅗ cwt.

Appearance: Smallish car with compact lines and rear-mounted engine. Blunt, rounded " bonnet " with oblong intake. Simple, plain bumpers front and rear. Straight-through wing line with air-intakes above rear wheel arches. Rounded tail houses air-cooled engine. Shallow windscreen and rear window. Disc wheels with plain hub-caps.

ZIL

U.S.S.R.

Zavod Imeni Likachev,
Moscow,
U.S.S.R.

Current Models: *111G*. Limousine. *111V*. Cabriolet.

ZIL-111V Cabriolet: Number of cylinders V8. Cubic capacity 5980 c.c. Compression ratio 9 : 1. B.H.P. 230. Max. m.p.h. 100. Overall length 20 ft. $1\frac{7}{10}$ in. Overall width 6 ft. $8\frac{3}{10}$ in. Height 5 ft. $4\frac{1}{2}$ in. Turning circle 52 ft. Wheel-base 12 ft. 4 in. Track 5 ft. $1\frac{4}{5}$ in. (front), 5 ft. 5 in. (rear). Fuel tank capacity 17·6 Imp. gals. Dry weight 5720 lb.

Appearance: Very large, heavy-looking car. Radiator air-intake with mesh grille which extends around front " corners " of body and incorporates oblong side-lamps. Heavy bumper features small intakes flanked by lamps. Heavily hooded headlamps, straight-through wing line to large, pointed tail-lamp clusters. Rear bumpers incorporate exhaust outlets at ends. Wrap-around windscreen and convertible fabric top. Note lavish use of bright trim. Plain, disc wheels.

NUMBER PLATES

INTERNATIONAL PLATES

THESE plates have one, two or three letters of the same size, usually in black, set on a white oval background. They indicate the country of origin as set out below, and are displayed by cars which are being driven in foreign countries.

Not all countries subscribe to this system of identification, however. For example, a plate bearing the letters TT (Titre Temporaire) shows that the owner has temporarily registered in France, though he may have come from another country originally. The letters following TT indicate the particular district of France where the registration was taken out.

Those plates with prefixes from QA to QS are issued by the R.A.C. or the A.A. in this country to vehicles temporarily imported from abroad. Numbers prefaced by EE indicate a first temporary registration for touring from Italy.

Cars used by High Commissioners in this country carry small plates bearing the letters HC, and those used by Foreign Embassies and Legations have a plate with the letters CD in addition to their registration plates.

A	Austria	CS	Czechoslovakia
ADN	Aden State*	CY	Cyprus*
AL	Albania	D	Germany (Federal Republic)
AND	Andorra	DK	Denmark, Faroe Islands
AUS	Australia*, Norfolk Islands*	DOM	Dominican Republic
B	Belgium	DY	Dahomey
BDS	Barbados*	DZ	Algeria
BG	Bulgaria	E	Spain, and Spanish Overseas
BH	British Honduras*		Territories
BL	Basutoland*	EAK	Kenya*
BP	Bechuanaland*	EAT	Tanzania (Tanganyika)*
BR	Brazil	EAU	Uganda
BRG	British Guiana*	EAZ	Tanzania (Zanzibar)
BRN	Bahrein*	EC	Ecuador
BRU	Brunei*	ET	Egypt
BS	Bahamas*	F	France, and French Overseas
BUR	Burma		Departments
C	Cuba	FL	Liechtenstein
CDN	Canada	GB	Great Britain and Northern
CGO	Congo (Leopoldville)		Ireland*
CH	Switzerland	GBA	Alderney*
CI	Ivory Coast	GBG	Guernsey*
CL	Ceylon*	GBJ	Jersey*
CNB	Sabah*	GBM	Isle of Man*
CO	Colombo	GBY	Malta*, Gozo*
CR	Costa Rica	GCA	Guatemala

279

GH	Ghana*	RCB	Congo (Brazzaville)
GR	Greece, Crete, Dodecanese Islands	RCH	Chile
H	Hungary	RH	Haiti
HK	Hong Kong*	RI	Indonesia
I	Italy, Sardinia, Sicily	RIM	Islamic Republic of Mauretania
IL	Israel	RL	Lebanon
IND	India*	RM	Malagasy Republic
IR	Iran	RMM	Mali
IRL	Republic of Ireland*	RNR	Zambia
IRQ	Iraq	RNY	Malawi*
IS	Iceland	RSM	San Marino
J	Japan	RSR	Southern Rhodesia*
JA	Jamaica*, Cayman Islands*, Turks and Caicos Islands*	RWA	Republic of Rwanda and Kingdom of Burundi
JOR	Jordan	S	Sweden*
K	Cambodia	SA	Saar
KWT	Kuwait	SD	Swaziland*
L	Luxembourg	SF	Finland
LAO	Laos	SGP	Singapore*
LT	Libya	SK	Sarawak*
MA	Morocco	SME	Surinam
MC	Monaco	SN	Senegal
MEX	Mexico	SU	U.S.S.R. (Union of Soviet Socialist Republics)
MS	Mauritius*		
N	Norway	SUD	Sudan
NA	Netherlands West Indies	SWA	South West Africa
NGN	West Irian (formerly Netherlands New Guinea)	SY	Seychelles*
		SYR	Syria
NIC	Nicaragua	T	Thailand*
NIG	Niger*	TG	Togo
NL	Netherlands	TN	Tunisia
NZ	New Zealand*	TR	Turkey
P	Portugal, Azores, Cape Verde Islands, Madeira, Mozambique, Portuguese Guinea, Portuguese Timor, Angola, Sao Joao Baptista de Ajuda, Sao Tome, and Principe Islands	TT	Trinidad and Tobago
		U	Uruguay
		USA	United States of America
		V	Vatican City
		VN	Viet-Nam
		WAG	Gambia*
PA	Panama	WAL	Sierra Leone*
PAK	Pakistan*	WAN	Nigeria*
PE	Peru	WD	Dominica (Windward Islands)*
PI	Philippine Islands	WG	Grenada (Windward Islands)*
PL	Poland	WL	St. Lucia (Windward Islands)*
PTM	Malaysia*	WS	Western Samoa
PY	Paraguay	WV	St. Vincent (Windward Islands)*
R	Rumania	YU	Yugoslavia
RA	Argentina	YV	Venezuela
RC	Formosa	ZA	Republic of South Africa
RCA	Central African Republic		

In the countries marked with an asterisk the rule of the road is Drive on the Left; in other countries it is Drive on the Right.

NUMBER PLATES OF THE BRITISH ISLES

Number plates are issued by a County Council, County Borough Council or Burgh Council (designated below—C.C., C.B.C. or B.C. respectively). Originally the plates consisted of one or two letters followed by a set of numbers. When all combinations of letters and figures had been exhausted, three letter marks followed by three figure sets of numbers were allocated. The three letter marks were formed by the addition of a prefix letter to the existing two letter mark allocated to an authority. Later, to provide yet another sequence of number plates, the positions of the letters and figures were reversed.

Despite these measures, by 1963 some authorities had exhausted all their available marks, and the feature of a "year letter" was introduced. This denotes the year of the vehicle's registration and is placed after the last figure, on plates bearing three letters followed by three figures, thus forming a seven symbol plate. Following years will be shown by successive letters of the alphabet.

An exception to the three letter system described above are the letters GPO. This is a mark issued by the London County Council to the General Post Office.

A	London C.C.	BL	Berks C.C.
AA	Hampshire C.C.	BM	Bedford C.C.
AB	Worcestershire C.C.	BN	Bolton C.B.C.
AC	Warwick C.C.	BO	Cardiff C.B.C.
AD	Gloucestershire C.C.	BP	West Sussex C.C.
AE	Bristol C.B.C.	BR	Sunderland C.B.C.
AF	Cornwall C.C.	BS	Orkney C.C.
AG	Ayr C.C.	BT	East Riding of Yorks C.C.
AH	Norfolk C.C.	BU	Oldham C.B.C.
AI	Meath C.C.	BV	Blackburn C.B.C.
AJ	North Riding of Yorks C.C.	BW	Oxfordshire C.C.
AK	Bradford C.B.C.	BX	Carmarthen C.C.
AL	Nottinghamshire C.C.	BY	Croydon C.B.C.
AM	Wilts C.C.	BZ	Down C.C.
AN	West Ham C.B.C.	C	West Riding of Yorks C.C.
AO	Cumberland C.C.	CA	Denbigh C.C.
AP	East Sussex C.C.	CB	Blackburn C.B.C.
AR	Hertford C.C.	CC	Caernarvon C.C.
AS	Nairn C.C.	CD	Brighton C.B.C.
AT	Kingston-upon-Hull C.B.C.	CE	Cambridge C.C.
AU	Nottingham C.B.C.	CF	West Suffolk C.C.
AV	Aberdeenshire C.C.	CG	Hampshire C.C.
AW	Salop C.C.	CH	Derby C.B.C.
AX	Monmouth C.C.	CI	Laoighis C.C.
AY	Leicestershire C.C.	CJ	Hereford C.C.
AZ	Belfast C.B.C.	CK	Preston C.B.C.
B	Lancashire C.C.	CL	Norwich C.B.C.
BA	Salford C.B.C.	CM	Birkenhead C.B.C.
BB	Newcastle-upon-Tyne C.B.C.	CN	Gateshead C.B.C.
BC	Leicester C.B.C.	CO	Plymouth C.B.C.
BD	Northamptonshire C.C.	CP	Halifax C.B.C.
BE	Parts of Lindsey (Lincs) C.C.	CR	Southampton C.B.C.
BF	Staffordshire C.C.	CS	Ayr C.C.
BG	Birkenhead C.B.C.	CT	Parts of Kesteven (Lincs) C.C.
BH	Bucks C.C.	CU	South Shields C.B.C.
BI	Monaghan C.C.	CV	Cornwall C.C.
BJ	East Suffolk C.C.	CW	Burnley C.B.C.
BK	Portsmouth C.B.C.	CX	Huddersfield C.B.C.

CY	Swansea C.B.C.	FJ	Exeter C.B.C.
CZ	Belfast C.B.C.	FK	Worcester C.B.C.
D	Kent C.C.	FL	Soke of Peterborough C.C.
DA	Wolverhampton C.B.C.	FM	Chester C.B.C.
DB	Stockport C.B.C.	FN	Canterbury C.B.C.
DC	Middlesbrough C.B.C.	FO	Radnor C.C.
DD	Gloucestershire C.C.	FP	Rutland C.C.
DE	Pembroke C.C.	FR	Blackpool C.B.C.
DF	Gloucestershire C.C.	FS	Edinburgh B.C.
DG	Gloucestershire C.C.	FT	Tynemouth C.B.C.
DH	Walsall C.B.C.	FU	Parts of Lindsey (Lincs) C.C.
DI	Roscommon C.C.	FV	Blackpool C.B.C.
DJ	St. Helens C.B.C.	FW	Parts of Lindsey (Lincs) C.C.
DK	Rochdale C.B.C.	FX	Dorset C.C.
DL	Isle of Wight C.C.	FY	Southport C.B.C.
DM	Flint C.C.	FZ	Belfast C.B.C.
DN	York C.B.C.	G	Glasgow B.C.
DO	Parts of Holland (Lincs) C.C.	GA	Glasgow B.C.
DP	Reading C.B.C.	GB	Glasgow B.C.
DR	Plymouth C.B.C.	GC	London C.C.
DS	Peebles C.C.	GD	Glasgow B.C.
DT	Doncaster C.B.C.	GE	Glasgow B.C.
DU	Coventry C.B.C.	GF	London C.C.
DV	Devon C.C.	GG	Glasgow B.C.
DW	Newport (Mon.) C.B.C.	GH	London C.C.
DX	Ipswich C.B.C.	GJ	London C.C.
DY	Hastings C.B.C.	GK	London C.C.
DZ	Antrim C.C.	GL	Bath C.B.C.
E	Staffordshire C.C.	GM	Motherwell and Wishaw B.C.
EA	West Bromwich C.B.C.	GN	London C.C.
EB	Isle of Ely C.C.	GO	London C.C.
EC	Westmorland C.C.	GP	London C.C.
ED	Warrington C.B.C.	GR	Sunderland C.B.C.
EE	Grimsby C.B.C.	GS	Perth C.C.
EF	West Hartlepool C.B.C.	GT	London C.C.
EG	Soke of Peterborough C.C.	GU	London C.C.
EH	Stoke-on-Trent C.B.C.	GV	West Suffolk C.C.
EI	Sligo C.C.	GW	London C.C.
EJ	Cardigan C.C.	GX	London C.C.
EK	Wigan C.B.C.	GY	London C.C.
EL	Bournemouth C.B.C.	GZ	Belfast C.B.C.
EM	Bootle C.B.C.	H	Middlesex C.C.
EN	Bury C.B.C.	HA	Smethwick C.B.C.
EO	Barrow-in-Furness C.B.C.	HB	Merthyr Tydfil C.B.C.
EP	Montgomery C.C.	HC	Eastbourne C.B.C.
ER	Cambridge C.C.	HD	Dewsbury C.B.C.
ES	Perth C.C.	HE	Barnsley C.B.C.
ET	Rotherham C.B.C.	HF	Wallasey C.B.C.
EU	Breconshire C.C.	HG	Burnley C.B.C.
EV	Essex C.C.	HH	Carlisle C.B.C.
EW	Huntingdon C.C.	HI	South Riding of Tipperary C.C.
EX	Great Yarmouth C.B.C.	HJ	Southend-on-Sea C.B.C.
EY	Anglesey C.C.	HK	Essex C.C.
EZ	Belfast C.B.C.	HL	Wakefield C.B.C.
F	Essex C.C.	HM	East Ham C.B.C.
FA	Burton-on-Trent C.B.C.	HN	Darlington C.B.C.
FB	Bath C.B.C.	HO	Southampton C.C.
FC	Oxford C.B.C.	HP	Coventry C.B.C.
FD	Dudley C.B.C.	HR	Wilts C.C.
FE	Lincoln C.B.C.	HS	Renfrew C.C.
FF	Merioneth C.C.	HT	Bristol C.B.C.
FG	Fife C.C.	HU	Bristol C.B.C.
FH	Gloucester C.B.C.	HV	East Ham C.B.C.
FI	North Riding of Tipperary C.C.	HW	Bristol C.B.C.

HX	Middlesex C.C.	KN	Kent C.C.
HY	Bristol C.B.C.	KO	Kent C.C.
HZ	Tyrone C.C.	KP	Kent C.C.
IA	Antrim C.C.	KR	Kent C.C.
IB	Armagh C.C.	KS	Roxburgh C.C.
IC	Carlow C.C.	KT	Kent C.C.
ID	Cavan C.C.	KU	Bradford C.B.C.
IE	Clare C.C.	KV	Coventry C.B.C.
IF	Cork C.C.	KW	Bradford C.B.C.
IH	Donegal C.C.	KX	Bucks C.C.
IJ	Down C.C.	KY	Bradford C.B.C.
IK	Dublin C.C.	KZ	Antrim C.C.
IL	Fermanagh C.C.	L	Glamorgan C.C.
IM	Galway C.C.	LA	London C.C.
IN	Kerry C.C.	LB	London C.C.
IO	Kildare C.C.	LC	London C.C.
IP	Kilkenny C.C.	LD	London C.C.
IR	Offaly C.C.	LE	London C.C.
IT	Leitrim C.C.	LF	London C.C.
IU	Limerick C.C.	LG	Cheshire C.C.
IW	Londonderry C.C.	LH	London C.C.
IX	Longford C.C.	LI	Westmeath C.C.
IY	Louth C.C.	LJ	Bournemouth C.B.C.
IZ	Mayo C.C.	LK	London C.C.
J	Durham C.C.	LL	London C.C.
JA	Stockport C.B.C.	LM	London C.C.
JB	Berks C.C.	LN	London C.C.
JC	Caernarvon C.C.	LO	London C.C.
JD	West Ham C.B.C.	LP	London C.C.
JE	Isle of Ely C.C.	LR	London C.C.
JF	Leicester C.B.C.	LS	Selkirk C.C.
JG	Canterbury C.B.C.	LT	London C.C.
JH	Hertford C.C.	LU	London C.C.
JI	Tyrone C.C.	LV	Liverpool C.B.C.
JJ	London C.C.	LW	London C.C.
JK	Eastbourne C.B.C.	LX	London C.C.
JL	Parts of Holland (Lincs) C.C.	LY	London C.C.
JM	Westmorland C.C.	LZ	Armagh C.C.
JN	Southend C.B.C.	M	Cheshire C.C.
JO	Oxford C.B.C.	MA	Cheshire C.C.
JP	Wigan C.B.C.	MB	Cheshire C.C.
JR	Northumberland C.C.	MC	Middlesex C.C.
JS	Ross and Cromarty C.C.	MD	Middlesex C.C.
JT	Dorset C.C.	ME	Middlesex C.C.
JU	Leicestershire C.C.	MF	Middlesex C.C.
JV	Grimsby C.B.C.	MG	Middlesex C.C.
JW	Wolverhampton C.B.C.	MH	Middlesex C.C.
JX	Halifax C.B.C.	MI	Wexford C.C.
JY	Plymouth C.B.C.	MJ	Bedford C.C.
JZ	Down C.C.	MK	Middlesex C.C.
K	Liverpool C.B.C.	ML	Middlesex C.C.
KA	Liverpool C.B.C.	MM	Middlesex C.C.
KB	Liverpool C.B.C.	MO	Berks C.C.
KC	Liverpool C.B.C.	MP	Middlesex C.C.
KD	Liverpool C.B.C.	MR	Wilts C.C.
KE	Kent C.C.	MS	Stirling C.C.
KF	Liverpool C.B.C.	MT	Middlesex C.C.
KG	Cardiff C.B.C.	MU	Middlesex C.C.
KH	Kingston-upon-Hull C.B.C.	MV	Middlesex C.C.
KI	Waterford C.C.	MW	Wilts C.C.
KJ	Kent C.C.	MX	Middlesex C.C.
KK	Kent C.C.	MY	Middlesex C.C.
KL	Kent C.C.	MZ	Belfast C.B.C.
KM	Kent C.C.	N	Manchester C.B.C.

NA	Manchester C.B.C.	PM	East Sussex C.C.
NB	Manchester C.B.C.	PN	East Sussex C.C.
NC	Manchester C.B.C.	PO	West Sussex C.C.
ND	Manchester C.B.C.	PP	Bucks C.C.
NE	Manchester C.B.C.	PR	Dorset C.C.
NF	Manchester C.B.C.	PS	Zetland C.C.
NG	Norfolk C.C.	PT	Durham C.C.
NH	Northampton C.B.C.	PU	Essex C.C.
NI	Wicklow C.C.	PV	Ipswich C.B.C.
NJ	East Sussex C.C.	PW	Norfolk C.C.
NK	Hertford C.C.	PX	West Sussex C.C.
NL	Northumberland C.B.C.	PY	North Riding of Yorks C.C.
NM	Bedford C.C.	PZ	Belfast C.B.C.
NN	Nottinghamshire C.C.	QA	London C.C.
NO	Essex C.C.	QB	London C.C.
NP	Worcestershire C.C.	QC	London C.C.
NR	Leicestershire C.C.	QD	London C.C.
NS	Sutherland C.C.	QE	London C.C.
NT	Salop C.C.	QF	London C.C.
NU	Derbyshire C.C.	QG	London C.C.
NV	Northamptonshire C.C.	QH	London C.C.
NW	Leeds C.B.C.	QJ	London C.C.
NX	Warwick C.C.	QK	London C.C.
NY	Glamorgan C.C.	QL	London C.C.
NZ	Londonderry C.C.	QM	London C.C.
O	Birmingham C.B.C.	QN	London C.C.
OA	Birmingham C.B.C.	QP	London C.C.
OB	Birmingham C.B.C.	QQ	London C.C.
OC	Birmingham C.B.C.	QS	London C.C.
OD	Devon C.C.	R	Derbyshire C.C.
OE	Birmingham C.B.C.	RA	Derbyshire C.C.
OF	Birmingham C.B.C.	RB	Derbyshire C.C.
OG	Birmingham C.B.C.	RC	Derby C.B.C.
OH	Birmingham C.B.C.	RD	Reading C.B.C.
OI	Belfast C.B.C.	RE	Staffordshire C.C.
OJ	Birmingham C.B.C.	RF	Staffordshire C.C.
OK	Birmingham C.B.C.	RG	Aberdeen B.C.
OL	Birmingham C.B.C.	RH	Kingston-upon-Hull C.B.C.
OM	Birmingham C.B.C.	RI	Dublin C.B.C.
ON	Birmingham C.B.C.	RJ	Salford C.B.C.
OO	Essex C.C.	RK	Croydon C.B.C.
OP	Birmingham C.B.C.	RL	Cornwall C.C.
OR	Hampshire C.C.	RM	Cumberland C.C.
OS	Wigtown C.C.	RN	Preston C.B.C.
OT	Hampshire C.C.	RO	Hertford C.C.
OU	Hampshire C.C.	RP	Northamptonshire C.C.
OV	Birmingham C.B.C.	RR	Nottinghamshire C.C.
OW	Southampton C.B.C.	RS	Aberdeen B.C.
OX	Birmingham C.B.C.	RT	East Suffolk C.C.
OY	Croydon C.B.C.	RU	Bournemouth C.B.C.
OZ	Belfast C.B.C.	RV	Portsmouth C.B.C.
P	Surrey C.C.	RW	Coventry C.B.C.
PA	Surrey C.C.	RX	Berks C.C.
PB	Surrey C.C.	RY	Leicester C.B.C.
PC	Surrey C.C.	RZ	Antrim C.C.
PD	Surrey C.C.	S	Edinburgh B.C.
PE	Surrey C.C.	SA	Aberdeenshire C.C.
PF	Surrey C.C.	SB	Argyll C.C.
PG	Surrey C.C.	SC	Edinburgh B.C.
PH	Surrey C.C.	SD	Ayr C.C.
PI	Cork C.B.C.	SE	Banff C.C.
PJ	Surrey C.C.	SF	Edinburgh B.C.
PK	Surrey C.C.	SG	Edinburgh B.C.
PL	Surrey C.C.	SH	Berwick C.C.

284

SJ	Bute C.C.
SK	Caithness C.C.
SL	Clackmannan C.C.
SM	Dumfries C.C.
SN	Dumbarton C.C.
SO	Moray C.C.
SP	Fife C.C.
SR	Angus C.C.
SS	East Lothian C.C.
ST	Inverness C.C.
SU	Kincardine C.C.
SV	Kinross C.C.
SW	Kircudbright C.C.
SX	West Lothian C.C.
SY	Midlothian C.C.
SZ	Down C.C.
T	Devon C.C.
TA	Devon C.C.
TB	Lancashire C.C.
TC	Lancashire C.C.
TD	Lancashire C.C.
TE	Lancashire C.C.
TF	Lancashire C.C.
TG	Glamorgan C.C.
TH	Carmarthen C.C.
TI	Limerick C.B.C.
TJ	Lancashire C.C.
TK	Dorset C.C.
TL	Parts of Kesteven (Lincs) C.C.
TM	Bedford C.C.
TN	Newcastle-upon-Tyne C.B.C.
TO	Nottingham C.B.C.
TP	Portsmouth C.B.C.
TR	Southampton C.B.C.
TS	Dundee B.C.
TT	Devon C.C.
TU	Cheshire C.C.
TV	Nottingham C.B.C.
TW	Essex C.C.
TX	Glamorgan C.C.
TY	Northumberland C.C.
TZ	Belfast C.B.C.
U	Leeds C.B.C.
UA	Leeds C.B.C.
UB	Leeds C.B.C.
UC	London C.C.
UD	Oxfordshire C.C.
UE	Warwick C.C.
UF	Brighton C.B.C.
UG	Leeds C.B.C.
UH	Cardiff C.B.C.
UI	Londonderry C.B.C.
UJ	Salop C.C.
UK	Wolverhampton C.B.C.
UL	London C.C.
UM	Leeds C.B.C.
UN	Denbigh C.C.
UO	Devon C.C.
UP	Durham C.C.
UR	Hertford C.C.
US	Glasgow B.C.
USN	London C.C.
UT	Leicestershire C.C.
UU	London C.C.
UV	London C.C.
UW	London C.C.
UX	Salop C.C.
UY	Worcestershire C.C.
UZ	Belfast C.B.C.
V	Lanark C.C.
VA	Lanark C.C.
VB	Croydon C.B.C.
VC	Coventry C.B.C.
VD	Lanark C.C.
VE	Cambridge C.C.
VF	Norfolk C.C.
VG	Norwich C.B.C.
VH	Huddersfield C.B.C.
VJ	Hereford C.C.
VK	Newcastle-upon-Tyne C.B.C.
VL	Lincoln C.B.C.
VM	Manchester C.B.C.
VN	North Riding of Yorks C.C.
VO	Nottinghamshire C.C.
VP	Birmingham C.B.C.
VR	Manchester C.B.C.
VS	Greenock B.C.
VT	Stoke-on-Trent C.B.C.
VU	Manchester C.B.C.
VV	Northampton C.B.C.
VW	Essex C.C.
VX	Essex C.C.
VY	York C.B.C.
VZ	Tyrone C.C.
W	Sheffield C.B.C.
WA	Sheffield C.B.C.
WB	Sheffield C.B.C.
WC	Essex C.C.
WD	Warwick C.C.
WE	Sheffield C.B.C.
WF	East Riding of Yorks C.C.
WG	Stirling C.C.
WH	Bolton C.B.C.
WI	Waterford C.B.C.
WJ	Sheffield C.B.C.
WK	Coventry C.B.C.
WL	Oxford C.B.C.
WM	Southport C.B.C.
WN	Swansea C.B.C.
WO	Monmouth C.C.
WP	Worcestershire C.C.
WR	West Riding of Yorks C.C.
WS	Edinburgh B.C.
WT	West Riding of Yorks C.C.
WU	West Riding of Yorks C.C.
WV	Wilts C.C.
WW	West Riding of Yorks C.C.
WX	West Riding of Yorks C.C.
WY	West Riding of Yorks C.C.
WZ	Belfast C.B.C.
X	Northumberland C.C.
XA	London C.C. (also Kirkcaldy B.C.)
XB	London C.C.
XC	London C.C.
XD	London C.C.
XE	London C.C.
XF	London C.C.
XG	Middlesbrough C.B.C.

XH	London C.C.	Y8	Glasgow B.C.
XI	Belfast C.B.C.	YT	London C.C.
XJ	Manchester C.B.C.	YU	London C.C.
XK	London C.C.	YV	London C.C.
XL	London C.C.	YW	London C.C.
XM	London C.C.	YX	London C.C.
XN	London C.C.	YY	London C.C.
XO	London C.C.	YZ	Londonderry C.C.
XP	London C.C.	Z	Dublin C.C.
XR	London C.C.	ZA	Dublin C.B.C.
XS	Paisley B.C.	ZB	Cork C.C.
XT	London C.C.	ZC	Dublin C.B.C.
XU	London C.C.	ZD	Dublin C.B.C.
XV	London C.C.	ZE	Dublin C.C.
XW	London C.C.	ZF	Cork C.B.C.
XX	London C.C.	ZH	Dublin C.B.C.
XY	London C.C.	ZI	Dublin C.B.C.
XZ	Armagh C.C.	ZJ	Dublin C.B.C.
Y	Somerset C.C	ZK	Cork C.C.
YA	Somerset C.C.	ZL	Dublin C.B.C.
YB	Somerset C.C.	ZM	Galway C.C.
YC	Somerset C.C.	ZN	Meath C.C.
YD	Somerset C.C.	ZO	Dublin C.C.
YE	London C.C.	ZP	Donegal C.C.
YF	London C.C.	ZR	Wexford C.C.
YG	West Riding of Yorks C.C.	ZT	Cork C.C.
YH	London C.C.	ZU	Dublin C.C.
YI	Dublin C.C.	ZW	Kildare C.C.
YJ	Dundee B.C.	ZX	Kerry C.C.
YK	London C.C.	ZY	Louth C.C.
YL	London C.C.		
YM	London C.C.		Dublin C.B.C.
YN	London C.C.	ZZ	The Council of any county which adjoins Northern Ireland; The Royal Irish Automobile Club, Dublin; The Automobile Association, Dublin.
YO	London C.C.		
YP	London C.C.		
YR	London C.C.		

NUMBER PLATES OF AUSTRALIA

These plates have a set of three letters and a set of three numbers. The colours of the letters and their backgrounds are varied and many depend on the State of origin.

Certain sets of letters are allocated to each authority so that no two plates are alike. This system replaces a coding of two letters that did allow for duplication. Before that, coding relied on numbers alone.

NUMBER PLATES OF EGYPT

These are oblong and bear a series of numbers and a set of letters. The digits are condensed, are half the height of the plate and may be five in number. The letters are larger and are Egyptian alphabet characters.

NUMBER PLATES OF FRANCE

These have a number of white letters and figures on a black ground. Each plate has a combination of two letters and two figures representing the issuing authority, followed by a serial number consisting of four figures.

NUMBER PLATES OF GERMANY

German Federal Republic and Western Sectors of Berlin

Under the recently introduced system of registration, number plates consist of two groups of letters and a serial number in black on a white background. The first group indicates the town or district of registration. The seal of the registration authority is also shown.

German Democratic Republic and Eastern Sector of Berlin

Number plates here have two letters indicating town or district, followed by serial number of two groups of two figures separated by a hyphen.

NUMBER PLATES OF ITALY

Italian number plates feature a line of letters of the issuing province, above a line of numbers. These are white on a black background. An exception to this is when the number exceeds four digits. In this case the fifth is placed to the right of the letters in the top line.

The plates are sold to car owners by the State through the War Wounded Association at prices fixed by the Ministry of Communications.

NUMBER PLATES OF THE NETHERLANDS

These feature a group of two letters and a number consisting of two groups of figures. Plates observed which have a group of two letters but a number of less than four digits belong to members of the Royal House or Foreign diplomats. Also, a plate bearing the letters C.D. and having a number of less than four digits preceded by the letter J belongs to a member of the International Court of Justice.

NUMBER PLATES OF NEW ZEALAND

Private vehicles have a set of numbers only on a coloured ground. The colour is changed every three years although a fresh windscreen label is issued every twelve months. Commercial vehicles carry a descriptive prefix letter.

NUMBER PLATES OF PORTUGAL

These number plates have white letters and numbers on a

black background. These are two letters, which represent the issuing authority, and the numbers are in two groups.

NUMBER PLATES OF SPAIN

These plates appear with a number of black letters representing the issuing province, followed by a group of figures also in black, the two groups separated by a hyphen and all on a white background. If a plate has five or more digits the symbolic letters of the authority may be above, but this will only be seen on rear plates.

When a vehicle is to be licensed it is taken to the authority where the letters and figures are affixed to the previously prepared plates.

NUMBER PLATES OF SWITZERLAND

Each Canton, which issues the licence, has two symbolic letters in black. To the left of these appears the federal shield and to the right the shield of the Canton both in their full colours. All are set on a white background.

Persons enjoying diplomatic privileges receive a plate bearing the letters C.D.

NUMBER PLATES OF THE PROVINCES OF CANADA, THE UNITED STATES OF AMERICA, CANAL ZONE, HAWAII, PUERTO RICO

Plates have numbers and letters of varying size, colour and arrangement. These are determined each year by the issuing authority, for the registration of vehicles expires annually and must be renewed. In so doing the car owner obtains a new plate, or " tag " as it is called, for the coming year from his traffic Registrar or Commissioner. Sometimes, however, a ruling is made to retain a plate for a further twelve months and a special supplementary label must be displayed in the windscreen. Some authorities require a re-registration of a vehicle if it undergoes a change of ownership, others allow the plates to remain on the car.

The origin of a car may be traced by observing the Province or State usually shown on the plate in an abbreviated form.

Printed in Great Britain by Butler & Tanner Ltd,
Frome and London
1647.1164